Race, Migration and Identity

The chapters in this collection cover diverse aspects of the changing meanings and boundaries of race, migration and identity in the contemporary United States of America. The situation in the USA has been the subject of intense policy and political debate over the past decades and the papers in this volume provide an important insight from a wide range of analytical perspectives. They provide an insight into the changing dynamics of race and migration in the contemporary environment, combining conceptual analysis with original empirical research. The concerns of this volume address global questions of relevance as well as those specific to the USA.

This book was originally published as a special issue of *Ethnic and Racial Studies.*

Martin Bulmer is Emeritus Professor of Sociology at the University of Surrey, UK. His research interests cover the methodology of social research, the history of the social sciences, the study of ethnicity and race, the application of sociology to public policy, and the sociology of social care.

John Solomos is Professor of Sociology and Head of Department at the University of Warwick, UK. His most recent publications are *Race, Multiculture and Social Policy* (2013, with Alice Bloch and Sarah Neal) and *Theories of Race and Ethnic Relations: Contemporary Debates and Perspectives* (2013, with Karim Murji).

Ethnic and Racial Studies

Series editors: Martin Bulmer, *University of Surrey, UK,* and John Solomos, *University of Warwick, UK*

The journal *Ethnic and Racial Studies* was founded in 1978 by John Stone to provide an international forum for high quality research on race, ethnicity, nationalism and ethnic conflict. At the time the study of race and ethnicity was still a relatively marginal sub-field of sociology, anthropology and political science. In the intervening period the journal has provided a space for the discussion of core theoretical issues, key developments and trends, and for the dissemination of the latest empirical research.

It is now the leading journal in its field and has helped to shape the development of scholarly research agendas. *Ethnic and Racial Studies* attracts submissions from scholars in a diverse range of countries and fields of scholarship, and crosses disciplinary boundaries. It is now available in both printed and electronic form. From 2015 it will publish 15 issues per year, three of which will be dedicated to *Ethnic and Racial Studies Review* offering expert guidance to the latest research through the publication of book reviews, symposia and discussion pieces, including reviews of work in languages other than English.

The *Ethnic and Racial Studies* book series contains a wide range of the journal's special issues. These special issues are an important contribution to the work of the journal, where leading social science academics bring together articles on specific themes and issues that are linked to the broad intellectual concerns of *Ethnic and Racial Studies*. The series editors work closely with the guest editors of the special issues to ensure that they meet the highest quality standards possible. Through publishing these special issues as a series of books, we hope to allow a wider audience of both scholars and students from across the social science disciplines to engage with the work of *Ethnic and Racial Studies*.

Titles in the series include:

The Transnational Political Participation of Immigrants
Edited by Jean-Michel Lafleur and Marco Martiniello

Anthropology of Migration and Multiculturalism
Edited by Steven Vertovec

Race, Migration and Identity
Shifting Boundaries in the USA

Edited by
Martin Bulmer and John Solomos

Routledge
Taylor & Francis Group

LONDON AND NEW YORK

ETHNIC
◄ AND ►
RACIAL
STUDIES

First published 2015
by Routledge

2 Park Square, Milton Park, Abingdon, Oxon OX14 4RN
711 Third Avenue, New York, NY 10017, USA

Routledge is an imprint of the Taylor & Francis Group, an informa business

First issued in paperback 2017

British Library Cataloguing in Publication Data
A catalogue record for this book is available from the British Library

ISBN 13: 978-1-138-85486-4 (hbk)
ISBN 13: 978-1-138-05920-7 (pbk)

Typeset in Times New Roman
by RefineCatch Limited, Bungay, Suffolk

Publisher's Note
The publisher accepts responsibility for any inconsistencies that may have
arisen during the conversion of this book from journal articles to book chapters,
namely the possible inclusion of journal terminology.

Disclaimer
Every effort has been made to contact copyright holders for their permission to
reprint material in this book. The publishers would be grateful to hear from any
copyright holder who is not here acknowledged and will undertake to rectify
any errors or omissions in future editions of this book.

Contents

CONTENTS

Citation Information

The chapters in this book were originally published in *Ethnic and Racial Studies*, volume 37, issue 3 (March 2014). When citing this material, please use the original page numbering for each article, as follows:

Chapter 1
Introduction
Martin Bulmer and John Solomos
Ethnic and Racial Studies, volume 37, issue 3 (March 2014) pp. 381–382

Chapter 2
Migrating race: migration and racial identification among Puerto Ricans
Carlos Vargas-Ramos
Ethnic and Racial Studies, volume 37, issue 3 (March 2014) pp. 383–404

Chapter 3
'I'm American, not Japanese!': the struggle for racial citizenship among later-generation Japanese Americans
Takeyuki Tsuda
Ethnic and Racial Studies, volume 37, issue 3 (March 2014) pp. 405–424

Chapter 4
Are second-generation Filipinos 'becoming' Asian American or Latino? Historical colonialism, culture and panethnicity
Anthony C. Ocampo
Ethnic and Racial Studies, volume 37, issue 3 (March 2014) pp. 425–445

Chapter 5
Mexican Americans as a paradigm for contemporary intra-group heterogeneity
Richard Alba, Tomás R. Jiménez and Helen B. Marrow
Ethnic and Racial Studies, volume 37, issue 3 (March 2014) pp. 446–466

Please direct any queries you may have about the citations to clsuk.permissions@cengage.com

Notes on Contributors

Richard Alba is Distinguished Professor of Sociology at the Graduate Center of the City University of New York, USA.

Martin Bulmer is Emeritus Professor of Sociology at the University of Surrey, UK.

Tomás R. Jiménez is Assistant Professor of Sociology at Stanford University, USA, and a Fellow at the Center for Social Cohesion.

Helen B. Marrow is Assistant Professor of Sociology and Latin American Studies at Tufts University, USA.

Douglas S. Massey is Professor of Sociology and Public Affairs at Princeton University, USA.

Jennifer Bickham Mendez is Associate Professor of Sociology at The College of William & Mary, USA.

Anthony C. Ocampo is Assistant Professor in the Department of Psychology and Sociology at Cal Poly Pomona, USA.

Jayanti Owens is a Doctoral Candidate in Sociology at Princeton University, USA.

Frank Samson is Assistant Professor of Sociology at the University of Miami, USA.

Deenesh Sohoni is Associate Professor of Sociology at The College of William & Mary, USA.

John Solomos is Professor of Sociology and Head of Department at the University of Warwick, UK.

Takeyuki Tsuda is Associate Professor of Anthropology in the School of Human Evolution & Social Change at Arizona State University, USA.

Carlos Vargas-Ramos is Research Associate in the Center for Puerto Rican Studies at Hunter College, City University of New York, USA.

Carol S. Walther is Assistant Professor in the Department of Sociology at Northern Illinois University, USA.

Cortney S. Warren is Associate Professor in the Department of Psychology at the University of Nevada, Las Vegas, USA.

Introduction

Over the five decades since its foundation, *Ethnic and Racial Studies* has provided a space for the publication of the latest research by scholars of race, ethnic relations and racism. In this *Themed Issue* of the journal, we have included nine papers which cover diverse aspects of the changing meanings and boundaries of race, migration and identity in the contemporary USA. Although we make no claim that the various papers share a common analytical frame or empirical focus we hope they highlight some key themes in the current scholarship and research. All the papers included here draw on original empirical research and address questions of relevance globally as well as in relation to the USA.

Race, migration and identity are common themes which run through all the papers in this thematic issue. The first paper by Carlos Vargas-Ramos provides an insight into the shifting patterns of racial identification among Puerto Rican migrants to the USA. Vargas-Ramos explores in particular the ways in which conceptions of whiteness and race are not fixed and change through the process of migration. This theme of shifting conceptions of race and migrant status is also addressed by Takeyuki Tsuda and Anthony Ocampo. Tsuda's paper focuses on the mobilisation of ideas of racial citizenship among later-generation Japanese Americans. Tsuda highlights the tension between the search for inclusion and the experience of being racialised others in American society. Ocampo's study of second-generation Filipinos links up in some ways with Tsuda's account, although it is interesting to note that there are differences in the experiences of Japanese and Filipino Americans.

This group of papers is followed by a study by Richard Alba, Tomas Jimenez and Helen Marrow on Mexican Americans and intragroup heterogeneity. The authors draw on the experience of Mexican Americans to emphasise the need to look at specific migrant groups as intrinsically diverse in both history and contemporary composition. Frank Samson's paper is also focused on Latino immigrants, in particular the ways in which their political opportunities are shaped by racialised processes. Samson's account outlines the importance of segmented political assimilation in the context of partisan political identification. The paper by Deenesh Sohoni and Jennifer Medez focuses on new areas of migrant settlement in order to explore the ways in which ethnic and migrant boundaries are being reconfigured.

A somewhat different angle is provided by Carol Walther's analysis of the role of ideas about skin tone in the selection of sperm donors. Although this paper is more specific in focus. it highlights the complexities of biracial and tri-racial stratification among sperm donors.

The final two papers in this issue focus on the shifting boundaries of race in contemporary US society. Cortney Warren focuses on ideas of physical body appearance among white, black and Latina college students. The final paper in the issue is by Douglas Massey and Jayanti Owens and focuses on an analysis of mediators of stereotype threat among black college students. These papers reflect the tendency of research to be conducted among ethnic minority students in the higher education sector.

This themed issue will be followed later in the year by another themed issue that will focus on questions about race and ethnicity in UK society. We hope that the two issues taken together will provide an opportunity for readers to think about similarities and differences between the two societies, thereby advancing the cause of comparative sociology.

Martin Bulmer
University of Surrey

John Solomos
University of Warwick

Migrating race: migration and racial identification among Puerto Ricans

Carlos Vargas-Ramos

Abstract

The pattern of racial identification among Puerto Ricans is not uniform. It varies depending on where they live. Most identify as white, but more do so in Puerto Rico than in the USA. This paper addresses the impact that living alternatively in the USA and in Puerto Rico has on racial identification among Puerto Ricans. Using Public Use Microdata Sample data from the American Community Survey and the Puerto Rico Community Survey 2006–2008, I find that while there is no single pattern of impact, those more grounded on the island's racial system are more likely to identify as white in the USA, while those less grounded in Puerto Rico are more likely to identify as multiracial or by another racial descriptor. On their return to the island, they revert to the prevalent pattern of racial identification, while still exhibiting effects of their sojourn on their racial identity.

Census data on Puerto Ricans and race manifest the contingent nature of racial identity and identification and how specific racial formations impact an individual's understanding of race and racial identification. Despite contemporary projections of Puerto Ricans as a multiracial people (Dávila 1997), in fact a mulatto nation (Torres 1998; Duany 2002), the majority of Puerto Ricans portray themselves as white in the context of official statistics. This is the case for both Puerto Ricans on the island and in the USA. Their location, however, determines the proportions by which they identify as white or as something else.

Presently, more than half of the 8.3 million people who identify as Puerto Ricans live in the USA. Moreover, there is a recurrent movement of migrants between the island and the USA, with net migration reaching the hundreds of thousands between decades (Rivera-Batiz and Santiago 1996; Duany 2002; Acosta-Belén and

Santiago 2006). Understandings of race and racial identification are likely to be challenged when migrants change social milieus with contrasting or conflicting racialization experiences. Considering the large and recurrent population movement between Puerto Rico and the USA, it is pertinent then to address how a people may be impacted when a large segment of the population is exposed to an alternative system of racial understanding.

Census data serve to illustrate how individuals adapt to different racial formations given the importance of census-based racial identification in shaping public policies and racial representations. These official statistics highlight how differently race is constructed by Puerto Ricans on the island and in the USA, and how specific individuals (i.e. migrants) behave when facing the census.

Responding to the race question in US Census Bureau questionnaires presents a specific contextual moment that reflects practices of racial self-representation in both Puerto Rico and the USA. Engaging this race question is a paradigmatic exercise in the process 'by which racial meanings are decided, and racial identities are assigned, in a given society' (i.e. racial formation) (Winant 1992, p. 183). Race has been a crucial factor in the USA since its founding. The question on race continues to be included in census questionnaires in the USA because of congressional mandates to monitor compliance with federal civil rights legislation (Nobles 2000). For Puerto Rico, the question on race was only incidentally reintroduced in census questionnaires in 2000 after the local government requested the US Census Bureau treat Puerto Rico as a state for the purposes of data collection and analysis, not because of specific concerns over the protection of civil rights of racial minorities. Consequently, the Census Bureau used the same questionnaire it used in the USA, but translated into Spanish.

In 2000, people in Puerto Rico had the first opportunity to engage in an extraneous bureaucratic process of racial self-representation in which they could declare, in the privacy of their own home, beyond immediate social scrutiny, their own racial identity but according to categories determined by governmental agencies outside their specific cultural setting. Prior to that year, race was established and recorded by a government agent (i.e. enumerator). In the USA, racial self-identification in the privacy of one's home was introduced in 1980. Under these circumstances, people on the island overwhelmingly identified as white; in the USA, people of Puerto Rican origin or descent responded differently.

A racial statistics puzzle

In 2010, more than three-quarters of people in Puerto Rico identified as white. Most Puerto Ricans in the USA also identified as white, but only among 53 per cent of the population (Table 1). The difference of more than twenty percentage points among those who identified as white on the island and in the USA is wide; just as wide as the difference among those who did not choose one of the racial categories offered by the Census Bureau in its questionnaires. Whereas only 8 per cent of Puerto Ricans on the island identified with *some other race*, 28 per cent did so in the USA. Much smaller differences were observed among those identifying as black, Asian or American Indian or with two or more races (i.e. multiracial).

One might argue that a larger proportion of non-whites migrated to the USA from the island after the Second World War. However, contemporary accounts point to the fact that 'a larger percentage of white than of colored Puerto Ricans came to the mainland' (Handlin 1959, p. 59). Alternatively, the settlement of people of foreign birth in Puerto Rico might provide an answer. Yet, the influx of largely white Cuban émigrés and largely non-white Dominican immigrants to Puerto Rico in the post-war era was too small to have a significant impact on the proportions of race in Puerto Rico. Collectively, these foreign-born residents have represented less than 3 per cent of the island's population. Given that the net migration of Puerto Ricans to the USA between 1950 and 2000 has been more than 950,000 people (cf. Rivera-Batiz and Santiago 1996; Vargas-Ramos 2008), it is unlikely that some 150,000 foreign-born island residents with a variety of racial identities would account for the differences in racial identification of Puerto Ricans in the USA and on the island.[1]

While the questionnaire used by the Census Bureau in Puerto Rico and in the USA may have been the same, the understanding of whiteness or blackness for a Puerto Rican who has lived for an extended period of time in the USA, in circumstances of poor

Table 1 *Racial identification among Puerto Ricans in the United States and for Puerto Rico*

	Total population	Per cent White	Per cent Black	Per cent Am. Indian	Per cent Asian/ PI	Per cent Other	Per cent Multi-Racial
Puerto Rico, 2010	3,725,789	75.8	12.4	0.5	0.1	7.8	3.3
Puerto Ricans in the U.S., 2010	4,623,716	53.1	8.7	0.9	0.8	27.8	8.7

Source: U.S. Bureau of the Census, Census 2010

5

employment, racial and ethnic residential segregation, and general social marginalization, in a society whose culture they may find foreign, may differ from that of a person in Puerto Rico who has never migrated or from their own once they return to Puerto Rico. The differences in racial identification among Puerto Ricans depending on their geographical location is to be accounted for by differences in racial formation in Puerto Rico and in the USA and by how this racial formation is internalized by them (Omi and Winant 1986).

Standard accounts of differences in race relations between the USA and Latin America have often been dichotomized between the polar binary based on hypodescent prevalent in the USA and the fluid racial continuum grounded in phenotype prevalent in Latin America. These differences set the stage for representations of state-sanctioned racism evident in the former and the more socially diffused discrimination in a comparatively more tolerant and benign environment in the latter (Blanco 1942; Degler 1971; Skidmore 1972; Freyre 1986; Wade 1997; Telles 2004).

Racial formation in Puerto Rico

The boundary between whiteness and intermediate groups in the racial continuum is so flexible in Puerto Rico that a person of African ancestry, and even certain phenotypic features associated with black-ness, may be accepted as white to an extent unlikely to occur in the USA (Hoetink 1967). The boundary between blackness and the intermediate group is also flexible so that only persons with the most stereotypically sub-Saharan African phenotype would be con-sidered black. Others may yet assert an intermediate identity and be recognized as such.

The social hierarchy that developed in Puerto Rico under the colonial control of Spain placed Spaniards in the upper echelons of governmental, military, commercial and religious institutions, with their *criollo* descendents occupying ancillary spaces (Picó 1988; Scarano 1993). At the bottom of the social scale were slaves, equated with blacks and their descendents after the effective elimination of indigenous labour, and the latter's devastation as a discrete social group (Kinsbruner 1996). Notable also was a sizeable segment of free blacks, either manumitted slaves or escapees from neighbouring islands under foreign control, as well as their descendents (Morales Carrión 1978). Most numerous was the population that resulted from the admixture of blacks and whites, historically termed *mulatos, pardos* or *coloureds*, in official records, and more colloquially *triguenos, jabaos*, and *morenos* at present.[2] This segment of the population has been the largest or second largest, after whites, during the past two and a half centuries. Their social standing and official treatment would vary, from being indistinguishable from blacks (whether free or slave) as subjects to discriminating state scrutiny in the form of reduced civil rights and arbitrary treatment for several decades in the aftermath of the Haitian revolution, to lesser social contempt from the white population with which it may even form social unions (e.g. marriages).

Ideologically, some leading local intellectuals, in an effort to accentuate its Spanish-origin whiteness in relation to the USA, after the transfer of the island's sovereignty in 1898, decried its mixed-race population for the backwardness of the Puerto Rican people, predicated on utter black inferiority (Pedreira 1973). Yet, as influential as these had been, contemporary and latter generations of intellectuals rejected these postulates. Instead, what flourished ideologically was an embrace of *mestizaje* (i.e. miscegenation) along with acceptance of *blanqueamiento* (i.e. whitening), concepts and practices that dated to Spanish colonial times. The discourse on *mestizaje* as a project of national identity construction may date to the middle of the nineteenth century elsewhere in Latin America (Martínez-Echazábal 1998); in Puerto Rico it took root in the first third of the twentieth century (Labrador-Rodríguez 1999). Alongside the resurgence of the ideology and social practice of whitening through racial mixing emerged a modern characterization of Puerto Rico that highlighted the multi-racial nature of the country, promoted by the government under the *criollo* Commonwealth regime starting in the 1950s (e.g. *Instituto de Cultura Puertorriqueña*) (Dávila 1997).

Underscoring this projection of a multiracial society was the racial democracy discourse that had surfaced throughout Latin America (Wade 1997; Duany 2002), at a time when Jim Crow discriminatory segregation reigned supreme in large swathes of the USA. There might exist social differences between the various racialized groups, but these were mostly class based, attributed to historical remnants of slavery that would ultimately disappear under modernization projects (Blanco 1942). Moreover, racial relations in Puerto Rico, the argument proceeded, were nevertheless better than in the USA (Duany 2002). Given this elite position, there was little use or desire for collecting data on race, racial identity and social disparities based on race. Consequently, the local government petitioned the US Census Bureau to remove questions on racial identification from census question-naires used in Puerto Rico.

The racial democracy discourse effectively silenced whatever grie-vances may have arisen from claims of racial inequality. It foreclosed the possibility of collectively advocating for redress, and furthered an individual-based solution centred on miscegenation. The logic under-scoring *blanqueamiento* was the intent to escape blackness, even if it required a 'browning' step. The treatment of the non-white population may be relatively benign, if condescending, but its insidiousness and effectiveness reside in its negrophobia and the discrimination against black Puerto Ricans. Substantial evidence of racial discrimination and prejudice against people of African descent in Puerto Rico exists (Godreau and Vargas-Ramos 2009); *blanqueamiento* facilitates an escape from abject blackness.

The characterization of a fluid Latin American racial continuum brings into relief another characteristic of such a racial system: its ambiguity. Yet, Gravlee (2005, p. 951) has demonstrated that instead of ambiguity there is rather 'a coherent and highly structured cultural model of *color* that appears to be shared across divisions of age, sex, class, and color' among Puerto Ricans, based on skin colour and hair form. Nevertheless, the system remains fluid. The boundaries between racial categories can and do in fact change over time, even rapidly. In accounting for the sudden increase in the number of whites from 1910 to 1920, Loveman and Muniz (2007, p. 934) conclude that 'boundary shifting was the most significant dynamic driving racial re-classification in the 1920 Puerto Rican census', and suggest that 'Puerto Rico whitened rapidly in the second decade of the twentieth century primarily through a shift in the social definition of whiteness itself' (Loveman and Muniz 2007, p. 935). This shift in the definition of whiteness, while socially pervasive, became operational at the level of the census enumerator, who was charged with ascertaining and recording a person's race.

More recently, 2010 decennial census results indicated that the proportion of whites declined while the proportion of blacks and *some other race* increased. Preliminary analysis and journalistic accounts indicate that Census 2000 results for Puerto Rico were so astounding in how people represented themselves racially that there was a reassessment of racial identity on the island in the intervening decade, accompanied by increased racial awareness and consciousness-raising campaigns sponsored by anti-racist organizations and advocates for equality for people of African descent, all of which resulted in a growing acceptance of either a black or non-white identity (Rivera Marrero 2011).[3]

Puerto Rican racial formation in the USA

Puerto Rican migration to the USA started in earnest after 1917, when the US Congress made US citizens out of these colonial subjects. However, emigration from the island took on massive proportions after the Second World War. Thomas (2009, pp. 9, 10) describes how Puerto Ricans were perceived by their new neighbours in the USA and how they reacted and internalized these perceptions:

Rejected by the increasingly white-seeming ethnics as not white; suspicious, themselves, of the Negro racial identity reflexively imposed on them by the white society; and seen by African-Americans as "Spanish" – or, at least, distinctly foreign – more than black, Puerto Ricans began to perceive the degree to which the intense and distinctive racisms of the United States would shape their experience as Americans. ... [A]s their foreignness and their inscrutable racial origins hindered them in their competition with other New Yorkers for jobs and a growing array of welfare benefits, and as their increasing numbers inspired intensifying prejudice on the part of whites, racial identity became a subject of intensely concerned debate within the Puerto Rican community.

The mixed-race segment of the population came to characterize Puerto Ricans in the USA. Early comparative studies on racial stratification in Puerto Rico and the USA noted the difference not between the treatment of blacks in both countries, as their life chances were similarly poor, but in the treatment of the mixed-race population (Duany 2002). In the USA since Reconstruction, those falling into such intermediate spaces have been treated socially, legally and politically as part of a larger black group (e.g. *Plessy v. Ferguson*), even when internally differentiated for census purposes. In Puerto Rico, on the other hand, they remained socially differentiated, even when reported alongside blacks (under a non-white or *coloured* category) for census purposes. Moreover, through *blanqueamiento*, this mixed-race segment could 'advance' towards whiteness in Puerto Rico, whereas in the USA this social advance was largely foreclosed.

Puerto Ricans may have been portrayed in press accounts and by local elites as a group that was suspect racially and culturally (Mills, Senior and Goldsen 1967; Pérez 2004; Thomas 2009). Yet, in official statistics, Puerto Ricans in the USA were to be represented as white. Thus, enumerators for the 1960 decennial census were instructed to '[m]ark "White" for such persons unless they are definitely of Negro, Indian, or other nonwhite race' as Puerto Rican was not a racial description (in Nobles 2000, p. 190).

Puerto Ricans, moreover, arrived in the USA with a distinct understanding of racial identity that, while originating on the island, fermented in an environment of racial discrimination and ethnocentrism, social marginalization and cultural contempt. The construction of a Commonwealth government-inspired Puerto Rican identity, based on a presumed racial triad whereby Puerto Rican culture was a creole mixture of three cultural influences (i.e. Spanish, Arawak and West African; privileged in that order), allowed individuals to racialize this cultural identity and assert that indeed a Puerto Rican person physically embodies this mixture of three ethnoracial groups. Being

Puerto Rican would embody for many not only a creole Spanish Caribbean culture, but indeed a mixed-race body as well. Thus, when Puerto Ricans in the USA self-identify with a racial descriptor not furnished by the Census Bureau, they may respond with terms denoting race mixture (e.g. *trigueño*, *mezclado*) but also by simply stating an ethnonational identity (e.g. *boricua*, Puerto Rican). Puerto Rican ethnicity in the latter case is effectively racialized and equated with phenotype (Berkowitz 2001). These changes in racial meaning and understanding, along with new procedures to collect decennial census data (e.g. self-identification, questionnaire mail-back), become manifest in the precipitous drop in the percentage of the Puerto Rican population in the USA that identified as white, from 93 per cent in 1970 to 48 per cent in 1980 and 46 per cent in 1990 (Duany 2002).

Choosing the residual category *some other race* becomes oppositional insofar as a substantial proportion of Puerto Ricans are rejecting categories that seem standard and indeed hegemonic in the USA but are not meaningful to this segment of the Puerto Rican population (Duany 2002). When results first appeared indicating that large proportions of Hispanics in the USA, including Puerto Ricans, were choosing another racial descriptor to those explicitly listed, analysts interpreted this as Latinos either misunderstanding the concept of race, or an option used by mixed-race individuals (Rodríguez 2000). Thirty years hence, the distinct terminology subsumed under the rubric *some other race* is a reflection of how Latinos in the USA are racialized as individuals, so that a Puerto Rican is stereotyped by social actors in the USA not simply as an ethnic or national type, but indeed as a specific phenotype identified geographically.

Migration and racial identification

The movement of people across borders to different cultural systems allows for dynamic changes in the process of assigning meaning to race and acquiring understandings of it that cannot be confined to independent occurrences in two separate geographical settings. The conveyance of different understandings of race through migration and settlement informs, affects and transforms in varying degrees the understanding of race in both the country of origin and the host country. The large proportion of Latinos that refuse to categorize themselves as either black or white (or Asian or Native American) is a case in which racial practices and bureaucratic understandings of race are challenged in the USA (Oboler 1995; Rodriguez 2000; De Genova and Ramos-Zayas 2003). Likewise return migration to countries of origins with altered understandings of race may also influence and change those understandings of race in their native countries (Torres 1998).

In travelling from Puerto Rico to the USA, migrants are likely to assert whiteness provided that their phenotype allows them to do so and they are so disposed ideologically. If phenotypically this is not possible, they may still attempt to escape blackness by asserting their identity as a mixed-race person with terms such as *trigueña*, *mestiza* or *mezclada*; emphasizing their ethnicity as a racial differentiator (e.g. *boricua*, Puerto Rican); or by marking on the census form that they are *other* without further explanation. They may still assert an inter-mediate racial status or racialize their ethnicity even if they see themselves as black in Puerto Rico, or they may yet opt to assert their blackness. On return, migrants who may have seen their aspirations for whiteness forestalled in the USA may opt for this option without the need to resort to intermediate categories or to a racialized ethnicity, especially if intermediate categories are not explicitly provided on the census form (Berkowitz 2001; Vargas-Ramos 2005). Alternatively, they may opt to continue identifying as black if their experience in the USA allowed them to witness and live in an environment where black identity is asserted, fostered and respected.

In the analysis that follows I identify factors that serve as proxy for the migration experience to ascertain the impact they may have on Puerto Rican racial identification in the USA. Furthermore, I examine what impact the migration experience may have on return migrants to Puerto Rico. These analyses rely on quantitative data from census sources to establish not only ways in which people identify themselves racially, but also how the migration experience plays a role in how those individuals identify themselves racially. Census data have a limited number of factors that may convey the inherently complex process of migrating and the socializing impact involved in settling in a new social and cultural system. Census data do no exhaustively capture the richness of this experience.[4] However, these data may yet provide enough indicators to allow us to make appropriate inferences applicable to large segments of the population.

Data and results

I explore these questions further but circumscribing my inquiry to the impact the migratory experience may have had on racial identification of Puerto Ricans. I observe Puerto Ricans in the USA and how their racial identification varies due to the impact of three factors that may be used as proxy for migration. I ascertain whether Puerto Ricans born on the island identify differently from Puerto Ricans born in the USA. Ability to speak English is another proxy of migration for Puerto Ricans as proficiency in English correlates with the length of time a Puerto Rican has lived in the USA (cf. Zentella 1997). Place of residence for Puerto Ricans the prior year is another way to gauge particularly how recent their migration has been. Lastly, I present data on how long these Puerto Rican migrants have lived in the USA since moving from Puerto Rico. The data for the analyses are based on separate samples of the population for the USA and Puerto Rico as collected by the US Census Bureau in the 2006–2008 American Community Survey public use microdata sets and packaged by University of Minnesota's Population Center as IPUMS (Ruggles et al. 2010).

I hypothesize that those Puerto Ricans in the USA more grounded in Puerto Rico, its society and its social conventions – operationalized by whether they were born in Puerto Rico, had recently migrated from the island, had lived in the USA for a shorter period of time and had a lower level of proficiency in English – are more likely to exhibit a pattern of racial identification similar to that of Puerto Rico; that is, with greater proportions identifying as white and lower proportions identifying as *other* or with more than one race as well as lower rates of identifying as black. On the other hand, those more grounded in the USA would be more likely to identify as white, but in lower proportions, more likely to identify as *other* in greater proportions and less likely yet to identify as black, but more likely to identify with several races.

Racial identification in the USA

A Puerto Rican born on the island but residing in the USA during the survey year was more likely to identify as white or *some other race* than those born in the USA. The latter were more likely to choose black or more than one race (Table 2). The pattern of racial identification is not as clear among those Puerto Ricans who changed residence from one year to the next (Table 3). As expected, a greater proportion of those who lived in Puerto Rico the year before but who were living in the USA at the time of the survey (59 per cent) identified as white than among those Puerto Ricans who simply moved between states in the USA or had not moved (52 per cent). Also, those who identified as black or with more than one of the racial options provided by the Census Bureau were more likely to reside in the USA the prior year than in Puerto Rico. However, there is hardly any distinction among those Puerto Ricans who chose another racial identification.

More consonant with the hypotheses are the results of ability to speak English. Those more proficient in English were more likely to choose black or two or more races (Table 4). On the other hand, those who were not as able to speak English well or at all were more likely to use white, but not by a great margin, while a greater proportion who

Table 2 *Racial identification in the US by birthplace (in percentage)*

	Born in US	Born in PR	Total
White	49.9	57.1	52.3
Black	7.2	3.1	5.8
OtherRace	31.9	36.1	33.3
Multi-racial	9.2	3.2	7.2

Source: 2006–2008 American Community Survey sample, IPUMS.
Chi-square = 48.13, p = .000

chose some other racial label to describe themselves were not as proficient.

Given that bivariate relations may incorporate or conceal other relations between variables, I proceed to regress these racial identification variables on migration variables. Table 5 shows the results of four regression models that highlight predictors of racial identification for Puerto Ricans in the USA based on their migration experience. Each logistic regression was run independently for black, *other*, two or more races (multiracial) and white. The purpose of running these regressions is to establish what independent impact these migration variables may have on racial identification while holding the other variables constant. The models also include socio-demographic characteristics, such as gender, age, educational attainment and whether a person is working or not, and their occupational industry, all of which may inform racial identification.[5] However, these latter socio-demographic characteristics will only be used as controls.[6] The emphasis of the analyses will be the effect of migration variables on racial self-identification.

Of all migration variables, birthplace is most consistent. Those born in Puerto Rico were more likely to identify as white and less likely to identify as black or by two or more races, as hypothesized. However, those born in Puerto Rico were also more likely to identify as *other*, contrary to expectations. Proficiency in English did not have any

Table 3 *Racial identification in the US by residence the prior year (in percentages)*

	In US prior year	In Puerto Rico prior year	Total
White	52.2	59	52.3
Black	5.9	3.8	5.8
Other Race	33	34	33.3
Multi-racial	7.3	2.8	7.2

Source: 2006–2008 American Community Survey sample, IPUMS.
Chi-square = 55.99, p = .000

Table 4 *Racial identification in the US by ability to speak English (in percentage)*

	Does not speak English	Speaks English, not well	Speaks English, well or very well	Total
White	53.4	52.6	52.4	52.7
Black	4.5	3.6	6.1	5.6
Other Race	38.7	39.4	32.7	33.9
Multi-racial	2.8	3.5	7.2	6.5

Source: 2006–2008 American Community Survey sample, IPUMS.
Chi-square = 681.75, p = .000

statistically significant impact for those who identified as white or multiracial, but it had a strong effect on those identifying as black. Those who did not speak English well, those who spoke it well, very well or exclusively were less likely to identify as black than those who did not speak English at all. English proficiency also had an impact on those who identified as *other*. Compared to those who did not speak English at all, those who spoke it but not very well and those who spoke it well were more likely to identify as *other*.

Table 5 *Migration predictors of racial identification for Puerto Ricans in the US (Logistic regression coefficients; standard error in parenthesis)*

	White	Black	Other Race	Multiracial
Constant	−.632***	− 1.299***	−.469***	−1.947***
	(.136)	(.297)	(.142)	(.336)
Speaks English:				
Not well	−.098	−.421*	.164*	.036
	(.097)	(.223)	(.099)	(.263)
Well	−.121	−.523**	.233**	−.08
	(.093)	(.211)	(.096)	(.253)
Very well/only	.004	−.402**	.067	.000
	(.092)	(.204)	(.094)	(.247)
In PR year before	.135	−.108	−.034	−.465*
	(.086)	(.224)	(.089)	(.259)
Yrs in US	−.004***	.001	.001	.006**
	(.001)	(.002)	(.001)	(.002)
Born in PR	.171***	−.671***	.19***	−.711***
	(.031)	(.078)	(.032)	(.075)
R-Square	.037	.028	.033	.025
-2 log likelihood	71130.44	20913.66	66257.54	21543.71
N	52583	52583	52583	52583
Chi-Square	1458.52***	500.951***	1260.27***	454.46***

* Coefficient significant at 0.1 level; **significant at 0.05 level; *** significant at 0.01 level

The length of the migration had some impact on some racial identification variables. The longer a Puerto Rican migrant had lived in the USA the less likely it was that they would identify as white and the more likely they would identify as multiracial, as expected. However, whether the migration was recent only had a statistical effect on those identifying with two or more races; if the migrant was residing in Puerto Rico the year prior to the survey, the less likely it was that they would identify as multiracial.

These results by and large support the hypotheses. Among those who identified as white, being born in Puerto Rico raised the probability of identifying as such. This probability diminished the longer such a person had lived in the USA. However, their ability to speak English or whether their migration was recent did not show a significant impact. For black identification, being born in Puerto Rico was a strong predictor for not identifying as such, while even a minimal ability to speak English also decreased the probability of identifying as black, compared to those who did not speak it at all. These findings are somewhat confounding. It seems as if Puerto Ricans born in the USA, but unable to speak English at all, were more likely to identify as black, suggesting a degree of marginalization. On the other hand, those who had an intermediate proficiency in English (i.e. speaks English but not very well, or speaks it well) were more likely to identify as *other*. Birthplace in Puerto Rico increased this likelihood further. But the findings for 'other racial identification' are the least supportive of the hypotheses, as it was expected that the longer a Puerto Rican had lived in the USA, exposing him/herself to that social environment, the more likely it would be that they would identify as *other*. Such an effect appeared to be slightly more evident on English proficiency, with those somewhat more grounded in the USA, but not necessarily fully immersed in it, more likely to identify as *other*. Yet, the racial identification category that fits the hypotheses most closely is for those who identified with more than one race. Those who were more grounded in Puerto Rico by virtue of birth, how recently they migrated from the island and the shorter sojourn in the USA, were less likely to identify multiracially. This identity was more consonant with being more grounded in the USA.

Racial identification in Puerto Rico

Most migrations generally, and the Puerto Rican migration specifically, are not unidirectional, but rather involve a return of a portion of the original migrants to the sending society. Based on three-year estimates from the 2006–2008 American Community Survey results for the island (i.e. Puerto Rico Community Survey (PRCS)), the hypothesis for how migration affects racial identification in Puerto

Rico is similarly based on the impact that acculturation in the social system of the USA and re-acculturation in Puerto Rico has had. Thus, how recently a migrant returned from the USA, the greater their ability to speak English and being born in the USA would lead to the expectation that the migrant would be more likely to identify as white, but to a lesser extent than Puerto Ricans who have not migrated.[7] These Puerto Ricans more grounded in the USA would also be more likely to define as *other* or with more than one race in greater proportions and less likely to identify as black.

Table 6 shows the difference in racial identification in Puerto Rico according to birthplace. Those born in the USA were slightly less likely to define as white and slightly more likely to identify with another racial descriptor. Those born in the USA were somewhat less likely to identify as black. Table 7 shows the results for racial identification in Puerto Rico based on whether a Puerto Rican residing on the island at the time of the survey was residing in the USA the prior year. Those who migrated recently to Puerto Rico from the USA were less likely to identify as white and black relative to those who were living in Puerto Rico the year before, and more likely to identify using other racial categories or using more than one racial category. Thus, among those whose migration from the USA was more recent, the greater their proportion identifying in these oppositional terms. However, these differences in proportions are not statistically significant and cannot be attributed exclusively to how recent the migration is, as the results may be given by chance.

Table 8 shows the results for racial identification based on a person's ability to speak English. These results show that those who had a greater command of English were more likely to identify as white, while those who did not speak English at all were more likely to identify with more than one racial category or as *other*. Considering these results on racial identification in the aggregate suggests that a sojourn in the USA has different outcomes on racial identification: those whose incorporation was more successful, measured by ability to speak English (as proxy for acculturation), were more likely to identify

Table 6 *Racial identification in PR by birthplace (in percentage)*

	Born in US	Born in PR	Total
White	75.9	77.3	77.3
Black	6.5	7.3	7.2
Other Race	11.8	10.1	10.1
Multi-racial	5.4	4.9	4.9

Source: 2006–2008 American Community Survey sample, IPUMS.
Chi-square = 27.93; p = .000

Table 7 *Racial identification in PR by residence the prior year (in percentage)*

	In US prior year	In Puerto Rico prior year	Total
White	74.7	77.3	77.2
Black	6.3	7.3	7.2
Other Race	11.7	10.1	10.2
Multi-racial	7	4.9	4.9

Source: 2006–2008 American Community Survey sample, IPUMS.
Chi-square = 9.022; p = .172

as white, while those whose incorporation may have been less successful were more likely to use racial descriptors that do not conform to the normative choices offered by the US Census Bureau.

In order to test these observations, while controlling for factors that may also have an effect on racial identification, I regress four separate measures of racial identification in Puerto Rico on migration-associated measures as well as other relevant socio-demographic variables. Table 9 shows the results of these logistic regression equations for identifying as black, *other*, two or more races (multi-racial) and white.

English proficiency appears to have the most consistent effect on racial identification throughout the equations. Those most proficient were more likely to identify as white and less likely to identify as black or *other*. Among respondents who chose two or more races, proficiency was more inconsistent. Those with the best ability to speak English were less likely to identify as multiracial, while those who spoke the least, but were still able to communicate in that language, were more likely to identify as multiracial relative to those who did not speak English at all or spoke it merely well. Birthplace was also a fairly consistent predictor, with those born in Puerto Rico more likely to identify as white, and less likely to identify as *other* or as multiracial. However, birthplace did not have any significant impact

Table 8 *Racial identification in PR by ability to speak English (in percentage)*

	Does not speak English	Speaks English, not well	Speaks English, well or very well	Total
White	75.2	76.4	81.4	77.2
Black	7.5	7.7	6.9	7.3
Other Race	11.7	6.8	7.4	10.1
Multi-racial	5	6.9	3.9	4.9

Source: 2006–2008 American Community Survey sample, IPUMS.
Chi-square = 408.5; p = .000

Table 9 *Migration predictors of racial identification for Puerto Ricans in Puerto Rico (Logistic regression coefficients; standard error in parenthesis)*

	White	Black	Other Race	Multiracial
Constant	.424*** (.161)	−2.229*** (.246)	−1.306*** (.223)	−2.556*** (.323)
Speaks English				
Not well	−.014 (.032)	.072 (.05)	−.119*** (.045)	.159*** (.061)
Well	.093*** (.036)	−.081 (.057)	−.102** (.049)	−.004 (.069)
Very well/only	.336*** (.035)	−.162*** (.055)	−.396*** (.05)	−.247*** (.069)
In US year before	−.064 (.138)	−.287 (.246)	.134 (.184)	.383* (.226)
Born in PR	.118** (.047)	.087 (.078)	−.196*** (.063)	−.158* (.088)
R-Square	.022	.007	.016	.011
-2 log likelihood	43732.024	22235.054	26995.94	16302.42
N	39428	39428	39428	39428
Chi-Square	591.691***	125.35***	324.36***	152.12***

* Coefficient significant at 0.1 level; **significant at 0.05 level; *** significant at 0.01 level

among those identifying as black. Neither did whether a migrant had returned recently to the island. In fact, only among those identifying as multiracial did recent arrival in Puerto Rico increase the likelihood of identifying thusly.

These results, by and large, do not consistently support the hypothetical expectations. Yet these results still present a clear effect of the migration between Puerto Rico and the USA on racial identification among Puerto Ricans. Those born in Puerto Rico were still more likely to identify as white, but those most proficient in English were even more likely to identify as such. Those migrants more grounded in the USA were not more likely to identify as *other*. On the contrary, it was those born in the USA, but who did not speak English, who were more likely to choose a racial descriptor not provided by the US Census Bureau. Although for those born in the USA and in that country the year before the survey was conducted, thus more grounded in the USA, the more likely it was that they would identify as multiracial.

Discussion

There is a preference for whiteness among Puerto Ricans. This is the case in both Puerto Rico and in the USA. However, this predilection is largely driven by island-born Puerto Ricans. When those island-born Puerto Ricans spend a number of years in the USA, their preference is met with a likely reality that their conception of whiteness does not match that of others who reside in the USA. Many Puerto Ricans may assert whiteness, but this assertion is challenged in the social environment they occupy. Many of these island-born Puerto Ricans in the USA then accommodate themselves in a residual and opposi- tional category – *other*. Many use this residual category to assert their mixed race with racial terms they relate to culturally (e.g. *trigueño*) or subsume their racially mixed ethnicity under nationality (i.e. Puerto Rican, *boricua*). But unexpectedly its use is not predicated by length of residence in the USA or how recently they arrived there. Using *other* is only influenced by a tenuous cultural integration in the USA evidenced by their limited command of English.

However, island-born Puerto Ricans in the USA rejected in greater likelihood other accommodations that the USA has made in its racial system. While allowing survey respondents to choose as many racial categories as they felt described them, only those much less grounded in Puerto Rico, by virtue of being born in the USA, a longer-term residence in the USA if they had migrated, and by not having migrated very recently, were likely to do so. This is a curious pattern given how prevalent the discourse of Puerto Rican miscegenation is on the island. It appears as though island-born Puerto Ricans related to this discourse when it is labelled with a culturally relevant term or subsumed under nationality. It seems that these mixed-race Puerto Ricans were largely unwilling to generically accept a multiracial label that may level their experience with that of other people in the USA who are not Puerto Rican or at minimum Hispanic. They chose to stand apart.

Blackness was certainly not a preference for the vast majority of Puerto Ricans in the USA and this was particularly the case for those born on the island, irrespective of their length of stay in the USA or how recently they may have lived there. Their cultural marginality in the USA, given by a lack of English proficiency, however, enhanced the likelihood of identifying as black. This is a marked contrast with those who identified as black in Puerto Rico for whom neither birthplace nor migration experience appeared to have any impact. In fact, only the very best command of English appeared to have any impact on this identity, and it is inversely related. The little variation in factors that may predict identifying as black in Puerto Rico also highlights the likelihood that this identity was highly influenced by both phenotype and an ideology that promotes acceptance or pride in blackness. In Puerto Rico, whitening as a practice and an ideology is pervasive. However, there is also evidence that among a non-trivial percentage of Puerto Ricans on the island there is a darkening process as well, whereby they will assume an identity that is darker than an observer may recognize (e.g. *trigueño* instead of white, or black instead of *trigueño*) (Vargas-Ramos 2005).

In Puerto Rico, whiteness prevails. It does so because the racial system encourages it in the midst of official and popular discourses that proclaim racial democracy and worthiness for all races, but concurrently encourages whitening. Not surprisingly, people born in Puerto Rico are more likely to latch on to this identity. This tendency to identify as white increases vastly when census instruments do not allow for locally meaningful categories that denote admixture (Berkowitz 2001; Vargas-Ramos 2005). Moreover, when these culturally grounded terms are not furnished in official documentation, people born on the island reject alternatives imposed on them by the US racial classification system that does allow for respondents to choose among multiple racial categories. Those people in Puerto Rico likely to use alternative forms of racial identification barring locally based terminology were those more grounded in the USA.

Conclusion

Puerto Rican migrants adapt to prevailing racial discourses, but do so on their own terms. They negotiate racial formations shaped by governmental policies they encounter at given points in time with understandings that they acquire and process along the way. Migrants bring with them perspectives from their country of origin, and are influenced by how their racial understandings coincide or differ from those in the county of settlement, and by their incorporation in a new settlement site. Those better grounded in the new social system are more likely to accept and adopt extant racial labels and concepts. Those less so grounded may resort to oppositional descriptors of racial identification. In the USA, these migrants have adopted forms of identity that often clash with extant understandings of race and racial identity in that country. Similarly, in Puerto Rico, evidence shows that sojourning in the USA also affects how migrants understand race once they return to their country of origin. Whether migrants accept or reject local understandings of racial identification also depends on whether these coincide with those understandings acquired or shaped during their sojourn and by their overall experience abroad – their life experience abroad matters.

Acknowledgements

I thank two anonymous referees for the valuable suggestions to earlier versions of this paper as well as Ana Y. Ramos-Zayas for her comments on a later version.

Notes

1.   Based on analysis of census data (Puerto Rico Community Survey 2006–2008, IPUMS), 94 per cent of Cubans in Puerto Rico identified as white, 3 per cent as black, 2 per cent as some other race, and 1 per cent with two or more races. Among Dominicans in Puerto Rico, 28 per cent identified as white, 35 per cent as black, 22 per cent as some other race, and 11 per cent with two or more races.

2.   *Trigueño, pardo* and *moreno* were often used either as euphemisms for or as alternatives to *mulato* or *negro*. The slave registry of 1872 contained more than 30 descriptors and adjectives to describe the skin colour of slaves, including *negro, mulato, moreno, pardo, trigueño* and *blanco*. (Negrón Portillo and Mayo Santana 2007). Terms such as *jabao* may not have been used in official documentation, but its use is recorded in the literary record as far as the middle of the nineteenth century (Álvarez Nazario 1974).

3.   In 2000, 80.5 per cent of the population identified as white, 8 per cent as black, 6.8 per cent as *other*, and 4 per cent as multiracial.

4.   Census data, for instance, do not include information on experience with racial discrimination in Puerto Rico and the USA; the race of most respondents' parents, unless they are children living in the parents' household; or length of sojourn in the USA for Puerto Rican return migrants residing on the island. All of these factors are likely to inform greatly a person's racial identity and identification.

5.   Most of these variables are categorical in nature. A dummy variable was created for each category. The omitted (reference) variables in the logistic equations in Tables 5 and 9 are: 'women', for Gender; 'did not attend school', for Educational Attainment; 'professional' for Occupation; 'out of the labour force', for Labour Force Participation; and 'not at all', for Speaks English.

6.   Results for these control variables are not presented in Tables 5 and 9, but are available from the author upon request.

7.   Data on the number of years persons born in Puerto Rico who resided in the USA but at the time of the survey resided in Puerto Rico are not available for analyses as they were not collected by the US Census Bureau in its American Community Survey or the Puerto Rico Community Survey.

References

ACOSTA-BELÉN, EDNA and SANTIAGO, CARLOS E. 2006 *Puerto Ricans in the United States: A Contemporary Portrait*, Boulder, CO: Lynne Reinner Publishers

ÁLVAREZ NAZARIO, MANUEL 1974 *El elemento afronegroide en el español de Puerto Rico: Contribución al estudio del negro en América*, San Juan: Instituto de Cultura Puertorriqueña

BERKOWITZ, SUSAN 2001 'Puerto Rico focus groups on the Census 2000 race and ethnicity questions, final report', *Census 2000 Evaluation* B.13 Washington, DC: US Census Bureau. Available from: http://www.census.gov/pred/www/rpts/B13.pdf [accessed 20 April 2012]

BLANCO, TOMÁS 1942 *El prejuicio racial en Puerto Rico*, San Juan: Biblioteca de Autores Puertorriqueños

DÁVILA, ARLENE M. 1997 *Sponsored Identities: Cultural Politics in Puerto Rico*, Philadelphia, PA: Temple University Press

DE GENOVA, NICOLAS and RAMOS-ZAYAS, ANA Y. 2003 *Latino Crossings: Mexicans, Puerto Ricans and the Politics of Race and Citizenship*, New York: Routledge

DEGLER, CARL 1971 *Neither Black nor White: Slavery and Race Relations in Brazil and the United States*, New York: Macmillan

DUANY, JORGE 2002 *The Puerto Rican Nation on the Move: Identities on the Island and in the United States*, Chapel Hill, NC: University of North Carolina Press

FREYRE, GILBERTO 1986 *The Masters and the Slaves*, Berkeley, CA: University of California Press

GODREAU, ISAR P. and VARGAS-RAMOS, CARLOS 2009 'Which box am I? Towards a culturally grounded, contextually meaningful method of ethnic and racial categorization in Puerto Rico', Cayey: Instituto de Investigaciones Interdisciplinarias, Universidad de Puerto Rico, Cuadernos de Investigación No. 8

GRAVLEE, CLARENCE C. 2005 'Ethnic classification in southeastern Puerto Rico: the cultural model of "color"', *Social Forces*, vol. 83, no. 3, pp. 949–70

HANDLIN, OSCAR 1959 *The Newcomers: Negroes and Puerto Ricans in a Changing Metropolis*, Cambridge: Harvard University Press

HOETINK, HARMANUS 1967 *The Two Variants in Caribbean Race Relations*, London: Oxford University Press

KINSBRUNER, JAY 1996 *Not of Pure Blood: The Free People of Color and Racial Prejudice in Nineteenth-Century Puerto Rico*, Durham, NC: Duke University Press

LABRADOR-RODRÍGUEZ, SONIA 1999 'Mulatos entre blancos: José Celso Barbosa y Antonio S. Pedreira. Lo fronterizo en Puerto Rico al cambio de siglo (1896–1937)', *Revista Iberoamericana*, vol. 65, no. 188–9, pp.713–31

LOVEMAN, MARA and MUNIZ, JERONIMO O. 2007 'How Puerto Rico became white: boundary dynamics and intercensus racial reclassification', *American Sociological Review*, vol. 72, no. 6, pp. 915–39

MARTÍNEZ-ECHAZÁBAL, LOURDES 1998 'Mestizaje and the discourse of national/cultural identity in Latin America, 1845–1959', *Latin American Perspectives*, vol. 25, no. 3, pp. 21–42

MILLS, C.WRIGHT, SENIOR, CLARENCE and GOLDSEN, ROSE K. 1967 *The Puerto Rican Journey: New York's Newest Migrants*, New York: Russell & Russell

MORALES CARRIÓN, ARTURO 1978 *Auge y decandencia de la trata negrera en Puerto Rico: 1820–1860*, San Juan: Centro de Estudios Avanzados de Puerto Rico y el Caribe, Instituto de Cultura Puertorriqueña
NEGRÓN PORTILLO, MARIANO and MAYO SANTANA, RAÚL 2007 *La esclavitud menor: La esclavitud en los municipios en el interior de Puerto Rico en el siglo XIX*, Río Piedras: Centro de Investigaciones Sociales, Universidad de Puerto Rico
NOBLES, MELISSA 2000 *Shades of Citizenship: Rance and the Census in Modern Politics*, Palo Alto, CA: Stanford University Press
OBOLER, SUZANNE 1995 *Ethnic Labels, Latino Lives: Identity and the Politics of (Re)presentation in the United States*, Minneapolis, MN: University of Minnesota Press
OMI, MICHAEL and WINANT, HOWARD 1986 *Racial Formation in the United States: From the 1960s to the 1980s*, New York: Routledge
PEDREIRA, ANTONIO S. 1973 *Insularismo*, Río Piedras: Editorial Edil
PÉREZ, GINA M 2004 *The Near Northwest Side Story: Migration, Displacement and Puerto Rican Families*, Berkeley, CA: University of California Press
PICÓ, FERNANDO 1988 *Historia general de Puerto Rico*, Río Piedras: Ediciones Huracán
RIVERA MARRERO, MILDRED 2011 '"Crece" la raza negra en el país', *El Nuevo Día*, 25 March. Available from: http://www.elnuevodia.com/crecelarazanegraenelpaís-923014. html [Accessed 23 March 2012] [in Spanish]
RIVERA-BATIZ, FRANCISCO L. and SANTIAGO, CARLOS E. 1996 *Island Paradox: Puerto Rico in the 1990s*, New York: Russell Sage Foundation
RODRIGUEZ, CLARA E. 2000 *Changing Race: Latinos, the Census and the History of Ethnicity in the United States*, New York: New York University Press
RUGGLES, STEVEN *et al.* 2010 *Integrated Public Use Microdata Series: Version 5.0*, Minneapolis, MN: University of Minnesota. Available from: http://usa.ipums.org/usa [Accessed 23 March 2012]
SCARANO, FRANCISCO A. 1993 *Puerto Rico: Cinco siglos de historia*, Bogotá: McGraw Hill Interamericana
SKIDMORE, THOMAS 1972 'Toward a comparative analysis of race relations since abolition in Brazil and the United States', *Journal of Latin American Studies*, vol. 4, no. 1, pp. 1–28
TELLES, EDWARD E. 2004 *Race in another America: The Significance of Skin Color in Brazil*, Princeton, NJ: Princeton University Press
THOMAS, LORRIN 2009 'Resisting the racial binary? Puerto Ricans' encounter with race in Depression-era New York City', *CENTRO Journal*, vol. 21, no. 1, pp. 5–35
TORRES, ARLENE 1998 'La gran familia puertorriqueña "ej prieta de beldá"' ['The great Puerto Rican family "is really really black"']', in Arlene Torres and N. E. Whitten (eds), *Blackness in Latin American and the Caribbean: Social Dynamics and Cultural Transformation*, Vol. II, Bloomington, IN: Indiana University Press, pp. 285–306
US CENSUS BUREAU 2011 *2010 Census National Summary File of Redistricting Data*. Retrieved from: http://factfinder2.census.gov/faces/nav/jsf/pages/index.xhtml [Accessed 23 March 2012]
VARGAS-RAMOS, CARLOS 2005 'Black, trigueño, white...?: Shifting racial identification among Puerto Ricans', *Du Bois Review: Social Science Research on Race*, vol. 2, no. 2, pp. 267–85
—————— 2008 'Migration and settlement patterns in Puerto Rico: 1985–2005', *Centro Policy Report*, vol. 2, no. 1, pp. 1–24
WADE, PETER 1997 *Race and Ethnicity in Latin America, Sterling*, VA: Pluto Press
WINANT, HOWARD 1992 'Rethinking race in Brazil', *Journal of Latin American Studies*, vol. 24, no. 1, pp. 173–92
ZENTELLA, ANA C. 1997 *Growing up Bilingual: Puerto Rican Children in New York*, Malden, MA: Blackwell Publishers

'I'm American, not Japanese!': the struggle for racial citizenship among later-generation Japanese Americans

Takeyuki Tsuda

Abstract

As one of the oldest Asian American groups in the USA, most Japanese Americans are of the third and fourth generations and have become well integrated in mainstream American society. However, they are still racialized as foreigners simply because of their Asian appearance. Their Asian phenotype continues to have a foreigner connotation because of large-scale immigration from Asia and an American national identity that is racially defined as white. This paper analyses how later-generation Japanese Americans are racialized as outsiders in their daily interaction with mainstream Americans, which is often accompanied by essentialized assumptions that they are also culturally foreign. In response, they engage in everyday struggles for racial citizenship by demanding inclusion in the national community as Americans despite their racial differences. It is uncertain whether such attempts to contest their racialization will cause current mono-racial notions of American identity to be reconsidered in more inclusive and multiracial ways.

Introduction

Japanese Americans are one of the oldest Asian American groups in the USA. Although most Asian Americans are primarily the product of the mass immigration of Asians to the USA after 1965, much of Japanese immigration occurred between the 1880s and 1924, when the USA prohibited further Asian immigration until after the Second World War. The descendants of this earlier wave of Japanese immigrants are now of the third and fourth generations (*Sansei* and *Yonsei*). The population of elderly second-generation *Nisei*, who were interned in concentration camps during the Second World War, has dwindled. Japanese immigration to the USA after the Second World War initially consisted of war-brides followed by businessmen, professionals and students. Their second-generation Japanese American descendants, called *shin-Nisei* or 'new *Nisei*', did not experience the internment and intense racial discrimination and grew up in an era of multiculturalism. As a result, they tend to be bilingual and maintain transnational social connections to their ethnic homeland.

Most Japanese Americans today are of the third and fourth generations, with a smaller population of second-generation descendants. Less than a quarter of the Japanese-descent community in the USA currently consists of first-generation immigrants (*Issei*) from Japan (Akiba 2006, pp. 159–60). In contrast, other Asian American communities are still primarily of the first and second generations, with immigrants outnumbering the American-born generations.

Japanese Americans have become socio-economically and culturally well integrated in mainstream American society with each successive generation. Because of their upward social mobility, they currently have higher educational levels on average than whites and a majority of them have become successful middle-class white-collar workers, professionals or business owners (Akiba 2006, pp. 163, 165). The cultural assimilation of later-generation Japanese Americans is also quite advanced because most of them are generations removed from their ancestral homeland of Japan and are born and raised in predominantly white, suburban communities (Akiba 2006, pp. 163, 165). In general, they cannot speak Japanese nor have retained any notable Japanese cultural customs, and most have lost their ancestral ties to Japan (see also Spickard 1996, pp. 145–7, 159; Tuan 2001, p. 106).[1]

Nonetheless, Japanese Americans continue to be racialized as perpetual foreigners simply because of their Asian appearance, an experience common among other Asian American groups (e.g. see Tuan 2001; Park 2005, pp. 6–8; Kim 2008, pp. 4–5, ch. 8). Unlike white ethnics of Southern and Eastern European descent, who disappeared into the majority white population and became ethnically unmarked Americans (Jacobson 1999; Roediger 2005), upward socio-economic mobility and cultural assimilation among Japanese Americans has not guaranteed them full acceptance as Americans for two reasons. Because of a US national ideology that equates Americanness with being white, racial minorities are more likely to be seen as foreign, or not really American. In addition, almost 70 per cent of Asian descendants in the USA are foreign-born (Min 2006, pp. 42–3). As a result, those with an Asian racial phenotype are often assumed to be immigrant foreigners (Tuan 2001, pp. 38–9). Although only a small minority of the Japanese descent community actually consists of immigrants, the 'Asian as immigrant' image is indiscriminately applied to them because of the tendency of mainstream Americans to view Asian Americans as a homogeneous ethnic group instead of recognizing internal differences within this panethnic community (see also Tuan 2001, pp. 21–2; Kibria 2002, pp. 70–5; Kim 2008, p. 210). The status of Asian Americans as non-white racial minorities is therefore fundamentally different from African Americans and Native Americans. Although the latter continue to experience socio-economic marginalization and serious discrimination and are positioned lower on the racial hierarchy than Asian Americans, they are not regarded as foreign because they have been in the USA for a much longer period of time.

It may not be that surprising that second-generation Asian Americans are often treated as racialized outsiders. However, the fact that third- and fourth-generation Japanese Americans continue to be subject to such exclusionary practices indicates that in many ways, their racial appearance is a much more socially visible marker than their social integration and cultural assimilation as Americans. In fact, other racial minorities of relatively recent immigrant origin seem to have similar experiences, such as South Asian Americans and to a lesser degree, Arab Americans (Purkayastha 2005; Naber 2008). Likewise, later-generation Mexican Americans (especially those who do not look white) are often mistaken as immigrant foreigners because of continued large-scale immigration from Mexico (Rosaldo 1994; Jiménez 2010, pp. 138–178). Later-generation Asian minorities in other countries are also marked as foreign, including Japanese descendants in Latin America (e.g. see Tsuda 2003, pp. 58–65).

This paper will examine the various ways in which later-generation Japanese Americans are racialized as perpetual foreigners in their daily interaction with mainstream Americans and how this leads to essentialized assumptions that they are also culturally foreign. In response, they contest their racialization in various ways in an attempt to change such hegemonic ethnic perceptions, although the effectiveness of such efforts is not always clear. The denial of their American-ness by virtue of their race ultimately brings their status as Americans citizens into doubt, making their daily lives a struggle for racial inclusion, or what I call 'racial citizenship'.

This paper is based on one and a half years of fieldwork and participant observation with Japanese American communities in San Diego and Phoenix between 2006 and 2009. I conducted fifty-five in-depth interviews with Japanese Americans of the second to fourth generations of all age groups. Initial contacts were made with Japanese American community organizations, but through snowball sampling, I also interviewed those who did not participate in these organizations. I also conducted extensive participant observation by attending meetings and events in the Japanese American community and socialized with various Japanese Americans on many occasions.

Racial citizenship and rights

The continued racial marginalization of later-generation Japanese Americans as immigrant foreigners indicates that despite their socio-economic and cultural incorporation into American society, they are still not considered full citizens by mainstream Americans. Citizenship is based on membership in social and national communities that leads to the conferral of basic rights to individuals and to groups. Although it is often associated with liberal universalism and equality, citizenship is based on an inherent tension between inclusion and exclusion (e.g. Joppke 1999, p. 660; Bloemraad, Korteweg and Yurdakul 2008), since definitions of who is a legitimate member of the nation (and deserving of rights) involves the marginalization and exclusion of those who do not belong to the national community.

Although American-born ethnic minorities have secured legal citizenship and civil rights in the USA through the country's *jus soli* nationality laws, where citizenship is granted by place of birth, this does not always guarantee them full social membership in the national community and access to equal social rights, or what can be called 'social citizenship' (Park 2005: p. 2–4; Kim 2008, p. 14). Since social citizenship is based on the socio-economic, cultural and racial criteria necessary for national belonging and membership, those who do not meet such criteria can therefore be excluded. For instance, the socio-economically dispossessed are not always granted full social rights in contrast to those who have attained upward economic mobility and better integration into mainstream society. Likewise, ethnic minorities are often socially excluded and marginalized from the national community because of their cultural and racial differences, leading to the denial of some basic social rights. Therefore, both social class and ethnic inequalities can become barriers to social citizenship. Although the classic work on social citizenship by T. H. Marshall focused on its social class aspects by examining the eventual expansion of social welfare rights to the British working class (1950), he did not consider the cultural and racial dimensions of social citizenship (Bloemraad, Korteweg and Yurdakul 2008, p. 157).

For ethnic minorities of immigrant origin, social citizenship and belonging in the national community often requires the adoption of what is considered the majority or dominant national culture (see Castles and Davidson 2000, p. 124). Such cultural membership in the nation can be acquired through cultural assimilation or externally imposed, for instance through what Ong (1996) calls 'cultural citizenship', the production of cultural beliefs and practices necessary for national belonging through the normative disciplinary forces of state and civil institutions that produce consenting subjects.[2] However, some form of assimilation is not the only pathway to cultural inclusion in the nation state. Marginalized ethnic minorities can also claim cultural citizenship by demanding recognition as legitimate members of the national community who deserve basic social rights despite their cultural differences from mainstream society (Rosaldo 1994; Flores 1997, p. 262). The possibilities of such cultural citizenship for ethnic minorities have become greater in countries like the USA that have adopted a multicultural ideology that allows cultural minorities to be accepted as social citizens without full cultural assimilation.

In contrast to social class and culture, race has not been seriously considered in theories of social citizenship as another factor that can determine who is included and excluded from the national community. National belonging is not only defined by socio-economic integration and cultural characteristics but also by race. Although some societies have multiracial conceptions of nationhood, others have more mono-racial notions of national membership. As a result, those who do not fit the dominant racial category are often not considered part of the nation and can be racially marginalized and deprived of fundamental social rights. However, unlike the social class and cultural dimensions of social citizenship, which allow ethnic minorities to strive for greater national inclusion through socio-economic mobility and cultural assimilation, the racial barriers to social citizenship are more difficult to overcome because of their apparently primordial nature.

Therefore, ethnic minorities who are marginalized on the basis of race must claim 'racial citizenship' by demanding inclusion in the national community and equal access to social rights despite their racial differences. In this sense, racial citizenship involves a type of claims-making like cultural citizenship and can involve collective mobilization and activism but is also a part of the daily struggle among minorities for racial belonging and social justice. If such struggles are successful, they can cause dominant notions of citizenship to be reconsidered in more inclusive and multiracial ways, leading to the conferral of equal social rights to racial minorities as full members of the nation.

Although Rosaldo (1994, p. 57) included race in his definition of cultural citizenship, others defined the concept mainly in cultural terms (Kymlicka 1995; Flores 1997). I argue that it is useful to keep the distinction between cultural and racial citizenship since not all ethnic minorities are defined and excluded from the national community by *both* cultural and racial differences. This is especially true for culturally Americanized later-generation ethnic minorities for whom only racial difference and not cultural difference prevents them from being accepted as real Americans. In other words, their struggle is for racial citizenship, and not cultural citizenship per se.

The relatively high rates of socio-economic success and cultural assimilation among later-generation Japanese Americans indicate that they have met the socio-economic and cultural criteria for social citizenship and national belonging. However, because American national identity continues to be racially defined as white, they lack the racial attributes necessary to be fully recognized as Americans and are often seen as foreigners. As one of my Japanese American interviewees succinctly put it: 'We have never been really accepted as American because we're not white. If you're not white, you're a foreigner.'

Japanese Americans as racialized foreigners

Most of the later-generation Japanese Americans I interviewed continued to be racialized as non-citizen outsiders, especially by those who were not acquainted with them personally. Their lack of racial citizenship and belonging is most often manifested by the ubiquitous question 'Where are you from?', which is sometimes asked when they encounter strangers or meet people for the first time. When the desired answer is not forthcoming, the follow-up question is often 'Where are you *really* (or originally) from?' (see also Kitano 1993, p. 5; Tuan 2001, pp. 141–2). Other variants are: 'Where were you born?'; 'How long have you lived in the USA?'; 'When did you come over [to the USA]?'

Such questions continued to be directed not only at second-generation Japanese Americans, but those of the third and fourth generations as well, solely on the basis of their physical appearance. In fact, Sherry Okamoto, a fourth-generation *Yonsei*, initially had trouble understanding the meaning behind such questions:

When I was asked where I was from at some cocktail party, I couldn't understand what people were getting at. So I thought maybe they wanted to know where I was raised, so I'd say "Los Angeles". Then, when they asked "No, where are you originally from?" I thought maybe I was being asked where I was born, so I'd say "Seattle". Recently, it finally began to dawn on me that maybe they thought I was from some Asian country because of the way I look. When I realized this, it really bothered me! I was like, my family has been here in the United States longer than many whites. Why do I continue to be seen as some kind of foreigner?

In this manner, Japanese Americans have come to realize that such questions are often based on mistaken assumptions that they are foreign nationals and not American citizens.

Even when Japanese Americans are not directly mistaken as non-citizen foreigners, mainstream Americans sometimes remain curious about their immigrant origins or ethnicity. In this regard, informants I interviewed were also asked 'What are you?' or 'Are you Chinese?', 'Are you Japanese?' and even 'Are you American?' Others were asked 'Where were your parents born (or where are they from)?'

In addition to these types of persistent questions, my interviewees gave other examples of how they were racialized by strangers as non-American foreigners simply because of the way they look. Dan Matsushita, who used to be part of the US volleyball team, recounted such an incident in Indianapolis:

> We were on tour and playing the Chinese national team. We were leaving the hotel and getting on the bus to play our match. When I walked up to the bus with my American teammates, the bus driver said, "The Chinese bus is over there." It was really surprising because I was wearing the American team jersey like the rest of my teammates!

Therefore, even when Japanese Americans display overt symbols of their Americanness, their foreign racial appearance can often have a greater impact on how they are ethnically perceived.

Likewise, Shannon Suyama, a third-generation *Sansei* who recently married a Caucasian man from New Zealand, told me that people always assume that her husband is the American, despite his accent, and that she is the immigrant, despite her lack of an accent. This was especially apparent when they both went to the local US Citizenship and Immigration Services (USCIS) office to fill out his immigration papers:

> So we go up to the window, [my husband] hands the form over to the man behind the glass, and he looks at it and says, "Oh, she left something blank. You need to talk to her..." He was speaking to my husband and saying, "What is her current address in the U.S.?" or something like that. And it became very apparent to me that he thought *I* was the immigrant filling out the form and my husband was the American who was helping me!

Therefore, although later-generation Japanese Americans are cultu-rally assimilated, they continue to be marked as foreign by their racial appearance. In fact, their unaccented English does not always guarantee that they will be regarded as real Americans. As is the case with other Asian Americans, a significant number of informants in my sample were told 'You speak English so well', or asked, 'Where did you learn to speak English so well?' In other words, it seems that some mainstream Americans still have difficulty reconciling someone with an Asian face speaking English like a native. Instead of concluding that such individuals must be Americans, the assumption sometimes seems to be that they are foreign nationals who learned to speak English surprisingly well. Again, race seems to matter more than cultural assimilation in the definition of who is American and who is not.

There are other cases when Japanese Americans are assumed to be foreign despite their cultural Americanization. A couple of interviewees reported instances when people wondered whether they celebrate American holidays. One third-generation Japanese American was asked by a woman at a Christmas party: 'Do they play Christmas carols in your country?' In this case, her husband interjected by saying: 'Honey, I think this *is* his country!' Likewise, another Japanese American recounted an experience at a grocery store during Thanksgiving:

> So I go up to the counter with a can of cranberry sauce and the clerk says, "Oh, I didn't know you people celebrated Thanksgiving!" Although I didn't bother to correct her, I was like, what do you mean "you people"? First of all, I'm American, and second of all, do you think Japanese Americans eat sushi for Thanksgiving? We eat turkey, just like other Americans!

Because of the tendency to conflate race and culture, those of Japanese phenotype or descent are naturally assumed to be culturally Japanese, even if they were born and raised in the USA. 'Japan is about as foreign of a country for me as Zimbabwe,' one *Sansei* remarked. 'But people continue to think I'm not truly Americanized yet and that somehow, I can't leave my culture behind, that I have some innate connection to Japan.' As a result, Japanese Americans are often expected to be familiar with the Japanese language and culture (Tuan 2001, pp. 78–9) or have a natural affinity with Japan. My interviewees reported numerous instances of strangers using Japanese words when interacting with them such as *konnichiwa* (hello), *domo arigato* (thank you) and *sayonara* (goodbye). Others simply assume Japanese Americans know a lot about Japan and ask them about the country or its culture or talk about prior experiences in Japan. Such treatment occurred especially in stores, restaurants and other businesses or agencies when their Japanese last names were revealed on their credit cards or documents.

Although such treatment of Japanese Americans as racialized outsiders is generally limited to first-time encounters with strangers, for some, it is persistent, whereas for others, it is less frequent. Nonetheless, relatively few Japanese Americans said that they are *not* racialized as foreigners or that it happened only a few times in the past, such as when they visited other parts of the USA where there are few Asian Americans.

In general, however, it is apparent that most Japanese Americans cannot escape their racial essentialization as foreigners despite their cultural assimilation and socio-economic integration into mainstream American society. Although they have become incorporated into the USA as cultural citizens, they are still not regarded as racial citizens simply because they lack the physical features needed to belong to the American nation. Therefore, despite being in the USA for many generations, they are still not seen as real Americans, demonstrating the power of race to define who is included in the national community as a social citizen and who is excluded. Of course, few white Americans would be asked questions about their foreign origins or be mistaken as non-American. 'It is pretty bothersome because I know with white Americans, they don't have to feel the pressure of being stereotyped even before you get to interact with someone,' Sherry Okamoto lamented.

Claiming racial citizenship: Japanese American reactions to racialization

When Japanese Americans find their status as Americans questioned because of their racial differences, they are forced to engage in everyday struggles to claim their racial citizenship by demonstrating that despite their apparently foreign appearance, they are American citizens by birthright and culture. However, the effectiveness of such Japanese American reactions to their racialization varies, and their ability to eventually expand dominant notions of American racial membership to include non-white ethnic minorities remains uncertain.

A majority of the Japanese Americans I interviewed were not that bothered by their racialization as foreigners and the constant questions they were asked about their supposed immigrant origins. They tended to explain such questions as a result of ignorance, confusion, simple curiosity or as inevitable because of the way they look, and did not take them personally or become offended and angry. However, a minority said they were bothered and really disliked such treatment, although most did not respond aggressively. In general, I found that the *shin-Nisei* are less bothered by the mistaken assumption that they are foreigners since their parents are from Japan and they are indeed more closely tied to their ethnic homeland and cultural heritage. In contrast, third- and fourth-generation Japanese Americans generally reacted more negatively to their foreignization, perhaps because of the absurdity of having to defend their Americanness when their family has been in the USA for generations. One *Sansei* described her reaction as follows:

> I got really tired of people coming up to me all the time and looking at me, and then asking "What are you?" I HATED that! And I knew exactly what they were asking. So when I got to college, I started to ask people, "What do you mean what am I? What are you asking?" And they said, "What's your nationality?" And so I gave them a hard time about that because it just bothered me that people didn't see me as American after three generations!

In this manner, although Japanese Americans realize that the 'What are you?' or 'Where are you from?' questions are about their assumed foreign origins, they somewhat defiantly refuse to give the answer that people are seeking. For instance, when asked 'Where are you from?', many of them simply state their city of residence or birth. 'I know what they are asking, but I don't give them what they want', Mike Oshima explained. 'When they ask this, I say "I'm from San Diego." Then they say, "No, where are you really from?," and I say, "I'm *really* from San Diego." The conversation more or less ends there!' By refusing to reveal their ethnic background, Japanese Americans are able to exercise their agency in a subtle way and actively subvert the implicit racism involved in such questions. Such evasive responses shift the power dynamic in their favour by preventing the interrogator from automatically excluding them as the racialized other, allowing them to insist on their racial citizenship as Americans.

Although this type of response is common among Asian Americans in general (e.g. see Tuan 2001, pp. 141–2; Kibria 2002, pp. 81–3), such implicit demands that their American citizenship be recognized may not always have the intended effect or actually change dominant perceptions of them as immigrant foreigners. For instance, when Japanese Americans state that they are from an American city, they can still be perceived as Asian immigrants who have been living in that city for a while. For instance, consider the following conversation I overheard at the San Diego airport between two white women:

Woman 1: So you ask these people where they are from and they say something like "San Francisco" and I'm like, that's not what I'm asking you, I want to know your country of origin. But they don't answer because maybe they are sick of answering this question. I don't know why they are like that.

Woman 2: Yeah, I know, it's strange. I don't know why they don't want to say where they're from. Asian countries are respected these days, so they shouldn't be embarrassed about it or anything.

Apparently, it had not occurred to these women that the apparent refusal of Asian Americans to 'properly' answer the 'Where are you from?' question is an attempt to assert their Americanness, not a wish to hide their Asian origins. Instead of realizing that 'these people' are real Americans because they are from the USA, they seemed to continue to conflate Asian Americans with Asian foreign nationals.

When this line of questioning is pursued further through follow-up questions, such as 'Where are you really (or) originally from?', Japanese Americans often engage in what Tuan (2001, pp. 141–2) calls an 'ethnic game' and continue to refuse to reveal their ethnic origins so that they cannot be racially categorized as foreign. A good example was given by Barbara Kitamura, a *Yonsei*:

> I was at this BBQ where I was the only Asian person, and someone comes up to me and asks, "Where are you from?" I said "Phoenix." Then she asks, "No, where are you originally from?" I said "I was born in Chicago." But then she asks, "Where are your parents from?" I said, "They were born in Seattle." "And what about your grandparents?" "They were born in California."

Again, Barbara's refusal to give the desired answer allows her to actively avoid the racialized exclusion implicit in such questions, thereby claiming her status as a native of the USA despite her apparently foreign phenotype.

When questioned about their supposed immigrant origins, some of my interviewees simply stated that they are Japanese Americans born in the USA. Others used the term, 'Americans of Japanese descent (or) ancestry.' However, a few informants cited examples where they continued to be treated as Japanese even after they clarified their status as Japanese Americans. 'Most Caucasians don't want to hear the "Japanese *American*" part,' one *Sansei* woman observed. 'They just want to hear the "Japanese" part.' For instance, Matt Honkawa gave an example of such treatment:

> So I go to this local Subway, the owner sees my name [on his credit card] and he starts with the whole "Oh, are you Japanese? *Konnichiwa*! *Genki desu ka*?" Then he starts saying he was in Japan, he really liked it, he has a good friend from Japan. I made it clear to this guy that I'm Japanese *American*, I was born here. But it doesn't seem to register in his head that I have nothing to do with the Japanese, and he keeps up the *"domo arigato, sayonara"* thing every time I go there and sometimes talks about Japan. It makes me feel uncomfortable, so I just stopped going there.

In this sense, instead of calling themselves 'Japanese American', some of my interviewees found it more effective to claim racial citizenship by simply insisting that they are 'Americans'. For example, according to Carol Hashimoto:

> I always say "I'm American." I never put "Japanese" in front of it. When people ask me, "Are you Chinese or Japanese?" I say "I'm American." I am really adamant about that. And when someone asks, "What are you?" I say, "I'm American."

Other later-generation Japanese Americans claim racial citizenship by demonstrating that they are culturally Americanized although they look Asian. As Kibria (2002, pp. 84–7) notes, Asian Americans attempt to neutralize or deflect assumptions of their foreignness by deploying cultural symbols of their Americanness such as language, dress and demeanour. For instance, Doug Ishimura, a *Sansei* living in Los Angeles, makes an effort to display his Americanness to counter the foreigner treatment he sometimes receives:

> When someone says, "Wow! You speak English so well!" it is quite jarring. So I think the way for me to approach people is to come off as more American than anything else. So, for instance, when I meet someone, I'll go "Hey! What's up!" That way, they won't say "Oh, are you from Japan?" because I'm more like them than not like them. So sometimes, I try to be more American than necessary.

Nonetheless, the perception of Japanese Americans as culturally Japanese sometimes continues to persist among acquaintances who know that they are Americans born in the USA. Therefore, they sometimes face continued pressure to be recognized as culturally American after initial greetings and introductions. According to Carol Hashimoto:

> When people ask me where I'm from, I always clear it up by saying I was born here and am a third-generation Japanese American. But I think they still can't get away from the "she's Japanese" notion. So in such cases, I try to speak a lot more [to show she doesn't have a foreign accent] and I just try to show that I'm very American. I make sure I don't mention things like Japan, sushi, or even my Toyota!

Some later-generation Japanese Americans contest their racial marginalization as non-American citizens more forcefully. When they are mistaken as Japanese immigrant foreigners or assumed to be culturally Japanese, not only do they correct the error, they use the occasion to 'educate' those who are apparently ignorant or misinformed. One

Yonsei described his reaction when someone approaches him and speaks Japanese: 'I say, "Well, if you want to practice your Japanese with someone, that is fine. But I am a fourth-generation American and don't speak the language. My parents did not speak Japanese either. Neither did my grandparents."' A few even strike back against their racial essentialization as foreigners, at the risk of being a bit rude. For instance, Bob Nakamura spoke about his *Sansei* daughter:

> My daughter, Wendy, teaches public speaking at a local community college and her students are always amazed they have this Asian teacher and say, "God Wendy, you speak English so well!" She responds by saying, "My family has been in the U.S. for three generations. That's why I speak it better than you!"

According to, Don Kushimura, another *Sansei*:

> The stuff you deal with every day when people say, "Where are you from?" I never took that very well when I was younger. I was more militant about it. I would get angry and say, "What do you mean?" And I'd lecture them about Japanese Americans, how we've been here since the late nineteenth century. Or I'd say, "So what's your name?" And then they'll tell me and I'd say, "Oh, is that Germanic?" And they'd say, "What?" and I'd say, "Well, since you were checking my ethnic background, I'm checking yours."

Like other Japanese Americans, Don asserts his agency by turning this type of racialized questioning against interrogators in order to demonstrate that he is just as American as they are.

Among my Japanese American interviewees, Bob Nakamura, the former president of a local Japanese American historical society, was probably the most effective in demanding his racial inclusion as an American. He described to me how he used invitations to speak at local San Diego high schools about his internment experiences during the Second World War as an opportunity to challenge students' racialized assumptions:

> There are still some of them that look at me like I'm not American. I spoke to a class a year ago, and afterwards, a couple of the students came up and said, "Mr. Nakamura, when you first came in, we thought you were Japanese. But you're more American than anyone I've seen!" I got my message across, I think! So when I speak at these high schools, I ask them: "What's an American supposed to look like? Tell me, what's an American supposed to look like? An American is what is in your head and your heart, not what you look

like or the color of your skin. Look around you, there are other types of Americans than just white ones." And they finally get it.

In contrast, a minority of the informants I interviewed responded to their racialization as 'Japanese' in ambiguous ways or chose not to actively contest their foreignization and demand racial citizenship as Americans. Some of them were young *shin-Nisei*, who felt more connected to Japan and their cultural heritage and were not as bothered or that conscious about being conflated with Japanese nationals. One *shin-Nisei* who spoke Japanese fluently actually told me that when someone speaks to her in Japanese, she actually responds in Japanese. 'If the person wants to practice some Japanese with me, I'm willing to oblige,' she said. Other informants (including a few who were later-generation) mentioned that they respond to questions about their immigrant origins or ethnicity by actually saying they are 'Japanese'. In other words, such individuals did not interpret such questions as a threat or affront to their status as Americans, but as a simple query about their ethnic background. 'I know they just want to know my heritage, so I just say "Japanese",' one of them explained. 'I guess I'm taking it for granted that they know I'm American so I'm just clarifying my ethnicity.' However, such responses may exacerbate the tendency to confuse Japanese Americans (including those of the later generations) with Japanese from Japan.

A few of my interviewees did not insist on their Americanness when they were clearly mistaken as Japanese foreigners because they figured it was not worth the hassle, especially in public, thus essentially forgoing their right to claim racial citizenship. This was the case with Sherry Okamoto, who is fourth generation:

> For instance, when I go to a store like Borders to buy something and the cashier looks at my name on my credit card and says, "Oh, *Okamoto*. You're from Japan! You guys have all that cool anime!" I mean, I don't even know how to react because the likelihood I'll ever see them again is very low. And there are people behind me in line, so I can't sit there and say, "No, I'm not Japanese" and go through the whole explanation. Even if I'm in a situation where I can talk about this, I feel that people don't want to hear me make a big fuss about it.

It is also important to note that the racialization of Japanese Americans as foreign was mostly limited to initial encounters with strangers and was often cleared up once they corrected such mistaken assumptions. Although their cultural essentialization as 'Japanese' may persist into later interactions, most Japanese Americans felt that those who eventually became close acquaintances and friends accepted them as American and did not treat them otherwise. According to Carol Hashimoto:

> When I meet someone or join a group or something and people initially think I'm an Asian foreigner, it gets cleared up quickly when I tell them I'm American and my family has been here for three generations. I think once people get to know me after a half hour or hour, it's fine and I feel accepted.

Likewise, Bob Nakamura acknowledged: 'Once people get to know us, they accept us as American. It's mainly the people that don't know me who look at me like I'm a foreigner.'

This is an indication that as more mainstream Americans interact with and befriend culturally Americanized, later-generation Japanese Americans and Asian Americans, they will gradually be accepted into the national community as full social citizens and Americans. However, since only a relatively small number of mainstream Americans currently have friends and close acquaintances who are later-generation Asian Americans, their racial foreignization will continue to persist. As a result, Japanese Americans must continue to struggle in their daily lives to be recognized as Americans despite their racial differences.

Conclusion: from racialized foreigners to Americans?

It is apparent that ethnic minorities can be denied full social citizenship and national belonging not only on grounds of cultural difference, but racial difference as well. Because Japanese Americans have been in the USA for generations and are well integrated in mainstream society, they wish to be seen and treated like other Americans instead of being forever tied to their Asian immigrant origins. However, large-scale immigration from Asia continues to give their racial phenotype a foreigner connotation, especially in a country where national membership as real Americans is often limited to those who look white. As a result, many Japanese Americans are racially essentialized as perpetual foreigners simply on the basis of their different Asian appearance and are excluded from the national community. Upon meeting people for the first time, even later-generation Japanese Americans are often asked a barrage of questions about their presumed immigrant origins.

Therefore, in contrast to white Americans, Japanese Americans must continue to endure the burden of race on a daily basis and must demand racial inclusion as Americans despite their status as a non-white minority. This ranges from refusing to answer questions about their foreign origins, clarifying their status as later-generation Americans, attempting to correct ethnic misconceptions, culturally demonstrating their Americanization, and educating other Americans about Japanese Americans. However, their struggles for racial citizenship and national belonging are uneven as some contest their racial marginalization more effectively, while others do so in more ambiguous ways with uncertain outcomes or decide to relinquish such efforts altogether. In fact, the power of race to exclude later-generation racial minorities as non-citizens is so strong that even when Japanese Americans challenge their racialization, they sometimes cannot fully shake the dominant perception that they are still essentially 'Japanese' and perpetually foreign.

What is at stake in such struggles for racial citizenship is not simply the right to be recognized as American. Because Japanese Americans are racially perceived as not truly belonging to the American nation, such denial of full social citizenship also indicates that they may be deprived of certain fundamental social rights as well, such as freedom from racial and ethnic discrimination (see Castles and Davidson 2000, pp. 105–6, 110). Although the amount of racial discrimination they experience has declined in recent decades, most Japanese Americans continue to report occasional instances of informal discriminatory behaviour in their daily lives. This includes racial slurs, derogatory remarks (such as about Pearl Harbor or the Second World War), harassment and ridicule when they were children, resentment for their economic success, and poor service at restaurants, stores or offices when they are the only Asian customers. Others report how they have been associated with negative images of Japan and Japanese ethnic stereotypes, or have been told in anger to go back to where they came from. However, I was also struck by the significant number of Japanese Americans who suspected they were subject to more formal employment discrimination when applying for jobs or promotions at work in the past and felt that they face a glass ceiling which prevents them from advancing to top management and administrative positions. Such persisting discrimination solely on the basis of race indicates that racial citizenship involves the demand not only for national belonging but also for equal social rights as Americans.

The USA has come to terms with its multicultural diversity as an integral part of its national identity, enabling culturally different ethnic minorities to claim membership in the nation and access to equal rights to a certain extent (that is, cultural citizenship). However, the country has yet to become a fully multi*racial* nation that accepts racially different, non-white minorities of immigrant origin as true Americans. In fact, because American national identity continues to be defined mono-racially as white, even when ethnic minorities become culturally assimilated over the generations, they can continue to be excluded as not American on the basis of racial difference. Although later-generation Japanese Americans speak fluent and unaccented

English and behave in Americanized ways, this has not been sufficient for them to be considered real American citizens and guaranteed full social rights, especially in parts of the USA where the population of Asian Americans is small. Because of the immediate social visibility of race, it remains the primary way that identities are initially judged and often overrides cultural markers of citizenship in determining who belongs to the American nation.

Will Asian Americans achieve racial citizenship by eventually becoming 'white' (or at least, honorary whites)? It is clear that the racial category of white is more a marker of social privilege and status than a purely biological phenotype (Zhou 2004, p. 30). Therefore, although Southern and Eastern European immigrants during the nineteenth century were initially seen as racially distinct and inferior,[3] their descendants were eventually incorporated into the majority white population through cultural assimilation and socio-economic mobility (Jacobson 1999; Roediger 2005). However, this was ultimately possible because of their phenotypic similarity to the dominant Anglo American population (Waters 1990, p. 2). In contrast, Asian Americans will continue to be racialized as non-white and foreign because of their greater perceived differences in physical appearance from white Americans.[4] As a result, their cultural Americanization and upward mobility will not lead to their eventual acceptance as 'white' and therefore as fully American (see Zhou 2004, p. 35; Kim 2007).

Therefore, in order for racial minorities like Asian Americans who are destined to be non-white to successfully become legitimate members of the nation, currently mono-racial and restrictive notions of Americanness must be replaced by more inclusive and multiracial conceptions of national belonging. Will Japanese Americans and other later-generation Asian Americans be able to eventually expand American national identity in ways that more fully accommodate racial difference? Since large-scale immigration from Asia will not decrease for the foreseeable future, an Asian phenotype will continue to be perceived as foreign. However, the population of later-generation Asian Americans will also continue to grow and eventually outnumber Asian immigrants in the USA, as happened for Japanese Americans decades ago. As Americans increasingly interact with a growing number of US-born, later-generation Asian Americans, they will become more accustomed to encountering people who look Asian but are fully Americanized, especially if Asian Americans continue to demand racial citizenship as true Americans. As a result, those with an Asian appearance may no longer be automatically associated with immigrant foreigners in the future and become more recognized as part of a multiracial American nation. Asian Americans may therefore eventually come to somewhat resemble African Americans, who comprise a racial minority but are regarded as Americans because of their long history in the USA.

In fact, in states such as California, where the population of Asian Americans is already high, there are already indications that their racialization as foreigners is somewhat abating. Some of my Japanese American interviewees in San Diego noted that they are mistaken less often as immigrant foreigners in California and that such treatment is more frequent in other parts of the USA where there are fewer Asian Americans. For instance, a *Sansei* in San Diego remarked:

> Japanese Americans have been very much accepted as part of the society here. People out here have met a lot of Asian Americans, so they kind of have that category for us. It's only out East or in the Midwest where people aren't used to us and don't understand who we are.

In fact, almost all of the relatively small number of Japanese Americans in my sample who claimed they were not regarded as foreigners lived in San Diego or southern California. In general, my interviewees in Phoenix (with a much smaller Asian American population) tended to report more instances of racialized exclusion. In addition, several informants noted that such treatment used to be more prevalent in the past. In contrast, younger Americans are becoming more aware of the growing population of Asian descendants in the USA who have become Americanized and therefore no longer automatically associate them with foreign immigrants. This may be the first step towards a more multiracial American nation where race is less of an obstacle to national inclusion for later-generation Asian Americans, or at least where culture, instead of race, is used to judge who belongs to the nation as a social citizen.

Notes

1. The only exception is the small number of post-war *shin-Nisei* who have retained the Japanese language and remain actively engaged in Japan.
2. It seems that this does not always produce culturally assimilated subjects since the dual process of self-making and being made involves both a subject that submits to power relations but also contests and resists them.
3. They were seen as shorter with darker complexions and distinct facial features and hair colour compared to Anglo Americans (Jacobson 1999, pp. 39–90).
4. Even the Japanese Americans of mixed racial descent whom I interviewed felt that they were perceived as racially different and were not considered white.

References

AKIBA, DAISUKE 2006 'Japanese Americans', in Pyong Gap Min (ed.), *Asian Americans: Contemporary Trends and Issues*, 2nd edn, Thousand Oaks, CA: Pine Forge Press, pp. 148–77

BLOEMRAAD, IRENE, KORTEWEG, ANNA and YURDAKUL, GOKÇE 2008 'Citizenship and immigration: multiculturalism, assimilation, and challenges to the nation-state', *Annual Review of Sociology*, vol. 34, pp. 153–79

CASTLES, STEPHEN and DAVIDSON, ALASTAIR 2000 *Citizenship and Migration: Globalization and the Politics of Belonging*, New York: Routledge

FLORES, WILLIAM 1997 'Citizens vs. citizenry: undocumented immigrants and Latino cultural citizenship', in William Flores and Rina Benmayor (eds), *Latino Cultural Citizenship: Claiming Identity, Space, and Rights*, Boston, MA: Beacon Press, pp. 255–77

JACOBSON, MATTHEW 1999 *Whiteness of a Different Color: European Immigrants and the Alchemy of Race*, Cambridge, MA: Harvard University Press

JIMÉNEZ, TOMÁS 2010 *Replenished Ethnicity: Mexican Americans, Immigration, and Identity*, Berkeley, CA: University of California Press

JOPPKE, CHRISTIAN 1999 'How immigration is changing citizenship: a comparative view', *Ethnic and Racial Studies*, vol. 22, no. 4, pp. 629–52

KIBRIA, NAZLI 2002 *Becoming Asian American: Second-Generation Chinese and Korean American Identities*, Baltimore MD: The Johns Hopkins University Press

KIM, NADIA 2007 'Critical thoughts on Asian American assimilation in the whitening literature', *Social Forces*, vol. 86, no. 2, pp. 561–74

—— 2008 *Imperial Citizens: Koreans and Race from Seoul to LA*, Stanford, CA: Stanford University Press

KITANO, HARRY 1993 *Generations and Identity: The Japanese American*, Needham Heights, MA: Ginn Press

KYMLICKA, WILL 1995 *Multicultural Citizenship: A Liberal Theory of Minority Rights*, Cambridge: Cambridge University Press

MIN, PYONG GAP 2006 'Settlement patterns and diversity', in Pyong Gap Min (ed.), *Asian Americans: Contemporary Trends and Issues*, 2nd edn, Thousand Oaks, CA: Pine Forge Press, pp. 32–53

NABER, NADINE 2008 'Introduction: Arab Americans and US racial formations', in Nadine Naber and Amaney Jamal (eds), *Race and Arab Americans before and after 9/11: From Invisible Citizens to Visible Subjects*, Syracuse, NY: Syracuse University Press, pp. 1–45

ONG, AIHWA 1996 'Cultural citizenship as subject-making: immigrants negotiate racial and cultural boundaries in the United States', *Current Anthropology*, vol. 37, no. 5, pp. 737–51

PARK, LISA SUN-HEE 2005 *Consuming Citizenship: Children of Asian Immigrant Entrepreneurs*, Stanford, CA: Stanford University Press

PURKAYASTHA, BANDANA 2005 *Negotiating Ethnicity: Second-Generation South Asian Americans Traverse a Transnational World*, New Brunswick, NJ: Rutgers University Press

ROEDIGER, DAVID 2005 *Working toward Whiteness: How America's Immigrants Became White: The Strange Journey from Ellis Island to the Suburbs*, New York: Basic Books

ROSALDO, RENATO 1994 'Cultural citizenship in San Jose, California', *PoLAR: Political and Legal Anthropology Review*, vol. 17, no. 2, pp. 57–63

SPICKARD, PAUL 1996 *Japanese Americans: The Formation and Transformations of an Ethnic Group*, London: Prentice Hall International

TSUDA, TAKEYUKI 2003 *Strangers in the Ethnic Homeland: Japanese Brazilian Return Migration in Transnational Perspective*, New York: Columbia University Press

TUAN, MIA 2001 *Forever Foreigners or Honorary Whites? The Asian Ethnic Experience Today*, New Brunswick, NJ: Rutgers University Press

WATERS, MARY 1990 *Ethnic Options: Choosing Identities in America*, Berkeley, CA: University of California Press

ZHOU, MIN 2004 'Are Asian Americans Becoming "White"?', *Contexts*, vol. 3, no. 1, pp. 29–37

Are second-generation Filipinos 'becoming' Asian American or Latino? Historical colonialism, culture and panethnicity

Anthony C. Ocampo

Abstract

This article examines how second-generation Filipinos understand their panethnic identity, given their historical connection with both Asians and Latinos, two of the largest panethnic groups in the USA. While previous studies show panethnicity to be a function of shared political interests or class status, I argue that the cultural residuals of historical colonialism in the Philippines, by both Spain and the USA, shape how Filipinos negotiate panethnic boundaries with Asians and Latinos, albeit in different ways. Filipinos cite the cultural remnants of US colonialism as a reason to racially demarcate themselves from Asians, and they allude to the legacies of Spanish colonialism to blur boundaries with Latinos. While the colonial history of Filipinos is unique, these findings have implications for better understanding racialization in an increasingly multiethnic society – namely, how historical legacies in sending societies interact with new racial contexts to influence panethnic identity development.

Introduction

During his 2011 visit to the Philippines, Pulitzer Prize-winning Latino author Junot Díaz (Matilla 2011) had this to say to a local reporter:

> You should come to the Dominican Republic because from what I've seen so far, Filipinos would have no problem over there. You wouldn't even notice you'd left . . .

We have certain strong similarities. Our countries have been colonized by both the Spanish and [American]. I feel the similarities very strongly.

Having grown up around Filipinos in New Jersey, Díaz is alluding to the history of Spanish and American colonialism shared by the Philippines and many Latin American societies. Díaz implicitly blurs the boundaries between Filipinos and Latinos by drawing from what Cornell and Hartmann (1998, p. 237) term a 'symbolic repertoire' – the stories, histories and cultural markers that bond different groups together. These historical and cultural connections between Filipinos and Latinos are echoed by scholars, historians and journalists (Pisares 2006; Morrow 2007; Guevarra 2012). However, within the US context, Filipinos are classified as Asian rather than Hispanic by including the US census. Filipinos were also involved in the establishment of the Asian American movement and continue to participate in pan-Asian organizations today (Espiritu 1992).

The links of Filipinos with both Latinos and Asians introduce an interesting question: how do second-generation Filipinos understand and negotiate their panethnic identity, given their connections to two of the largest panethnic groups in the USA? In everyday life, race involves the complex negotiation of factors beyond institutional designations, including outsiders' perceptions, cultural knowledge and ways of behaving (Jackson 2001). Racial categorizations constantly evolve, and groups may develop a panethnic consciousness that transgresses 'official' designations. To address my question, I use multiple data sources that elucidate Filipino panethnic identity patterns. First, I draw from in-depth interviews and surveys of 50 second-generation Filipino adults from Los Angeles, a multiethnic city and the primary destination of Filipino immigrants. Second, I analyse two large-scale surveys of the immigrant second generation – the Immigrant and Intergenerational Mobility in Metropolitan Los Angeles (IIMMLA) and Children of Immigrants Longitudinal Study (CILS) – which provide a baseline of panethnic identity patterns of Filipinos and other Asians.

Although it was not the original intent of the study to examine how colonialism affects panethnicity, the majority of interview respondents themselves brought up both Spanish and US colonialism in the Philippines when discussing identity. Previous research highlights colonialism as an important historical backdrop for understanding assimilation (Portes and Rumbaut 2001). As Massey and colleagues (1993) have argued, colonialism matters because it creates cultural links between members of the sending and receiving countries. However, past studies mainly consider how colonialism links immigrant groups to *mainstream* members of the host country.[1] As such, this study focuses on the way that colonialism shapes how immigrant groups relate with *minority* members of society. Additionally, this study also examines how colonialism might affect assimilation outcomes specifically among *children of immigrants* in a multiethnic society. Although children of immigrants may not have been socialized within the colonized society, colonialism has an enduring imprint on the culture passed on to them by their parents, which in turn affects identity (Kasinitz et al. 2008). Filipinos draw on their colonially influenced culture when negotiating boundaries between themselves and other groups.

Classical assimilation models once posited that immigrants and their children would assimilate into a white middle-class mainstream (Gordon 1967), but contemporary frameworks have shown them now being incorporated into diverse segments of US society (Portes and Zhou 1993). Ongoing Latino and Asian migration is dramatically changing the US racial landscape, which in turn is reshaping immigrant assimilation processes. For example, in Los Angeles, among the top destinations for Latino and Asian immigrants, nearly half of the residents are of Latino descent, and non-Hispanic whites constitute a mere 28 per cent of the population (Census 2010). Children of immigrants living in such multiethnic contexts might find more incentive in identifying with their minority peers, rather than align themselves with groups associated with the white mainstream.

Understanding panethnic identity through a cultural lens, Filipinos cited US colonialism as a reason to demarcate themselves from Asians while alluding to the cultural legacies of Spanish colonialism to blur boundaries with Latinos. While existing scholarship has explained panethnicity as a function of shared class status or political interests (Espiritu 1992), I find that the cultural legacies of Spanish and US colonialism play a defining role for Filipinos' panethnic identity development. These findings challenge studies that suggest that children of immigrants prefer identities associated with upward mobility (in this case, Asian over Latino) and highlight the mechanisms that facilitate panethnic consciousness *across* class lines, a phenomenon less discussed in previous research. This study also considers how identity is shaped by the negotiation of cultural aspects associated with both the pre-migration society and the multiethnic landscape of contemporary US society.

Assimilation theory and panethnicity

Identity has long been considered a mechanism of immigrant-group assimilation. Early scholars asserted that immigrants and their children identify as unhyphenated Americans to fully assimilate into US society (Park 1950; Gordon 1964). However, contemporary reformulations of assimilation suggest that children of immigrants are incorporated into different segments of society due to a constellation of structural, economic and cultural factors, a perspective known as segmented

45

assimilation (Portes and Zhou 1993). Notably, this framework posits that connections to *ethnic* identity allow children of immigrants to acquire social and economic resources that facilitate upward mobility (Zhou and Bankston 1998). However, studies in this tradition say relatively less about the mechanisms shaping *racial* or *panethnic* identification. Some have critiqued these studies for overemphasizing the negative aspects associated with ascribing to racial identities that are externally imposed (Neckerman, Carter and Lee 1999).

Theories of panethnicity have highlighted the social, economic and political advantages of identifying with one's racial group (Espiritu 1992). Recent studies discuss the viability of panethnic identification, highlighting how children of immigrants seamlessly switch between ethnic and panethnic labels depending on the situation (Kasinitz et al. 2008), rather than viewing them as mutually exclusive options. However, intragroup dynamics and racialized constructions in mass media often prompt individuals to develop culturally based notions of panethnicity (Dhingra 2007). When these individuals feel that they do not fit the 'rules' for panethnic 'membership', they in turn express ambivalence or resistance to being lumped into these racial categories (Kibria 1998).

Colonialism and assimilation

Some scholars have argued that assimilation, identity and panethnicity models are implicitly US-centric and overlook the transnational nature of these processes (Espiritu 2004). Recent studies show that assimilation and identity formation of immigrant groups are influenced by US economic or military presence in the home country (Espiritu 2007; Kim 2008), transnational media (Roth 2009) and migratory flows between sending and host societies (Jiménez 2010). Focusing on colonialism can highlight how historical and contemporary relations *between* sending and receiving nations interact with immigrant experiences in the US context to shape assimilation.

The effect of colonialism on immigration and assimilation patterns is multi-layered. Colonial regimes exploit the natural resources and labour of the colonized society, and the resulting economic underdevelopment of the latter creates the impetus for members of its society to migrate in the first place. Second, colonial relationships influence policies that facilitate the socio-economic selectivity of individuals who migrate even in the post-colonial period (Choy 2003). Third, the institutional and cultural influences of colonial regimes 'prepare' members of the colonized society to migrate. Potential migrants in these societies possess cultural and institutional familiarity with the colonizing nation long before crossing international borders. This familiarity in turn facilitates the decision to migrate and the ability to assimilate into mainstream jobs, neighbour-hoods and organizations (Portes and Rumbaut 2001). Such findings should not at all suggest that colonialism should be framed in any positive light. Scholars show that colonialism breeds feelings of racial inferiority among immigrant groups even after the colonial period has ended, which in turn can lead to detachment from one's co-ethnic community (David and Okazaki 2006).

While studies have examined how colonialism affects the immigrant generation, few address how it distinctly influences second-generation outcomes. As Jiménez (2010) argues, immigration scholars should be more precise about colonialism's effects across generations, rather than assume that it permanently relegates immigrants with colonial histories to second-class status. Without discounting the exploitative history of colonialism, Waters (1999) notes that European colonialism has served as a basis of panethnic consciousness among second-generation West Indians from different societies – although Waters' study is among the few that considers how colonialism creates connections with other *minority* populations. Building on this research, this study shows how Filipino children of immigrants negotiate their colonial history when navigating panethnic boundaries with other ethnic groups. Warikoo (2011) provides a template of how this might occur. Her research shows that second-generation Indo-Caribbeans inherit South Asian cultural practices from their immigrant parents' society, but the degree to which it shapes their identity depends on the value that Indian culture carries within their racial context.

Historical context

The Philippines became part of the Spanish Empire during the early sixteenth century, the period when Spain established *Nueva España* in modern-day Mexico. Considered an extension of its empire in Latin America, Spain established the Acapulco–Manila galleon trade, which facilitated extensive cultural exchange between Filipinos and Mexicans for three centuries (Guevarra 2012). The Spanish period ended in 1899 but left enduring imprints on modern-day Philippine society. Spanish language has had a strong influence on Tagalog, which along with English is the current lingua franca of Philippine society (see Table 1). Filipinos were also given Spanish surnames (e.g. Torres, Rodríguez, Santos) during the colonial period. And similar to Spain's Latin American colonies, the Philippines remains a predominantly Catholic society, one of only two throughout Asia.[2] Over 80 per cent of Filipinos living in the Philippines and abroad are Catholic (Rodríguez 2006).

Despite Filipino revolutionary efforts in 1899, the Philippines was acquired by the USA following the Spanish–American War. Under the guise of 'benevolent assimilation', the Americans used cultural

Table 1 *Everyday words in English, Spanish, and Tagalog*

English	Spanish	Tagalog
Household		
Table	mesa	mesa
Living room	sala	sala
Chair	silla	silya
Kinship		
Uncle	tío	tito
Aunt	tía	tita
Godfather	nino	ninong
Godmother	nina	ninang
Clothing		
Pants	pantalones	pantalon
Jacket	chaqueta	dyaket
Shoes	zapatos	sapatos
Food-related		
Fork	tenedor	tinidor
Spoon	cuchara	kutsara
Snack	merienda	meryenda
Days		
Monday	Lunes	Lunes
Tuesday	Martes	Martes
Wednesday	Miércoles	Miyerkoles

imperialism to subjugate the native population, establishing US-style schools and English as the medium of instruction and national language (Choy 2003). Colonial policies granted Filipinos the status of US 'nationals', a legal status created by the US government specifically to facilitate large-scale migration of mostly male labourers to low-wage agricultural and factory work. Despite their ability to migrate, Filipino workers encountered violent resistance from white nativists, who eventually helped lobby Congress to pass the 1936 Tydings-McDuffie Act,[3] which granted the Philippines independence and effectively halted Filipino migration (Baldoz 2011).

Ironically, the legacies of the American colonial period set the stage for a highly selective group of Filipinos to migrate when the Hart-Cellar Act reopened US borders to non-white immigrants in 1965. US-modelled schools socialized Filipinos to American ways of life and provided widespread access to higher education. Filipinos had access to health care training institutions, initially established to aid US military stationed in the Philippines (Choy 2003). After US colonialism, the Philippine economy remained underdeveloped, and unemployment was rampant, creating a surplus pool of highly educated, English-speaking Filipino workers. During the 1970s, the Philippine government implemented aggressive labour emigration policies, transforming the country into a 'labor brokerage state' (Rodríguez 2010, p. 6). Millions within the surplus labour pool were primed to fill shortages in US professional sectors, particularly within health care.

These legacies explain why Filipinos are more linguistically and residentially assimilated than their Asian counterparts. Over two-thirds of Filipino migrants speak English 'very well', in contrast to less than a third of other Asian migrants (Portes and Rumbaut 2006). In addition, there are no culturally homogenous ethnic enclaves for Filipinos that compare to Chinatown, Koreatown or Little Saigon, as they generally reside in racially integrated neighbourhoods (Vergara 2009). These factors also explain why higher proportions of Filipinos enter main-stream, English-speaking occupations versus ethnic economies. Filipi-nos are actively recruited by US employers into health care, teaching and other professional sectors (Ong and Azores 1994). However, the language barriers and residential concentration more common among Chinese, Korean and Vietnamese mean that these groups can remain in occupational sectors that are ethnically insular (Zhou 2009).

Like their parents, Filipino children of immigrants are distinct from their second-generation Asian peers. Among second-generation Asians, Filipinos by far have the highest rates of being monolingual English speakers (Zhou and Xiong 2005). Interestingly, while Filipino migrants generally have more mainstream occupational pathways than other Asian migrants, their children fare less well in their educational outcomes than their other Asian peers. While most second-generation Filipinos pursue higher education, they are less likely than their Chinese, Korean and Vietnamese counterparts to attend four-year universities, more likely to opt for less prestigious institutions and less likely to graduate with a four-year degree (Teranishi et al. 2004; Zhou and Xiong 2005). Moreover, research by Teranishi (2002) shows that Filipinos are treated like remedial students, while their East Asian counterparts are automatically perceived as more high achieving – all part of what Espiritu and Wolf (2001, p. 157) have termed a 'paradox of assimilation'.

Espiritu (1992) argues that the cultural differences rooted in colonialism also explain why Filipinos of different generations have faced challenges in developing panethnic consciousness with other Asians. She suggests that the history of Spanish colonialism presents the possibility for Filipinos to build panethnic alliances with Latinos, or in the least can be utilized as political leverage within pan-Asian organizations (Espiritu 1992, p. 172). While Asian cultures and experiences are indeed heterogeneous, there are cultural distinctions unique to Filipinos historically rooted in their dual colonial past.[4] This article explores how the cultural residuals of this past influence how Filipinos negotiate panethnic boundaries between themselves and other ethnic groups.

Methodology

In-depth interviews

This study draws from in-depth interviews with 50 second-generation Filipinos from two middle-class, multiethnic neighbourhoods in Los Angeles: Eagle Rock and Carson. Unlike other Asian immigrants in Los Angeles, there are no ethnically homogenous Filipino neighbourhoods in the region comparable to Chinatown, Koreatown and Little Saigon. Filipinos live in multiethnic neighbourhoods and are often the primary Asian-origin group in the area (Census 2010). Eagle Rock and Carson are two such neighbourhoods that are also well-known Filipino settlements (Gorman 2007; Ibañez and Ibañez 2009). There are Filipino restaurants, community centres and immigrant service centres, although they do not dominate the neighbourhood landscape in the same fashion as other Asian ethno-burbs (Zhou 2009).

Eagle Rock and Carson are majority–minority neighbourhoods that are also middle class – the median household income in both Eagle Rock and Carson is about $67,000, well above the national average (Census 2010). In both neighbourhoods, 20 per cent of residents are Filipino and over 35 per cent are Mexican. However, in Eagle Rock, the remaining population is white, whereas in Carson, it is mostly African American with a small, but visible number of Samoans (about 3 per cent). Lacy (2008) suggests that comparing neighbourhoods with distinct racial contexts yields insights into the heterogeneous identity trajectories of middle-class minorities. While neighbourhood racial context is not the central focus of this article, I do examine how it may mitigate the relationship between colonialism and identity.

Officially, Eagle Rock is characterized as a neighbourhood with a population of about 34,000, and Carson is considered a city with a population of 90,000. However, individuals rarely conceptualize the areas in which they live by official government designations (Gottdiener and Hutchinson 2010). This was the case with Filipinos in the study, who referred to Eagle Rock and Carson as 'neighbourhoods' without hesitation. In using the term 'neighbourhood' to describe Eagle Rock and Carson, I am choosing to remain consistent with respondents' particular use of the term.

The interviews were conducted between March 2009 and January 2010, and each lasted approximately ninety minutes. Half of the respondents were recruited through messages distributed on an online networking website. One fourth of respondents were recruited through contacts established during casual interactions in coffee shops, churches, parks and shopping centres in the neighbourhoods. The remaining were referred by those already interviewed. Respondents in the study each had Philippine-born migrant parents, were born in the

USA (or had migrated by age five) and were between twenty-one and thirty years old at the time of the interview.

Several interview questions addressed panethnic identity. I asked respondents: (1) What would you consider to be your racial identity? (2) Which ethnic and racial groups do you feel you and other Filipinos are most similar to? (3) Have you ever identified as Asian American? I also asked *why* Filipinos might or might not identify with certain panethnic labels or groups. The interview included topics that previous studies have linked to identify formation, such as neighbourhood experiences, school experiences, and interactions with family and friends. I noted moments when respondents discussed panethnic identity both explicitly (e.g. 'I am Asian American') and implicitly (e.g. 'We [Filipinos and another group] are the same.').

While the scope of the article discusses colonialism, this was not a theme originally included in the interview protocol, nor was it a topic that I introduced during the conversation. However, the majority of respondents brought up the theme of colonialism of their own accord when discussing Filipino identity. When they did, I probed further into the way they used this frame when negotiating panethnic boundaries. I also paid attention to whether the association between colonialism and identity was mitigated by other factors, such as neighbourhood context, socio-economic status or interracial encounters.

Following each interview, respondents were asked to fill out a brief demographic survey with questions about their level of education, socio-economic status (SES), and ethnic and racial identity choices. Respondents first answered the open-ended question: 'How do you self-identify?' For a subsequent question – 'What is your racial background?' – respondents were asked to indicate whether they identified as white, African American, Latino, Asian or Pacific Islander.

Quantitative data

Immigrant and Intergenerational Mobility in Metropolitan Los Angeles (IIMMLA)

The IIMMLA is a cross-sectional survey of second-generation adults in the greater Los Angeles area conducted in 2004. Researchers targeted adult children of immigrants[5] of Latino and Asian origin. Participants were surveyed during a thirty-five-minute telephone interview and asked questions related to their incorporation and mobility, including national origin, SES, educational background, occupation and cultural involvements. In this article, I draw only from surveys of the 1,617 respondents of the four primary Asian groups included – Filipino, Chinese, Vietnamese and Korean – also the four largest Asian ethnicities in Los Angeles (Census 2010). To examine panethnic identity, I focus on their responses to the question: 'For classification purposes, we'd like to know what your racial background is. Are you White, Black or African American, Asian, Pacific Islander, American Indian, Alaskan native, or member of another race, or a combination of these?'

Children of Immigrants Longitudinal Study (CILS)

The CILS is a longitudinal survey of second-generation immigrants from San Diego, California and Fort Lauderdale/Miami, Florida. Three waves of the survey were conducted in 1992, 1995 and 2001–03, when respondents' average age was about fourteen, seventeen and mid-twenties, respectively. The CILS shares similar objectives to the IIMMLA in that it aims to elucidate the mechanisms underlying second-generation assimilation and acculturation. Key variables included language, educational achievement, SES, and ethnic and racial identification. I draw only from the San Diego sub-sample because the number of Filipino-origin respondents in Miami is negligible. My analysis is limited to the four primary Asian descent subgroups included in the survey – Filipino, Vietnamese, Laotian and other Southeast Asian (mainly Hmong and Cambodian). Because wave two of the study (1995) was the only one that asked respondents to both self-identify[6] and choose from a discrete set of racial categories, my analysis is based on the 921 Asian-origin respondents surveyed during this wave. To examine panethnic identity, I focus on their responses to the question: 'Which of the races listed do you consider yourself to be – White, Black, Asian, Multiracial, Other?'

Although the interviews are not from respondents of the IIMMLA and CILS, the surveys provide a baseline comparison of panethnic identity patterns among second-generation Filipinos and Asians, which complement the qualitative findings. In addition, both are based in southern California, where Filipinos negotiate ethnic boundaries vis-à-vis the large numbers of Latinos and Asians in the region. While surveys may not address respondents' reasons for selecting panethnic labels or may not show implicit forms of panethnic consciousness, they illustrate how Asian panethnicity resonates differently among Asian-origin groups.

Cultural marginalization within Asian America

> Author: Do you ever identify as Asian American?
> Ronald: Not really. It's like denying what I am. It's like denying that I'm Filipino, like not really acknowledging my *culture*.

Despite its political origins, Asian panethnicity has evolved to take on cultural meanings, as Ronald's remarks indicate. When presented with the question 'What groups are Filipinos most similar to?', respondents interpreted this to mean 'Whose *culture* is most similar to that of Filipinos?'. Filipinos were generally reticent about identifying as Asian, and this had to do with cultural factors. Few felt cultural connections between themselves and other Asians, and the ones they noted were superficial at best, such as food or geography. As one respondent noted: 'Filipinos' diet is very Asian, like rice, fish, and stuff a normal American wouldn't eat.' Beyond this, most associated Asian American identity with East Asian cultural stereotypes, which they felt did not fit Filipinos. As Kevin asserted: 'The face of Asian Americans is an East Asian face, literally. Not a Filipino one.'

Respondents referred to the Americanization of Filipino culture as a reason to demarcate themselves from other Asians. Some felt different from other Asians because the latter had a 'real history and therefore, had a real culture.' Jenn noted that, in contrast to other Asians, Filipino culture was associated with hybridity because of the colonial influences throughout Philippine history:

> We're not really Asian. I feel like on a cultural level, we don't relate. The Chinese have this long history that's very established, and it's written. We've been colonized like how many times? Where's the identity in that? Are we Spanish, Muslim, Chinese, and now, are we American? Because if you go to Manila, it's practically like Los Angeles. It's so Americanized.

Echoing Jenn's remarks, others felt that this colonial history was antithetical to being Asian American because 'real' Asian culture is 'untouched by Western influences'.

Others framed the post-colonial American influence as an advantage that made Filipinos 'less foreign' than other Asians. Franky noted: 'When whites see other Asian groups, they seem them as being "fobbier" [more "fresh off the boat"]. But then they see Filipinos and we're more assimilated to American culture.' Eddie pointed to the Americanized aspects of Philippine media: 'A lot of the popular culture and styles and music are based on [America]. When you watch Filipino variety shows, what do you see? They're playing Usher, Lady Gaga, and American pop and hip hop.' Implicit in such comments is the assumption that Asian culture is inherently foreign, while Filipino culture is more westernized, and thus, *not* Asian. By contrasting up-to-date trends in Philippine culture with a 'fobbier' Asian culture, these remarks also imply that Asian identity is 'uncool', which may further explain Filipinos' aversion to pan-Asian identity.

Respondents also said that the English proficiency of Filipinos in the USA – an outgrowth of American colonialism – distinguished them from Asians. Lynette recalled an uncomfortable moment in an Asian American studies course in college when her class had a discussion about the typical Asian American experience:

> I felt like there was a difference between those who were Chinese, Korean, and those who were Filipino. It just *felt* different. I think because a lot of the "Asian American experiences" that we read about in our class talked about language. The other Asians would talk about their parents only being able to speak Mandarin or Vietnamese and having to be the mediator between two cultures – *that* was the Asian American experience. But I felt that wasn't the case for me. I was like, "You know, my parents speak English just fine."

Ironically, while Asian American studies was created to foster a shared sense of panethnic identity among different Asian ethnicities, Lynette's experience served the opposite function – it highlighted differences between Filipinos' experiences from those of East Asians, who many felt dominated mainstream Asian American narratives.

Several noted the cultural construction of Asian panethnicity on a global level. They recounted times when others referred to Filipinos as the 'wetback Asians' or the 'Mexicans' or 'blacks' of Asia. Raymond said: '[Filipinos] do the manual labor all over the world.' Kevin, in turn, argued that when people think of Asians, they automatically refer to China, Japan and Korea, or as he noted: 'The three countries that have power.' While Raymond and Kevin grew up middle class and have professional parents, their remarks show how their sense of pan-Asian identity is influenced by the international community of Filipino labourers. Their comments illustrate that panethnicity is not entirely a US-based construction, but rather, at least in part, a transnational ideological construction (Espiritu 2004; Roth 2009).

The lack of other Asian ethnicities in their childhood neighbourhoods also explains why Filipinos expressed weak panethnic ties. Proximity facilitates opportunities for people to identify commonalities across ethnic lines and develop a panethnic consciousness.

In Eagle Rock and Carson, Filipinos had minimal opportunity to interact with other Asians. Most did not interact with Asians until their college years. As Jacob noted: 'College was the first time I really was around a bunch of Asians!' Grace described her first days at UC Irvine (where non-Filipino Asians are 40 per cent of the student body) as a 'culture shock' because 'everyone is super Asian'. Such characterizations imply how both felt that Filipinos were not part of the pan-Asian collective.

Post-colonial panethnicity: Filipino and Latino cultural connections

Even though respondents used colonialism to distance Filipinos from other Asians, they used the colonialism frame to blur boundaries with

Latinos. While no respondent identified as Latino outright, many more closely associated Filipinos with Mexicans and other Latinos because of the shared history of Spanish colonialism, including some who checked 'Asian' on the post-interview survey. Lia noted the 'Latinizing' effect of this history on Filipino culture, saying that Filipinos 'have more similarities with Latin culture than other Asians'.

Some felt Filipinos 'must have Spanish blood' because both co-ethnics and Latinos commonly mistook them as Mexican due to their phenotype (e.g. they 'looked' Mexican) or their Spanish surname. Nearly half of respondents recalled being spoken to in Spanish by Latinos, and some were even mistaken as Latino by other Filipinos. In her first days working as a nurse, Adriana recalled that her Filipina co-workers spoke Tagalog to each other yet conversed with her in English. When Adriana replied in Tagalog, one co-worker expressed her surprise: 'I didn't know you were Filipina. I thought you were Hispanic!'

Respondents bonded with Latinos based on three main cultural similarities: language, surnames and Catholicism. Jon, a hotel manager, recalled being mistaken as Latino by the Mexican immigrants he worked with:

> When they see me in the hall, they speak to me in Spanish. Then I tell them, "No hablo español," and they're like, "Why don't you speak Spanish?" and then I tell them I'm Filipino. And then they insist, "Well, some Filipinos speak Spanish. You have Spanish last names, right?"

Respondents recalled efforts by Filipino and Latino immigrants to communicate with each other when interacting in the neighbourhood, given the heavy overlap in everyday words in Spanish and Tagalog (see Table 1). When I asked him whether he saw Filipinos and Latinos interact much, Jayson answered:

> All the time! My mom, for example, whenever she goes to the market, she [and the Latino workers] will be like, "Hola, amigo. Hola, amiga." Because of the similarities in our language, you can communicate in [each others'] native tongue.

While language bridged Filipinos with Latinos, it created further rifts with Asians. Ronald said that interacting with other Asian immigrants was relatively more difficult 'because there's virtually no overlap between Tagalog and say, Chinese or Vietnamese.'

Catholicism was another colonial legacy that Filipinos used to liken themselves with Latinos. Diana said Filipinos were 'definitely' more similar to Latinos because:

> [My] parents have *santos* and the Virgin Mary all around the house, and that's just like Latinos. I'd go to my Guatemalan friend's house, and you'd see the same thing. There's a lot of religion intermingled with her culture and my culture.

Many Filipino and Latino ethnic practices also have a religious component. Alma noted how religion was embedded in rites of passages for Filipina and Mexican young women (debuts and *quinceañeras*, respectively). She added: 'When you hear Filipino and Latino, you think Catholic automatically. I don't think religion when I think of Asians. Or if I do, maybe I think of Buddha, but not Jesus or Mary.' Although Catholicism might not have prompted outsiders to racialize respondents as Latino, it nonetheless affected how Filipinos racially positioned themselves vis-à-vis Latinos and other Asians.

This cultural closeness became evident in situations where other Filipinos were not even present. Alex attended a private college with many East Asians and Latinos, but few Filipinos. Coming from Eagle Rock, he initially felt disconnected from his Asian classmates, yet noted a sense of closeness with his Latino peers, who also invoked the colonial frame. At a party sponsored by one of the Latino organizations, Alex recounted:

> I never felt out of place at the party, even though it was all Latinos. Funny enough. My one friend who was half-Mexican, but looked more white and was from like a bougie [rich], all-white town got flack for being there. They kept calling him "white boy." But with me, a bunch of the guys would come up to me and be like, "Oh what? You're Filipino? It's practically the same thing [as Latino]. We all got punked by Spain anyway, right?" Most of my friends in college ended up being Latino because they were the next closest thing to Filipinos.

Alex's experience shows that the negotiation of panethnic boundaries is not determined solely by national origin – otherwise his 'white-looking' friend should have felt more at home at the predominantly Latino event. Alex's comfort stemmed from his experiences growing up with Latinos, which allowed him to fit in more than someone who was 'biologically' Mexican. Alex also noted that Latino events were 'more fun' and 'cooler' than those sponsored by other Asians, whom he and other Filipinos stereotyped as studious and bookish.

This idea that Filipinos and Latinos were 'the same thing' was echoed in conversations about interracial dating. While having dated Mexican women in the past, Nelson expressed a new-found anxiety about dating a Vietnamese woman:

> Nelson: I'm kind of nervous about the girl I'm dating. She's Vietnamese, so this is the first time I'm dating someone from a different culture.
> Author: Didn't you say that you dated a bunch of Mexican girls before?
> Nelson (laughing): Ha, that doesn't count. Mexicans are the same as Filipinos!

For Nelson, cultural differences between Filipinos and Latinos are less salient than those between Filipinos and Asians. Such comments illustrate how the cultural boundaries of racial categories subconsciously influence Filipinos' sense of 'we-ness' with Asians and Latinos.

Respondents' identification with Latinos is interesting given that Filipinos, on the aggregate level, have a higher SES than Latinos. At the same time, Eagle Rock and Carson have a large minority middle class, including middle-class Mexican Americans. The narratives suggest that there was more class convergence between Filipinos and Mexicans in these neighbourhoods than statistical data might indicate. While nearly every respondent identified as middle class, most noted having close connections with relatives who were working class (both in the USA and abroad) or recalled having been working class earlier in life. As such, class differences did not necessarily disrupt the connections they felt with Latinos who lived in the 'less nice parts' of Eagle Rock or Carson. However, Filipino–Latino connections did weaken when negative media stereotypes of Latinos were discussed. Franky said that while he felt close with Latinos in terms of religion and culture, he did not relate to the 'stereotypical Cholo [gangster] looking ones'. In addition, Filipino–Latino connections seemed to break down in the school context. Those attending public high schools said that while teachers viewed Filipinos as high-achieving students,[7] 'Latinos weren't seen as honors students by school officials'. These findings suggest that Filipinos' connection with Latinos might decline if the association potentially compromised their middle-class standing or mobility.

Filipino panethnic identity patterns

Post-interview survey

Respondents filled out a brief survey that asked an open-ended question about identity and then chose a racial identity from a set of discrete options. I had the opportunity to observe respondents as they answered these questions. For the open-ended question, every respondent wrote 'Filipino' without hesitation. However, when asked to select their racial background, many vacillated between the given options. Half inquired whether they could write in 'Filipino' as their race. Table 2 shows that respondents were split between choosing 'Asian' and 'Pacific Islander'. There was also a clear relationship between panethnic identification and neighbourhood.

Given the racial ambivalence of Filipinos in both neighbourhoods, what explains this difference? The interviews suggest that choosing 'Pacific Islander' was a function of not wanting to choose 'Asian'. Eagle Rock respondents selected Pacific Islander, but had few concrete notions of what this identity 'meant'. When prompted about why he felt Filipinos were 'more Pacific Islander than Asian', Vince said:

Table 2 *Panethnic identification of respondents (N =50)*

	Neighbourhood		
	Eagle Rock	Carson	All
Asian	20%	84%	52%
	(5)	(21)	(26)
Pacific Islander	80%	16	48%
	(20)	(4)	(24)
	100%	100%	100%
	(25)	(25)	(50)

'I don't know. Probably because the Philippines are islands in the Pacific?' Others displayed the same lack of investment, noting merely that it was 'better than choosing Asian'. Carson respondents had more concrete ideas of Pacific Islander identity because of their interactions with Samoans. Bryan said: 'Pacific Islander is for the Samoans. And there's no Asians in Carson besides Filipinos, so I guess we can fill that in.' Such responses illustrate that Carson Filipinos did not necessarily express strong attachments to Asian identity, even if they chose it on the form. These findings show that Filipinos' identity options depend largely on the availability and meaning of categories within their local context.

IIMMLA and CILS

Filipino identity patterns on the IIMMLA and CILS parallel those from my interview respondents. Less than one half (47 per cent) and two-thirds (63 per cent) of Filipino IIMMLA and CILS respondents, respectively (see Tables 3 and 4), identified as Asian, in contrast to about 90 per cent of other Asians. These findings are interesting given

Table 3 *Panethnic identification by ethnicity, second-generation Asians (N =1,617)*

	Filipino	Chinese	Vietnamese	Korean
Asian	47%	96%	98%	98%
	(189)	(395)	(393)	(393)
Pacific Islander	45%	1%	1%	1%
	(182)	(5)	(4)	(2)
Other	8%	3%	1%	2%
	(31)	(13)	(4)	(6)
	100%	100%	100%	100%
N	(402)	(413)	(401)	(401)

Source: IIMMLA 2004

Table 4 *Panethnic identification by ethnicity, second-generation Asians (N = 921)*

	Filipino	Vietnamese	Laotian	Southeast Asian
Asian	63%	91%	93%	89%
	(351)	(172)	(98)	(59)
National origin	22%	5%	4%	2%
	(121)	(9)	(4)	(1)
Other	15%	4%	3%	9%
	(89)	(8)	(3)	(6)
	100%	100%	100%	100%
N	(561)	(189)	(105)	(66)

Source: CILS 2001–03

that 'Asian' is stereotyped as a middle-class or upwardly mobile identity (Zhou 2009). One might expect that Southeast Asians, the most socio-economically disadvantaged subgroup, would be least inclined to identify as Asian, given that studies show panethnicity to be a function of class commonality (Carter 2005). Ultimately, these findings complement the interview data by illustrating that Filipinos' panethnic ambivalence occurs across different contexts (Los Angeles and San Diego) and ages (adults and teenagers[8]).

Conclusion

Despite linguistic, socio-economic and cultural differences, ethnic groups develop panethnic consciousness by organizing for political interests, emphasizing cultural commonalities or highlighting shared racial experiences. Filipinos have done all these things with both Asians and Latinos, and thus can justifiably be categorized as either. Ultimately, they are officially Asian, according to the US census. Despite this, individuals do not always ascribe to the panethnic labels imposed on them, and the unique colonial history of the Philippines has prompted Filipinos to be vocally ambivalent about their racial designation. In Espiritu's (1992, p. 107) seminal book *Asian American Panethnicity*, one Filipino despondently asserted that Filipinos were Asian because of a 'geographical accident'. Espiritu has noted the possibility of Filipinos joining Latino panethnic coalitions, but ultimately acknowledges that both the pan-Asian and pan-Latino option bring significant challenges.

If these historical and cultural connections mean that Filipinos are 'kinda Asian and kinda Latino', as one respondent put it, how did the young adults in this study negotiate panethnic identity? The term 'Asian American' was born as a politicized identity, yet it was not a lack of political engagement that prompted their ambivalence. Rather, the cultural legacies of Spanish and US colonialism in the Philippines played a more significant role in how respondents negotiated panethnic boundaries. It is worth nothing that despite the cultural links between US and Philippine societies, no respondent identified as an unhyphenated American, signalling the continued significance of race in American society.

As the narratives revealed, the cultural hybridity resulting from Spanish and US colonialism was a central part of Filipino ethnic identity. Whether talking about culture, language or religion, respondents would embed them within colonial contexts. This culturally based understanding of ethnicity extended to their negotiation of panethnicity. US colonialism created a rift between Filipinos and other Asians. Their experiences of feeling more Americanized, having English-speaking households, and being less bicultural than other Asians prompted their feelings of disconnection. This social distancing was further amplified by their internalization of the Asian 'forever foreigner' stereotype and lack of interaction with other Asians in their neighbourhoods. Moreover, the surveys reflected the lukewarm resonance of Asian panethnicity for Filipinos, relative to other Asian ethnicities.

In turn, Spanish colonialism bonded them with Latinos, a sentiment that at times was mutual, as the opening quote from Junot Díaz illustrates. In their everyday lives, reminders of Spanish colonialism are present in their parents' language, surnames and religion. The presence of Latinos in their neighbourhood further 'replenished' the Spanish aspects of Filipino ethnic culture (Jiménez 2010), making the Filipino–Latino link especially salient. These findings challenge previous studies that suggest that Filipinos should align themselves with Asians, a group stereotyped as upwardly mobile. Within the context of a middle-class neighbourhood, colonial commonalities prompt Filipinos to blur boundaries with Latinos (except in situations where it compromised their social standing).

Are Filipino Americans a unique case? Certainly the extensive colonial history in the Philippines distinguishes them from other Asians. Nonetheless, colonialism also represents an extreme case of cultural shifts in pre-migration societies that persist today, due to US militarism, foreign policy, transnational media and migration-related cultural exchanges (Kim 2008). Cultural shifts in the pre-migration society shape the identity 'toolkit' that children of immigrants use to relate with groups in a multiethnic society (Warikoo 2011). However, the use of this toolkit is also contingent on the value of 'symbolic repertoires' that children of immigrants possess. In a 'Latinized' city like Los Angeles, there is symbolic value to aligning oneself with Latinos rather than Asians, particularly for young adults who at the time may be more concerned with social standing than economic mobility. Although a study of Los Angeles may not be generalizable to second-generation experiences across the country, the choice of research site elucidates important social phenomena bound to take place in other parts of the country affected by migration: negotiation of race beyond the black–white binary, the emergence of new panethnic categories, and the interaction of historical legacies with new racial contexts. Ultimately, the Filipino case highlights the ever-evolving process of panethnic identity construction – a process that is not US-centric in nature, but one shaped heavily by the interaction of historical legacies with the changing racial landscape of American society.

Acknowledgements

I am grateful to Min Zhou, Roger Waldinger, Wendy Roth, Jennifer Jones, Kerry Ann Rockquemore, Anthony Alvarez and the reviewers for their feedback throughout various stages this manuscript.

Notes

1.   Studies of European migration have more thoroughly detailed how colonialism affects assimilation among post-colonial migrants. Studies of the Indian migration in the British colonial era show how colonial policies facilitated the movement of Indian professionals to East Africa during the early twentieth century (Poros 2010). British–Indian colonial relations allowed Indians in East Africa to then migrate to the UK when African societies later gained independence. While their colonial status allowed them entry into Britain, it also became a marker of their second-class citizenship in their new host society (Dhingra 2012).
2.   East Timor, a former Portuguese colony of one million people (1 per cent the size of the Philippines), is the only other Catholic society in Asia.
3.   Filipino migrants of the early twentieth century encountered hostility and violence from white nativists hoping to halt Filipino migration. However, it was not until 1934 that nativists coalesced with Midwestern agribusiness players who were worried about competition with Philippine agricultural products. These constituencies lobbied Congress to pass the Tydings-McDuffie Act in 1936 and grant the Philippines independence following a ten-year transition period succeeding its passage (Baldoz 2011, pp. 156–193).
4.   The Philippines is not the only Asian country with a colonial past. While countries, like Korea, experienced colonialism, they are qualitatively different in many respects. First, the Philippines was colonized for longer than most other Asian countries. Second, the legacies of both Spanish and US colonialism are more deeply embedded within the mainstream culture of contemporary Philippine society. The closest parallel is British colonialism in India, which lasted nearly as long as in the Philippines. This partly explains why besides Filipinos, there are challenges to including Indians within the pan-Asian collective (Kibria 1998).
5.   Second-generation studies generally includes both 1.5 and second-generation individuals.
6.   Before asked about panethnic identity, respondents were asked the open-ended question: 'How do you identify, that is what do you call yourself?'
7.   Teranishi (2002) revealed that Filipinos were treated as remedial students while Chinese were dubbed model minorities. In this study, Filipinos were the only Asians present in the

school, leading teachers to designate them model minorities relative to the other groups present.

8. When surveyed, IIMMLA respondents were adults, while CILS respondents were teenagers.

References

BALDOZ, RICK 2011 *The Third Asiatic Invasion*, New York: NYU Press

CARTER, PRUDENCE 2005 *Keepin' It Real*, New York: Oxford University Press

CENSUS BUREAU OF THE UNITED STATES. 2010. *Census of Population and Housing*. Washington, DC: Government Printing Office.

CHOY, CATHERINE 2003 *Empire of Care*, Durham, NC: Duke University Press

CORNELL, STEPHEN and HARTMANN, DOUGLAS 1998 *Ethnicity and Race*, Thousand Oaks, CA: Pine Forge

DAVID, E. and OKAZAKI, SUMIE 2006 'The colonial mentality scale for Filipino Americans', *Journal of Counseling Psychology*, vol. 53, no. 2, pp. 241–52

DHINGRA, PAWAN 2007 *Managing Multicultural Lives*, Stanford, CA: Stanford University Press

—— 2012 *Life behind the Lobby*, Stanford, CA: Stanford University Press

ESPIRITU, YEN LE 1992 *Asian American Panethnicity*, Philadelphia, PA: Temple University Press

—— 2004 'Asian American panethnicity', in Nancy Foner and George Frederickson (eds), *Not Just Black and White*, New York: Russell Sage, pp. 217–36.

—— 2007 'Gender, Migration, and Work', in Min Zhou and James Gatewood (eds), *Contemporary Asian America*, New York: NYU Press, pp. 207–32.

ESPIRITU, YEN LE and WOLF, DIANE 2001 'The paradox of assimilation', in Ruben Rumbaut and Alejandro Portes (eds), *Ethnicities*, Berkeley, CA: University of California Press, pp. 157–86

GORDON, MILTON 1964 *Assimilation in American Life*, New York: Oxford University Press

GORMAN, ANNA 2007 'Mall anchors thriving Filipino community', *Los Angeles Times*, 22 August. [Available from: http://articles.latimes.com/2007/aug/22/local/me-filipino22 [Accessed 11 January 2013]]

GOTTDIENER, MARK and HUTCHINSON, RAY 2010 *The New Urban Sociology*, Boulder, CO: Westview

GUEVARRA, RUDY 2012 *Becoming Mexipino: Multiethnic Communities and Identities in San Diego*, New Brunswick, NJ: Rutgers University Press

IBAÑEZ, FLORANTE and IBAÑEZ, ROSEYLN 2009 *Filipinos in Carson and the South Bay*, Mt Pleasant, SC: Arcadia

JACKSON, JOHN 2001 *Harlemworld*, Chicago, IL: University of Chicago Press

JIMÉNEZ, TOMAS 2010 *Replenished Ethnicity*, Berkeley, CA: University of California Press

KASINITZ, PHILIP *et al.* 2008 *Inheriting the City*, New York: Russell Sage

KIBRIA, NAZLI 1998 'The contested meaning of "Asian American"', *Ethnic and Racial Studies*, vol. 21, no. 5, pp. 939–58

KIM, NADIA 2008 *Imperial Citizens*, Stanford, CA: Stanford University Press

LACY, KARYN 2008 *Blue-Chip Black*, Berkeley, CA: University of California Press

MASSEY, DOUGLAS, *et al.* 1993 'Theories of international migration', *Population and Development Review*, vol. 19, no. 3, pp. 431–66

MATILLA, DEXTER 2011 'Pulitzer Prize-winning novelist Junot Díaz', *Philippine Daily Inquirer*, 26 December. [Available from: http://lifestyle.inquirer.net/28907/pulitzer-prize-winning-novelist-junot-diaz [Accessed 11 January 2013]]

MORROW, PAUL 2007 'Mexico is just not a town in Pampanga', *Pilipino Express*, 1 October. [Available from: http://www.pilipino-express.com/history-a-culture/in-other-words/225-mexico-is-not-just-a-town-in-pampanga.html [Accessed 11 January 2013]]

NECKERMAN, KATHERINE, CARTER, PRUDENCE and LEE, JENNIFER 1999 'Segmented assimilation and minority cultures of mobility', *Ethnic and Racial Studies*, vol. 22, no. 6, pp. 945–65

ONG, PAUL and AZORES, TANIA 1994 'The migration and incorporation of Filipino nurses', in Paul Ong, *et al.* (eds), *New Asian Immigration in Los Angeles and Global Restructuring*, Philadelphia, PA: Temple University Press, pp. 164–95

PARK, ROBERT 1950 *Race and Culture*, Glencoe, IL: Free Press

PISARES, ELIZABETH 2006 'Do you (mis)recognize me? in Antonio Tiongson, *et al.* (eds), *Positively No Filipinos Allowed*, Philadelphia, PA: Temple University Press, pp. 172–98

POROS, MARITSA 2010 *Modern Migrations*, Stanford, CA: Stanford University Press

PORTES, ALEJANDRO and RUMBAUT, RUBEN 2001 *Legacies*, Berkeley, CA: University of California Press

——— 2006 *Immigrant America*, Berkeley, CA: University of California Press

PORTES, ALEJANDRO and ZHOU, MIN 1993 'The new second generation', *Annals of the American Academy of Political and Social Science*, vol. 530, no. 1, pp. 491–522

RODRíGUEZ, EVELYN 2006 'Primerang Bituin', *Asia Pacific Perspectives*, vol. 6, no. 1, pp. 4–12

RODRíGUEZ, ROBYN 2010 *Migrants for Export*, Minneapolis, MN: University of Minnesota Press

ROTH, WENDY 2009 'Latino before the world', *Ethnic and Racial Studies*, vol. 32, no. 6, pp. 927–47

TERANISHI, ROBERT 2002 'Asian Pacific Americans and critical race theory', *Equity and Excellence in Education*, vol. 35, no. 2, pp. 144–54

TERANISHI, ROBERT, *et al.* 2004 'The college-choice process for Asian Americans', *Review of Higher Education*, vol. 27, no. 4, pp. 527–51

VERGARA, BENITO 2009 *Pinoy Capital*, Philadelphia, PA: Temple University Press

WARIKOO, NATASHA 2011 *Balancing Acts*, Berkeley, CA: University of California Press

WATERS, MARY 1999 *Black Identities*, Cambridge, MA: Harvard University Press

ZHOU, MIN 2009 *Contemporary Chinese America*, Philadelphia, PA: Temple University Press

ZHOU, MIN and BANKSTON, CARL 1998 *Growing Up American*, New York: Russell Sage

ZHOU, MIN and XIONG, YANG 2005 'The multifaceted American experience of children of Asian immigrants', *Ethnic and Racial Studies*, vol. 28, no. 6, pp. 1119–52

Mexican Americans as a paradigm for contemporary intra-group heterogeneity

Richard Alba, Tomás R. Jiménez and Helen B. Marrow

Abstract

Racialization and assimilation offer alternative perspectives on the position of immigrant-origin populations in American society. We question the adequacy of either perspective alone in the early twenty-first century, taking Mexican Americans as our case in point. Re-analysing the child sample of the Mexican American Study Project, we uncover substantial heterogeneity marked by vulnerability to racialization at one end but proximity to the mainstream at the other. This heterogeneity reflects important variations in how education, intermarriage, mixed ancestry and geographic mobility have intersected for Mexican immigrants and their descendants over the twentieth century, and in turn shaped their ethnic identity. Finally, based on US census findings, we give reason to think that internal heterogeneity is increasing in the twenty-first century. Together, these findings suggest that future studies of immigrant adaptation in America must do a better job of accounting for heterogeneity, not just between but also *within* immigrant-origin populations.

Introduction

In every immigration era, certain groups are taken as emblematic of the period's problems and successes. What the Irish were to the second half of the nineteenth century in the USA, the Eastern European Jews and Italians were to the first half of the twentieth. Today it is the turn of the Mexicans. At 30 per cent of the total foreign born, they are the largest group in the contemporary immigrant stream. When their US-born generations are included, they are the second largest non-European ethno-racial group in the country.

There is irony in this new attention to Mexicans because they have been an immigrant group for more than a century, and before then, they were a large part of the original population resident on territory that was incorporated into the USA by conquest. This long history means that Mexicans belong not just to the immigrant and second generations, but also to the third and later ones, as well to a group that cannot be classified in generational terms because their ancestors were never immigrants.

This complex history of conquest *and* immigration affects current sociological accounts of the fortunes of contemporary Mexican immigrants and their descendants. These accounts vacillate between the more optimistic – drawing analogies between Mexicans and earlier immigrant groups (Perlmann 2005; Park and Myers 2010) – and the more pessimistic – arguing that Mexican Americans of all generations are stymied by an inability to compete in a post-industrial economy, historical and present-day racism, and the humble socio-economic position – and often unauthorized status – of their parents (López and Stanton-Salazar 2001; Portes and Rumbaut 2001). Racialization theories play a dominant role in the latter accounts, depicting Mexican Americans as systematically and enduringly disadvantaged by processes of racial exclusion (Massey 2007; Chavez 2008). The racialization account has been advanced by the seminal book *Generations of Exclusion* (Telles and Ortiz 2008), which draws on a longitudinal data set tracking Mexican Americans in San Antonio and Los Angeles from the mid-1960s to late-1990s.

Given the group's emblematic status and large presence, it is important to get the Mexican American story right. We argue that neither the optimistic nor pessimistic accounts do justice to the diversity of the Mexican American experience in the twenty-first century. Instead, we argue that its *internal heterogeneity* is a key and potentially paradigmatic aspect. Heterogeneity is reflected along a broad spectrum that includes vulnerability to racialization on one end – anchored in a combustible mix of factors including undocumented parental status, a concentrated Mexican American social milieu, residential segregation, and persistently low educational attainment – and assimilation to the mainstream[1] on the other – evinced by ethnically mixed ancestry, intermarriage, movement away from established Mexican American areas of concentration, and post-secondary education. Of course, many Mexican-origin individuals fall in between.

To uncover this diversity, we draw on the rich data assembled by Telles and Ortiz (2008) for *Generations of Exclusion*, supplementing it with 1970 and 2000 census data.[2] Our analysis of Telles and Ortiz's Mexican American Study Project (MASP) data unpacks key dimensions of *intra-group diversity*, such as educational attainment, mixed ancestry and geographic mobility. Our procedures are mainly correlational because we are interested in identifying the characteristics associated with location along the mainstream/racialization spectrum.

We show that during the late decades of the twentieth century the concentration of Mexican-origin individuals at the less racialized end of the spectrum was already appreciable. We give reasons to think that this concentration continues to grow, but that so too does the concentration at the other end. Increasing heterogeneity indicates that what it means to be Mexican American is far from uniform. It is ever more contingent on other characteristics, such as how much education Mexican-origin individuals have, whether they are endogamously or exogamously married, and how close to or far from established Mexican American concentrations they live. Together, our findings suggest that future studies of intergenerational immigrant adaptation in America must account for heterogeneity, not just between but also *within* immigrant-origin populations.

Racialization and assimilation: an unresolved tension

Racialization refers to social processes that create and maintain systematic, unequal life chances between hierarchically ordered populations, where the superior one is generally described as the majority (whatever its numerical size) and the inferior one as a minority (Bonilla-Silva 1997). In race theory, the minority is seen as determined by exclusion from the majority group, which imposes on others descent-based categories that are invested with ideological content explaining inferiority (e.g. stereotypes) and justifying disparate treatment and outcomes (Omi and Winant 1994; Winant 2000; Massey 2007).

Race theories are not monolithic. Some put more emphasis on ideology and politics (e.g. Omi and Winant 1994); others on social structure (e.g. Bonilla-Silva 1997). Some see inequality, once generated, as systemic and durable; others allow for some individual mobility within a relatively stable group order. Some even envision shifts in the position of groups within a racial hierarchy (e.g. Bonilla-Silva 2004). What these theories share, however, is a primary focus on the mechanisms that produce and maintain unequal life chances, and therefore a suspicion about widespread assimilation as a mechanism that might bring about parity with the mainstream for many members of a racially defined minority. Absent large-scale social movements or overt political protest, race theories presume that it is difficult for most members of a minority to escape the negative impacts of categorical ordering and the 'definite social relations between the races' that it entails (Bonilla-Silva 1997, p. 469; see also Feagin 1991). Consequently, Omi and Winant (1994) insist on the strict theoretical separation of race from 'ethnicity', with its historical connections to assimilation.[3]

Such ideas are illustrated in several major studies of Mexican Americans including, most recently, *Generations of Exclusion* (Telles and Ortiz 2008). The book mainly casts Mexican Americans as a racialized group suffering from a 'social stigmatization that is entwined in a series of economic, political, and social processes and practices', such as 'institutional discrimination' that 'includes the under-financing of public schools which mostly Mexican origin students attend' (Telles and Ortiz 2008, pp. 285, 288; see also Kozol 1992). Telles and Ortiz (2008, p. 265) acknowledge that assimilation to the mainstream is possible, but they argue that it is 'slow' and uncommon and, moreover, that later-generation Mexican Americans continue to 'experience a world largely shaped by their race and ethnicity'. Above all, they show that the assimilation problems of Mexican Americans register in an educational gap from white Americans, which persists into the third and later generations.

A sceptical stance towards large-scale assimilation puts racialization theory in a bind, just as the stubbornness of racial inequality is problematic for assimilation theories. Older conceptions of assimilation included the eradication of the social distinction and differences between two populations (e.g. Gordon 1964; cf. Brubaker 2001). But assimilation is better conceptualized as the decline – not disappearance – of a distinction for some portions of a racial, or ethnic, minority group (Alba and Nee 2003). The distinction declines when it becomes restricted to fewer, and more private, social domains. For members of groups undergoing assimilation, the social and cultural distance to the mainstream decreases, and life chances come to closely approximate those held by their peers in the dominant group who are similar in socio-economic origin, birth cohort and so forth. Assimilation in this sense is contingent rather than universal, and may produce heterogeneity within minority groups, as opposed to uniform racial exclusion (Brubaker 2001).

We demonstrate here the substantial scale of Mexican American assimilation in the late twentieth century and give reasons to think it is increasing over time. This assimilation, however, does not negate the potency of racialization for many Mexican Americans. In light of assimilation theory, our focus is mainly on the variations in social context associated with intermarriage, mixed ancestry and geographical mobility, and on their joint relationship to educational attainment, a primary measure of Mexican Americans' social status. Since racialization theory presumes that racial categories are hard to escape while assimilation theory argues that they can become 'blurred', we also consider dimensions of ethnic identity.

The paradoxes of generations for Mexican Americans

A first step in assessing the situation of people of Mexican descent is to be clear about the appropriate temporal measures of change. Because this group includes individuals who were colonized, descendants of immigrants from different historical periods, and contemporary immigrants, measuring change over time is not straightforward. Immigrant *generation*, the most frequently used temporal marker of assimilation, refers to an individual's family distance from the point of immigration, where the immigrants make up the first generation, the US-born children of immigrants constitute the second generation, and so forth. Generation was the temporal measure of choice for studies of European-origin groups. Mass immigration of the canonical groups in the literature took place during a compact period that extended from roughly 1890 to 1920, creating a strong correlation between the generational status of individuals and the time period of their birth, or *birth cohort*.

Thus, individuals of the same generation – for instance, the offspring of immigrants – also experienced major historical events – the Great Depression and the Second World War – at similar points in their life cycle. For them, generation simultaneously captured the effects of birth distance since immigration *and* historical events.

Because Mexican immigration has been 'replenished' for the last century (Jiménez 2010), its continuous nature complicates the logic of using generation in the conventional way. Comparing Mexican Americans across generations without accounting for cohort misses important *intra*generational differences (Park and Myers 2010; Bean et al. 2013). For example, second-generation Mexican Americans growing up in the 1920s and 1930s attended highly segregated schools, came of age during the Great Depression and the Second World War, and entered the middle-adult years during a booming post-war economy. The second-generation children of post-1965 Mexican immigrants may also attend segregated schools, but they have come of age at the time of a globalized post-industrial economy, affirmative action and massive unauthorized immigration.

A related shortcoming of the conventional approach is that it fails to capture the effects of changes in the characteristics of Mexican immigrants over time. The average educational attainment in Mexico rose over the twentieth century, and educational attainment has been higher among Mexican immigrants in each successive cohort (Smith 2003). Thus, Mexican Americans who descend from earlier waves of immigrants trace their roots to immigrant populations who were more disadvantaged (in absolute terms) than those who come to the USA today. The disadvantaged position of these Mexican Americans is owed partly to differences in the educational and socio-economic status of immigrant forebears.

Finally, there is the problematic inclusion of the descendants of non-immigrant Mexicans in a generational classification. One cannot make sense of their experience with concepts derived from immigration because that experience more resembles those of so-called colonized groups (Lieberson 1961) – one, at least initially, of dispossession and exclusion and bereft of the optimism about social and material advance that is typically part of the immigrant's baggage. The colonial experience is especially relevant to the Mexican American communities near the Texas–Mexican border, including San Antonio, one of the two research sites for the MASP.

The MASP in geographical and historical context

To meet the challenges of identifying true change, we draw on the data and analyses presented in *Generations of Exclusion* (Telles and Ortiz 2008). The extraordinary data in the book come from a 1965 study of Mexican Americans in Los Angeles and San Antonio, the basis of the classic book, *The Mexican American People* (Grebler et al. 1970). Telles and Ortiz tracked down many of the original respondents and their now-grown children, making possible a view of intergenerational change among Mexican Americans during the late twentieth century.

Like many data sets intended for the study of ethnicity and race, the MASP data need to be set within their historical and geographical context in order to establish the valid range of the conclusions that can be drawn. It is important to begin with the sampling design for the original 1965 study. Since it focused on collecting data from individuals who were identifiably of Mexican descent, the ethnically focused design risks built-in biases against the more assimilated members of a group.

Implications of this sampling design are evident in two ways. First, for the sake of sampling efficiency, the original study was geographically confined to two cities with very large populations of Mexican Americans. Such cities offer more institutionally complete communities than do places with much smaller group populations, and therefore exert a stronger hold on group members, who have on average fewer socially intimate relationships with non-group members (Breton 1964). By contrast, in studies of cities and rural areas with smaller Mexican-origin populations, researchers have uncovered more contact between new immigrants and natives (Erwin 2003), and more social and other forms of assimilation among later-generation Mexican Americans (Jiménez 2010).

Second, the original sampling strategy within Los Angeles and San Antonio focused on individuals with so-called 'Spanish surnames'.

Counts of people with such surnames, provided by the 1960 census, were the only means available at that time for identifying the locations of Mexican American individuals and creating a sampling frame (Grebler et al. 1970, pp. 601–8, 631–47). The study design stratified census tracts by these counts, and within tracts of low and intermediate concentration, interviewers were instructed to pass by households with non-Spanish surnames. Intermarried Mexican Americans, particularly women, are thus likely to be under-represented in the original 1965 study (Telles and Ortiz 2008, pp. 50–1).

Finally, putting the original study in historical context, it was conducted in 1965–66, at almost exactly the moment when the civil rights movement was achieving its greatest legislative successes. Since Mexican Americans in some areas, especially in Texas, were forced to attend segregated schools prior to this point, the education of many were truncated, and the new generation of children had a socio-economic starting point not immediately much better than their parents had experienced. According to Grebler and colleagues (1970, p. 152), the educational attainment of Mexican Americans in 1960 was lower in Texas than in any other south-western state by a sizeable margin, and the educational gap separating the group from Anglos was the largest there. The role of pre-civil-rights-era institutional discrimination, and of school segregation in particular, did not affect only the parent sample of the MASP data; since the members of the child sample were born between 1947 and 1965, it is likely to have hampered some of them, too.

Intra-group heterogeneity and intergenerational change in the late twentieth century

Our analysis begins with markers of heterogeneity along three social-context dimensions – mixed ancestry, intermarriage and geographic mobility – using findings from *Generations of Exclusion* plus our own analyses of the MASP and US census data. We then show how these markers reveal heterogeneity in terms of two other dimensions: the first socio-economic (education) and the second identificational (ethnic identity).

Intermarriage and mixed ancestry

One of the most significant contributions of the MASP data concerns the children of intermarriages. Although there is an under-representation of intermarriages in the MASP data, the linkage of members of the MASP child sample to the family contexts in which they grew up is a significant advantage over more conventional sources. Telles and Ortiz demonstrate that intermarriage has been increasing intergenerationally (i.e. between parents and their children) among Mexican Americans in Los Angeles and San Antonio. For instance, 15 per cent of the original second-generation respondents and 32 per cent of their third-genera-tion children are intermarried. Almost all of these intermarriages involve Anglos/whites (Telles and Ortiz 2008, p. 176).

Intermarriage is selective of Mexican Americans who are distant in other ways from the core of the group. Having higher levels of education, growing up in less Hispanic neighbourhoods and being interviewed by phone (a proxy for geographic mobility) increase the odds of intermarriage with a non-Hispanic for Mexican Americans in the child sample (Telles and Ortiz 2008, p. 179). Thus, the children who are raised in intermarried families not only have a non-Mexican American parent but a Mexican American parent who is atypical for the group.

The children of intermarriages form a distinctive sub-population, which Telles and Ortiz (2008, p. 281) describe as follows:

> The 9% of children with a non-Hispanic parent were less likely to know Spanish, were more likely to intermarry themselves, identified less with their Mexican origin, and were more likely to call themselves American. Such children were often perceived as and understood themselves as less Mexican.[4]

Being the child of intermarriage raises the odds of marriage to a non-Hispanic fivefold (Telles and Ortiz 2008, p. 180), suggesting strongly that the children of intermarriages are integrated into non-Mexican as well as Mexican social circles.

Children with mixed Mexican ancestry were, moreover, more common in the 1960s than the MASP data can reveal because of the limitations of the original sample. Consider the national marriage data for Mexican Americans in Table 1, which we constructed from the 1970 census. It was the first census to use a Hispanic-origin question, making it possible to identify Mexican Americans of all generations, not just those with Spanish surnames. In Table 1, we focus on marriages in which the woman was under forty years of age in 1970 in order to capture the family settings in which Mexican American children were then growing up. Otherwise, we try to match the population of marriages that Grebler et al. (1970) would have observed in Los Angeles and San Antonio in 1965–66: one or both partners must be Mexican immigrants or US-born Mexican Americans who were at least eighteen years old in 1965–66.

Since couples produce children, what matters for the composition of the child generation in the MASP data is the intermarriage rate in 1970 based on marriages, not individuals. This rate of intermarriage by Mexican

Table 1. *Marriage patterns of Mexican-descent individuals in the United States, 1970 US census (in percentages based on table total; shaded cells represent exogamous marriages)*

		Wife's origin					
		Mexican (born in Mexico)	Mexican (born in USA)	Other Spanish origin	White, non-Spanish	Other, non-Spanish	**Total (*n*) marriages**
	Mexican (born in Mexico)	10.4	4.9	0.8	1.0	0.0	**57,800**
	Mexican (born in USA)	6.7	50.4	1.7	10.0	0.6	**234,200**
Husband's origin	Other Spanish origin	0.7	1.7	0.0	0.0	0.0	**7,800**
	White, non-Spanish	2.1	8.7	0.0	0.0	0.0	**36,300**
	Other, non-Spanish	0.1	0.3	0.0	0.0	0.0	**1,400**
	Total (*n*) marriages	**67,400**	**222,500**	**8,500**	**36,900**	**2,200**	**337,500 (100.1%)**

Note: Restrictions: Mexican-born individuals must have entered the country no later than 1966 to be included, and wives must be between the ages of twenty-two and forty in 1970; individuals who married for the first time after 1966 are excluded.
Source: 1970 US Census, 1% Public Use Microdata Sample.

Americans in the 1970 census is 23 per cent (the sum of the shaded boxes in Table 1). Therefore, even if we assume that the fertility of the endogamous marriages is substantially higher than those of the exogamous ones, we should expect the percentage of mixed-ancestry Mexican Americans in the nationwide child generation in 2000 to be about twice as large[5] as the percentage reported in the MASP data in that year.

As our analysis shows, intermarriage, arguably *the* yardstick of assimilation, was a significant aspect of the Mexican-American experience at the time that Grebler et al. (1970) collected the first wave of the MASP data, and the contribution of individuals with mixed ancestry to Mexican American assimilation patterns have been consequential. In light of the continued rise in intermarriage noted by Telles and Ortiz (2008) and other studies (e.g. Duncan and Trejo 2007), mixed ancestry, particularly with Anglo/white parentage, is certain to have become even more prevalent among later-generation Mexican Americans today.

Geographic mobility

Another benefit of the MASP data is that they allow for an analysis of how geographic mobility within the USA affects Mexican Americans' prospects for economic progress and social assimilation. Interest in geographic mobility has been increasing, given the dispersion of recent Mexican immigrants and Mexican Americans away from 'traditional' destinations in the south-west and southern California into 'new' ones, where the social contexts in which they and their children live are different (Zúñiga and Hernández-León 2005; Massey 2008; Marrow 2011). *Generations of Exclusion* documents a small degree of geographic mobility among original respondents living in Los Angeles and San Antonio between 1965 and 2000, but much more geographic mobility among their adult children as of 2000. While 2 per cent of the original respondents had moved out of the San Antonio metropolitan area by 2000 and 15 per cent out of Los Angeles, 11 per cent of their adult children had left San Antonio by 2000 and 22 per cent had moved away from Los Angeles (Telles and Ortiz 2008, pp. 58–9).[6]

Geographic mobility is strongly related to mixed ancestry and intermarriage, as is indicated in Table 2, which we compiled from the MASP child sample. This table reveals that the least geographically mobile groups are those with unmixed ancestry who are endogamously married or still single. Even when they leave the core counties of Los Angeles and San Antonio they tend to stay close by, relocating to a suburban county in the same metropolitan region. Exogamous

Table 2. *Geographic mobility patterns by marriage and ancestry types, child sample of the Mexican American Study Project (in percentages)*

	Child's ancestry			
	Unmixed Mexican			Mixed
	Marital status/type			
Geographic mobility	Single	Married (endogenous)	Married (exogamous)	
Still within the core county	74.1	77.0	44.7	56.3
Has moved to a suburban county	7.8	10.4	20.7	16.7
Has moved outside the metro area	18.0	12.6	34.6	27.0
Total (*n*) individuals (unweighted)	**189** (99.9%)	**345** (100.0%)	**149** (100.0%)	**68** (100.0%)

Note: $\chi^2 = 59.91$, d.f. $= 6$, $p < .001$

73

marriage, however, is associated with greater mobility, as many individuals move out of these metropolitan regions entirely.

Mobility is associated with surprisingly large and positive effects on assimilation indicators. This finding emerges from the multivariate analyses of the MASP data, in which Telles and Ortiz regularly include a telephone interview (versus one conducted face to face) as a proxy measure of geographic mobility. This proxy is one of the strongest determinants of earnings, income and net worth in 2000, increasing earnings by $7,479, income by $7,816, and net worth by $25,650, net of other factors (Telles and Ortiz 2008, p. 153). It is also one of the strongest determinants of not living in a Hispanic neighbourhood in 2000, decreasing the percentage of Hispanics in respondents' neighborhood by 14 per cent (Telles and Ortiz 2008, p. 170). Finally, it is a significant determinant of intermarriage, limited Spanish proficiency and reporting no discrimination in 2000 (Telles and Ortiz 2008, p. 235; see also Appendix Tables B.3–6, pp. 299–306).

These findings suggest that while a substantial fraction of Mexican Americans and their descendants are at risk of racial discrimination and stunted social mobility within two of the most concentrated metropolitan areas of traditional Mexican settlement, a theoretically important – and numerically significant – proportion is in a more advantageous position by virtue of its geographic mobility. The extent of this geographic mobility has not only increased over generations for the specific cohorts of Mexican Americans in the MASP data, it has also increased more generally as the newest Mexican immigrant arrivals have dispersed outside of traditional areas of Mexican settlement.

Education

Telles and Ortiz (2008, pp. 274–7) rightly place education at the centre of their analysis of Mexican American disadvantage, showing that it is powerfully related to numerous socio-economic and other assimilation indicators. However, their conclusions that their 'evidence shows no educational assimilation' and that 'the third and fourth generation do worst of all, suggesting downward assimilation in education' (Telles and Ortiz 2008, p. 131) are too pessimistic a reading of their data. Analysing changes in educational levels by the combination of generation *and* birth cohort actually reveals consistent and positive progress. For instance, Telles and Ortiz (2008, p. 111, Figure 5.2) show that average years of education rose from 4.1 among first-generation parents of original respondents (who attended school in the 1900s–30s) to 10.0 among second-generation original respondents (who attended school in the 1930s–50s) and to 13.1 among their third-generation children (who attended school during the 1950s–80s).

Mexican Americans in the sample have also made progress to narrow the educational gap with non-Hispanic whites across these historical generations. The gap between whites and all second-and-later-generation Mexican Americans who attended school in the 1900s–30s was roughly 3.4 years, but 2.3 years for the Mexican Americans who attended school in the 1930s–50s, and just 1.3 for all third-and-later-generation Mexican Americans who attended school in the 1950s–80s.

Our concern here is with unpacking educational heterogeneity among later-generation Mexican Americans, the group for whom educational stagnation appears to set in. Hence, we show how respondents' average years of education vary by original location, mixed ancestry and intermarriage. The data we have tabulated in Table 3 for the third and later generations demonstrate that the core of the educational problem in the MASP data is found among the endogamously married and single Mexican Americans of unmixed ancestry who grew up in San Antonio. Their education averages between 12.2 and 12.4 years; their counterparts who grew up in Los Angeles are not far above this range. All other categories of later-generation Mexican Americans have average educational attainments that are higher, generally by about a year.

Educational attainment is also related to whether later-generation Mexican Americans remain close to or within residential concentrations of the group. Decomposing categories of unmixed ancestry by geographic mobility, it appears that those who remain in San Antonio have the lowest education levels – although the numbers for the mobile are too small to be confident (data not shown). A similar connection

Table 3. *Educational attainment of the third- and later-generation child sample of the Mexican American Study Project, by marriage and ancestry types and region of origin (in mean years of education)*

	Child's ancestry			
	Unmixed Mexican			Mixed
	Marital status/type			
Region of origin	Single	Married (endogenous)	Married (exogamous)	
Los Angeles (unweighted n)	13.2 *(56)*	12.7 *(99)*	13.4 *(74)*	13.2 *(35)*
San Antonio (unweighted n)	12.2 *(62)*	12.4 *(117)*	14.1 *(25)*	13.2 *(11)*

Note: $F(7, 471) = 3.58$, $p < .001$

to mobility does not appear among those who grew up in Los Angeles, but the average levels of education are higher there.

This brief analysis points to the link between higher educational attainment, mixed ancestry, intermarriage and geographical mobility. As individuals distance themselves from the group's core, by marrying non-Mexicans or moving away from Mexican American concentrations, their education rises – and vice versa. This nexus carries important implications for the mechanisms of racialization, which are connected to spatial disparities in educational institutions. *Barrio* communities are also drained of the more successful Mexican Americans who, like all highly educated Americans compared with their less educated counterparts (Wozniak 2010), have more transferable skills and greater information about job opportunities in distant labour markets, and are more likely to move long distances to family and community settings that provide better opportunities.

Our analysis also indicates that, in the closing decades of the twentieth century, low educational attainment among later-generation Mexican Americans was most problematic in San Antonio, which is emblematic of communities strongly impacted by conquest and colonization. In Texas, this experience coloured the relations between Mexican Americans and Anglos well into the twentieth century, and the subordination of later-generation Mexican Americans was reflected in segregated school systems and unusually low educational attainment in the early 1960s, when the Grebler et al. (1970) study was launched. This experience should not be confused with the immigration experience, which characterizes the overwhelming majority of Mexican Americans nationwide.

Ethnic identity

Diversity among people of Mexican descent also registers in the form and salience of ethnic identity, which, because of factors such as replenishment of the immigrant population, the history of colonization and geographic dispersion, hinge on axes of both time and space. Across generations, Spanish-language use fades, intermarriage rates increase, and observance of Mexican customs and holidays declines, as does an affinity for Mexican music (Telles and Ortiz 2008). However, the replenishment of an immigrant population provides individuals who are generationally distant from the immigrant point of origin with new exposure to the symbols and practices that define Mexican ethnicity, while also reinforcing the racialization of Mexican-origin individuals, regardless of their generation, as perpetual foreigners (Jiménez 2010). Moreover, profit-making and political groups increasingly court Mexican Americans for their growing economic and political power, while an anti-Mexican-immigrant backlash racializes the whole group as illegal and foreign (Chavez 2008). This ambivalence, particularly towards immigrants, intensifies variation in the form and salience of Mexican-origin ethnic identity nationwide.

Importantly, intermarriage has produced a Mexican-origin population that includes a large number of individuals for whom Mexican ancestry is one of many components of a multiethnic ancestral heritage. These individuals show flexibility in constructing their ethnic identity that does not exist for their 'unmixed' counterparts (Jiménez 2004; Lee and Bean 2010). In the MASP data, the odds that Mexican Americans with one non-Hispanic parent identify as 'American' or 'other' are more than twice that of their unmixed co-ethnics (Telles and Ortiz 2008, p. 305). In addition, the types of identity labels that Mexican Americans use to describe their ethnic origin display geographic variation. Mexican Americans in San Antonio are unusually likely to choose pan-ethnic labels, like 'Hispanic', and avoid ethnic-specific labels like 'Mexican' (Telles and Ortiz 2008, pp. 238–63). These choices likely reflect the fact that Mexican Americans in San Antonio have had to fashion ethnic identities in the face of a persistently strong hostility typical of the Texas border region.[7]

Our analysis focuses on two indictors related to social boundaries: how individuals present themselves and how they are likely to be perceived by others. One is the salience of a Mexican American identity (we contrast those who say that they 'hardly ever' or 'never' think of themselves as Mexican origin or as Chicano against everyone else); the other, the perceived likelihood that persons meeting respondents for the first time will think of them as having Mexican origin (we contrast those who say 'probably not' or 'definitely not' against all others). In the MASP data, about one sixth of Mexican Americans rarely think of themselves as Mexican (17 per cent), and more than a quarter believe that others are unlikely to perceive them as Mexican (29 per cent).

Having mixed ancestry powerfully and positively affects rarely thinking of oneself as Mexican or Chicano. Table 4 shows that mixed ancestry increases the odds of such a weak identity by more than 2.5 times. There is something of a countervailing tendency in the effect of age on the frequency of thinking of oneself as Mexican: Table 4 shows that younger respondents are, all other things being equal, more likely to identify in this way, perhaps reflecting the growing salience of Mexican ethnicity in contemporary America (Jiménez 2010). Education has no effect either way.

Believing oneself to be not easily identifiable as a Mexican American is positively related to education, intermarriage and geographic mobility. According to Table 4, a four-year increase in education – the difference between high school and a college degree – almost doubles the chances that respondents believe that they are *not* easily spotted as having Mexican ancestry. Intermarriage also more than

Table 4. *Logistic regression analysis of factors shaping self- and external identification as Mexican, child sample of the Mexican American Study Project (odds ratios)*

	Rarely think of oneself as Mexican/Chicano	Unlikely to be identifiable as Mexican
Education (years)	1.01	**1.16**
Mixed ancestry	**2.60**	1.56
Marital status		
Single	1.01	**2.13**
Exogamous	1.14	**2.32**
Endogamous	–	–
Geographical mobility		
Still within the core county	–	–
Has moved to a suburban county	1.37	1.02
Has moved outside the metro area	0.86	**1.56**
Gender (female)	1.11	1.24
Year born	**0.96**	1.00
Raised in San Antonio	**2.36**	**0.57**

Numbers in bold are statistically significant (.05 level).

doubles these chances, and moving away from Los Angeles or San Antonio lifts them, too. Skin colour, although not shown in Table 4, may also play a role, with darker respondents believing that they are more likely to be identifiable as Mexican Americans. However, since skin colour was only measured in face-to-face interviews in the MASP, we cannot meaningfully compare its effect between the 'stayers' and 'movers' independently of geographic mobility.

The weakening of ethnic identity among Mexican Americans who are distant from the group's core may even remove some individuals from the group, at least in a statistical sense. Alba and Islam (2009; see also Emeka and Agius Vallejo 2011) found that, across censuses, sizes of US-born cohorts of Mexican Americans declined to a degree unexplained by mortality. Presumably, some individuals who identified themselves on a census form as Mexican American at one point in time did not do so at a later point. This phenomenon does not mean that all of these 'disappearing' individuals have detached themselves entirely from a Mexican American identity, but rather that their attachment to it is no longer regular and reliable.

Conclusion

Our findings based on the MASP and supplemental census data paint a complex picture of the Mexican American situation. Racialization is an appropriate characterization of the disadvantage faced by a large portion of the group, including many whose family roots in the USA extend back more than two generations. Although we cannot fully assess the role of skin colour, the disadvantages experienced by many Mexican Americans do arise from spatially concentrated forms of institutionalized discrimination, such as poor schools, and are buttressed by stigmatizing ideologies.

However, we find that another substantial portion of the group is in the process of assimilating into the mainstream in significant ways and does not face such extreme racialization. This portion is detectable through a series of markers on various economic, social and identificational dimensions, including high educational attainment, geographic mobility away from regions of Mexican American concentration, intermarriage and mixed ancestry. If we count those members of the MASP child sample who are intermarried, have mixed ancestry or who have moved away from their metropolitan region of birth, we arrive at 41.7 per cent of the total. This minority is not small, even without adjusting for the under-representation of mixed ancestry among them.

In addition, it is almost certain that this portion of the group is growing in size among later-generation Mexican Americans. In the 2000 census, Duncan and Trejo (2007, p. 246) found that nearly 50 per cent of the marriages involving at least one US-born Mexican American were to non-Mexicans, the lion's share of whom were non-Hispanic whites. Even if the fertility of the endogamous is higher than that of the exogamous, the high frequency of Mexican American intermarriage implies a substantial increase of mixed ancestry among later generations of the group compared to the situation in 1965 – the baseline year for the MASP data.

Other forces are likely to increase the size of the movement in an assimilatory direction. One is the ongoing geographic dispersal of immigrants away from regions of Mexican American concentration. Recent research shows that, unlike their counterparts in traditional destinations, Mexicans' place in the local racial hierarchies of new destinations has not yet crystallized (Hernández-León and Zúñiga 2005; Smith 2005; Marrow 2011). Also, despite rising segregation, largely due to new immigration, Hispanics in new destination metros are significantly less segregated and isolated from both whites and blacks than they are in traditional metros (Fischer and Tienda 2006).

But the concentration of Mexican Americans at the other end of the spectrum may also be growing. One reason is the large proportion of the Mexican immigrant population that has long-term unauthorized status – currently estimated at 6.7–7 million (Passel and Cohn 2011). Even as assimilation siphons off Mexican Americans who are advancing socio-economically and integrating socially, credible evidence shows that the mobility of a large part of the contemporary second generation – including those who are US citizens born to unauthorized immigrant parents (Yoshikawa 2011) – is hampered because of the increasingly consequential effects of unauthorized status (Abrego 2006; Gonzales 2011). New research from Los Angeles suggests that for this very disadvantaged portion of the group, the negative legacy effects of nativity or legal status discrimination – rather than group-level racial discrimination – may better account for patterns of 'delayed' – rather than 'blocked' – intergenerational educational and residential incorporation (Brown 2007; Bean et al. 2011, 2013). Still, the strong association of unauthorized status with 'Mexicanness' helps to racialize the entire group as 'illegal', and therefore unfit for full membership in US American society (Chavez 2008; Jiménez 2010).

The heterogeneity of experience and social position is likely to be salient for Americans of Mexican descent in the early twentieth century and possibly paradigmatic for numerous other non-white immigrant-origin groups. For one thing, the ethno-racial turnover that will be produced in the labour market by the baby boomers' retirement during the next quarter-century will create unusual opportunities for minority-group advancement and assimilation (Alba 2009). Simultaneously, many second- and third-generation members of contemporary immigrant groups will be held back by racial disadvantages, especially the inferior life chances associated with growing up in segregated neighbourhoods.

The results will seem paradoxical, as does the status of Mexican Americans in the MASP data. While there is the social acceptability signalled by relatively high intermarriage rates, there are also the high dropout rates and persistently low educational attainment of young people in some Mexican American communities. As Telles (2010) argues, and as recent empirical accounts suggest (Brown 2007; Bean et al. 2011; Vasquez 2011; Agius Vallejo 2012; Bean et al. 2013), no single existing theoretical model will capture this diversity, for both racialization and assimilation characterize the Mexican American group – and others. For example, some members of the West Indian community are well educated and economically successful, while others are downwardly mobile and geographically concentrated (Waters 1999; Portes et al. 2005). Many members of the traditional Dominican and Puerto Rican communities in New York City are hampered by persistent low education and high poverty rates, but newer arrivals exhibit greater class differentiation (Aranda 2008), and geographic dispersion into newer gateway settlements is taking place (Itzigsohn 2009; Oropesa and Jensen 2010). Racialization and assimilation *divide* these groups, too – highlighting intra-group diversity as potentially one of the defining features of patterns of immigrant-group incorporation in the twenty-first century.

Notes

1. Following Alba and Nee (2003, p. 12), we understand the 'mainstream' as 'that part of American society within which ethnic and racial origins have at most minor impacts.'
2. We thank Edward Telles and Vilma Ortiz for sharing the child sample of the MASP data. We take responsibility for any errors committed in our analysis of the data.
3. While scholars heavily debate the distinction between these two terms both in the USA and abroad, for our purposes it suffices to say that the boundaries around ethnic groups often derive more strongly from 'insiders'' claims to perceived common ancestry, whereas those around racial groups often derive from 'outsiders'' imposition of a social distinction based on perceived phenotypical and other differences (Cornell and Hartmann 2006).
4. Lee and Bean (2010) report similar findings from interviews with the offspring of Mexican–white intermarriages.
5. The children in these families generally belong to the baby boom cohorts, when fertility of non-Mexican women was very high. Assuming that the average exogamous family had 3.0 children and the average endogamous one 4.0, we would expect about 18 per cent of Mexican Americans born in this period to come from intermarriages.
6. These are likely to be underestimates of mobility since the mobile are harder to find in a follow-up study than are those who have remained in place.
7. There is, to be sure, variability in the racialization patterns of Mexicans over time and place within Texas (Montejano 1987).

References

ABREGO, LEISY JANET 2006 '"I can't go to college because I don't have papers": incorporation patterns of Latino undocumented youth', *Latino Studies*, vol. 4, no. 3, pp. 212–31

AGIUS VALLEJO, JODY 2012 *Barrios to Burbs: The Making of the Mexican-American Middle Class*, Stanford, CA: Stanford University Press

ALBA, RICHARD 2009 *Blurring the Color Line: The New Chance for a more Integrated America*, Cambridge, MA: Harvard University Press

ALBA, RICHARD and ISLAM, TARIQUL 2009 'The case of the disappearing Mexican Americans: an ethnic-identity mystery', *Population Research and Policy Review*, vol. 28, no. 2, pp. 109–21

ALBA, RICHARD and NEE, VICTOR 2003 *Remaking the American Mainstream: Assimilation and Contemporary Immigration*, Cambridge, MA: Harvard University Press

ARANDA, ELIZABETH M. 2008 'Class backgrounds, modes of incorporation, and Puerto Ricans' pathways into the transnational professional workforce', *American Behavioral Scientist*, vol. 52, no. 3, pp. 426–56

BEAN, FRANK, *et al.* 2011 'The educational legacy of unauthorized migration: comparisons across US immigrant groups in how parents' status affects their offspring', *International Migration Review*, vol. 45, no. 2, pp. 348–85

BEAN, FRANK, *et al.* 2013 'The implications of unauthorized migration for the educational incorporation of Mexican-Americans', in Bryant Jensen and Adam Sawyer (eds), *Regarding Educacion: Mexican-American Schooling, Immigration, and Bi-national Development*, New York: Teachers' College Press, pp. 43–65

BONILLA-SILVA, EDUARDO 1997 'Racism: toward a structural interpretation', *American Sociological Review*, vol. 62, no. 3, pp. 465–80

—— 2004 'From bi-racial to tri-racial: towards a new system of racial stratification in the USA', *Ethnic and Racial Studies*, vol. 27, no. 6, pp. 931–50

BRETON, RAYMOND 1964 'Institutional completeness of ethnic communities and the personal relations of immigrants', *American Journal of Sociology*, vol. 70, no. 2, pp. 193–205

BROWN, SUSAN K. 2007 'Delayed spatial assimilation: multigenerational incorporation of the Mexican-origin population in Los Angeles', *City & Community*, vol. 6, no. 3, pp. 193–209
BRUBAKER, ROGERS 2001 'The return of assimilation? Changing perspectives on immigration and its sequels in France, Germany, and the United States', *Ethnic and Racial Studies*, vol. 24, no. 4, pp. 531–48
CHAVEZ, LEO 2008 *The Latino Threat: Constructing Immigrants, Citizens, and the Nation*, Stanford, CA: Stanford University Press
CORNELL, STEPHEN and HARTMANN, DOUGLAS 2006 *Ethnicity and Race: Making Identities in a Changing World*, Newbury Park, CA: Pine Forge Press
DUNCAN, BRIAN and TREJO, STEPHEN 2007 'Ethnic identification, intermarriage, and unmeasured progress by Mexican Americans', in George J. Borjas (ed.), *Mexican Immigration to the United States*, Cambridge, MA: National Bureau of Economic Research, pp. 229–67
EMEKA, AMON and AGIUS VALLEJO, JODY 2011 'Non-Hispanics with Latin American ancestry: assimilation, race, and identity among Latin American descendants in the US', *Social Science Research*, vol. 40, no. 6, pp. 1547–63
ERWIN, DEBORAH O. 2003 'An ethnographic description of Latino immigration in rural Arkansas: intergroup relations and utilization of healthcare services', *Southern Rural Sociology*, vol. 19, no. 1, pp. 46–72
FEAGIN, JOE 1991 'The continuing significance of race: antiblack discrimination in public places', *American Sociological Review*, vol. 56, no. 1, pp. 101–16
FISCHER, MARY J. and TIENDA, MARTA 2006 'Redrawing spatial color lines: Hispanic metropolitan dispersal, segregation, and economic opportunity', in Marta Tienda and Faith Mitchell (eds), *Hispanics and the Future of America*, Washington, DC: National Academies Press, pp. 100–37
GONZALES, ROBERTO G. 2011 'Learning to be illegal: undocumented youth and shifting legal contexts in the transition to adulthood', *American Sociological Review*, vol. 76, no. 4, pp. 602–19
GORDON, MILTON M. 1964 *Assimilation in American Life: The Role of Race, Religion, and National Origins*, New York: Oxford University Press
GREBLER, LEO, *et al.* 1970 *The Mexican-American People: The Nation's Second Largest Minority*, New York: The Free Press
HERNÁNDEZ-LEÓN, RUBÉN and ZÚÑIGA, VICTOR 2005 'Appalachia meets Aztlán: Mexican immigration and intergroup relations in Dalton, Georgia', in Victor Zúñiga and Rubén Hernández-León (eds), *New Destinations: Mexican Immigrants in the United States*, New York: Russell Sage, pp. 244–73
ITZIGSOHN, JOSÉ 2009 *Encountering American Faultlines: Race, Class, and the Dominican Experience in Providence*, New York: Russell Sage
JIMÉNEZ, TOMÁS R. 2004 'Multiethnic Mexican Americans and ethnic identity in the United States', *Ethnicities*, vol. 4, no. 1, pp. 75–97
—— 2010 *Replenished Ethnicity: Mexican Americans, Immigration, and Identity*, Berkeley, CA: University of California Press
KOZOL, JONATHAN 1992 *Savage Inequalities*, New York: HarperCollins
LEE, JENNIFER and BEAN, FRANK D. 2010 *The Diversity Paradox: Immigration and the Color Line in 21st Century America*, New York: Russell Sage
LIEBERSON, STANLEY 1961 'A societal theory of race and ethnic relations', *American Sociological Review*, vol. 26, no. 6, pp. 902–10
LÓPEZ, DAVID E. and STANTON-SALAZAR, RICARDO D. 2001 'Mexican Americans: a second generation at risk', in Rubén G. Rumbaut and Alejandro Portes (eds), *Ethnicities: Children of Immigrants in America*, Berkeley, CA: University of California Press, pp. 57–90
MARROW, HELEN B. 2011 *New Destination Dreaming: Immigration, Race, and Legal Status in the Rural American South*, Stanford, CA: Stanford University Press

MASSEY, DOUGLAS S. 2007 *Categorically Unequal: The American Stratification System*, New York: Russell Sage
——— (ed.) 2008 *New Faces in New Places: The Changing Geography of American Immigration*, New York: Russell Sage
MONTEJANO, DAVID 1987 *Anglos and Mexicans in the Making of Texas, 1836–1986*, Austin, TX: University of Texas Press
OMI, MICHAEL and WINANT, HOWARD 1994 *Racial Formation in the United States: From the 1960s to the 1990s*, 2nd edn, New York: Routledge & Kegan Paul
OROPESA, R. S. and JENSEN, LEIF 2010 'Dominican immigrants and discrimination in a new destination: the case of Reading, Pennsylvania', *City & Community*, vol. 9, no. 3, pp. 274–98
PARK, JULIE and MYERS, DOWELL 2010 'Intergenerational mobility in the post-1965 immigration era: estimates by an immigrant generation cohort', *Demography*, vol. 47, no. 2, pp. 369–92
PASSEL, JEFFREY S. and COHN, D'VERA 2011 *Unauthorized Immigrant Population: National and State Trends, 2010*, Washington, DC: Pew Hispanic Center
PERLMANN, JOEL 2005 *Italians then, Mexicans now: Immigrant Origins and Second-Generation Progress, 1890 to 2000*, New York: Russell Sage
PORTES, ALEJANDRO, *et al.* 2005 'Segmented assimilation on the ground: the new second generation in early adulthood', *Ethnic and Racial Studies*, vol. 28, no. 6, pp. 1000–40
PORTES, ALEJANDRO and RUMBAUT, RUBÉN G. 2001 *Legacies: The Story of the Immigrant Second Generation*, Berkeley, CA: University of California Press
SMITH, JAMES P. 2003 'Assimilation across the generations', *American Economic Review*, vol. 93, no. 2, pp. 315–9
SMITH, ROBERT C. 2005 'Racialization and Mexicans in New York City', in Victor Zúñiga and Rubén Hernández-León (eds), *New Destinations: Mexican Immigration to the United States*, Russell Sage, pp. 220–43
TELLES, EDWARD 2010 'Mexican Americans and immigrant incorporation', *Contexts*, vol. 9, no. 1, pp. 28–33
TELLES, EDWARD E. and ORTIZ, VILMA 2008 *Generations of Exclusion: Mexican Americans, Assimilation, and Race*, New York: Russell Sage
VASQUEZ, JESSICA 2011 *Mexican Americans across Generations: Immigrant Families, Racial Realities*, New York: New York University Press
WATERS, MARY C. 1999 *Black Identities: West Indian Immigrant Dreams and American Realities*, Cambridge, MA: Harvard University Press
WINANT, HOWARD 2000 'Race and race theory', *Annual Review of Sociology*, vol. 26, pp. 169–85
WOZNIAK, ABIGAIL 2010 'Are college graduates more responsive to distance labor market opportunities?', *Journal of Human Resources*, vol. 45, no. 4, pp. 944–70
YOSHIKAWA, HIROKAZU 2011 *Immigrants Raising Citizens: Undocumented Parents and their Young Children*, New York: Russell Sage
ZÚÑIGA, VICTOR and HERNÁNDEZ-LEÓN, RUBÉN (eds) 2005 *New Destinations: Mexican Immigration to the United States*, New York: Russell Sage

Segmented political assimilation: perceptions of racialized opportunities and Latino immigrants' partisan identification

Frank Samson

Abstract

To account for Latino immigrants' assimilation into the American political mainstream, I derive social psychological factors from the contextual notion of 'modes of incorporation' in the segmented assimilation literature. These social psychological factors, perceptions of racialized opportunities (PROPs), relate to immigrants' adoption of political party identities (i.e. Democrat, Republican). I test these PROPs factors utilizing the 2006 Latino National Survey ($N = 5,717$ immigrant Latino respondents). Multinomial logistic regressions predicting party identification, compared to either 'Don't Know' or 'Don't Care' options, indicate that PROPs are significantly related to Latino immigrants' identification as either Democrats or Republicans. High levels of identification with perceived white opportunities are related to Republican identity and high levels of identification with perceived black opportunities differentiate Democrats from Republicans.

Introduction

Latino support will progressively determine the two major US political parties' futures.[1] Increased Latino political power swayed elections in 2004, 2006, 2008 and 2010 (Barreto et al. 2008; Leal et al. 2005; Leal et al. 2008; Gomez and Amor 2011). Former Florida governor Jeb Bush stated:

> It's a question of political math...If Hispanic voters are increasingly the swing voters in the swing states, it cries out for common sense to make an effort on an on-

going basis to assure that Hispanics know that the Republican Party or that the conservative cause wants them. (Gomez 2011; see also Gimpel and Kaufmann 2001)

Identifying factors related to Latino immigrant partisan identification become important as their population numbers continue to rise.

This paper views political party identification as an identity into which immigrants assimilate. The segmented assimilation literature, with its focus on modes of incorporation (Portes and Zhou 1993; Zhou 1997; Portes, Fernández-Kelly and Haller 2005; Stepick and Stepick 2010), can help detail not only the dynamics of ethnic identity retention, but also partisan identification. Because modes of incorporation place various constraints on immigrants' opportunities and structure a particular locale's mobility pathways, which in turn shape ethnic identification, these trajectories could also affect partisan identity adoption.

This paper proposes that perceptions of racialized opportunities (PROPs) inform Latino immigrants' partisan identification. PROPs refer to estimations of racialized and differentiated life chances to attain a desired living standard, based upon conventional socio-economic factors that improve life chances (jobs, education, income), as well as the political influence that secures or further improves life chances. Using the 2006 Latino National Survey's sample of 5,717 immigrants, I use multinomial logistic regression to estimate the probability of identifying as Democrat, Republican or Independent compared to two categories: (1) those who 'Don't Care' about party identification; and (2) those who either 'Don't Know' their party identification (perhaps due to indecision or unfamiliarity with US partisan politics) and those who profess an 'Other Party' identification. The results indicate that high PROPs associated with whites are related to Republican identity and high PROPs associated with blacks differentiate Democrats from Republicans.

Theoretical background

Prior research on Hispanic partisan identification accounted for demographic factors, socio-economic background, experiences, ideology and policy attitudes. Cain, Kiewiet and Uhlaner (1991) documented the effects of income and union membership (economic advancement), years in the USA (assimilation into minority group status) and foreign policy concerns. Wong (2000) detailed the importance of media exposure and English language skills. Alvarez and García Bedolla (2003) explored policy attitudes (e.g. beliefs about affirmative action, school vouchers, government-supported health care, etc.). Dutwin et al. (2005) explored self-identification as Latino/Hispanic (versus American), political trust and national origins.

85

Uhlaner and Garcia (2005) drew attention to ancestry (e.g. Cuban, Mexican, Puerto Rican). Moreover, conventional political socialization models founded upon intergenerational transfer and early socialization may have limited purchase due to recent, large Latino immigration (Campbell et al. 1960).

The present research identifies a set of social contexts-conditioned racial attitudes that may also prove influential: perceptions of racialized opportunities (PROPs). While immigrants negotiate mobility structures demarcated by the mode of incorporation, immigrants associate the opportunities available to them with the opportunities available to whites, blacks or co-ethnic immigrants. This paper tests whether these PROPs relate to partisan identification.

Modes of incorporation and perceptions of racialized opportunities

Three contextual factors (government policy, host society acceptance, and the co-ethnic community's size and character) largely shape immigrants' modes of incorporation and partially determine their segmented mobility trajectories (Portes and Rumbaut 2001). Government policy towards immigrants can be hostile (e.g. exclusion or undocumented status), neutral (documented process but no additional governmental support) or favourable (additional programmes targeted to ease the transition of immigrants such as refugees. Likewise, host society acceptance can be hostile/prejudiced or neutral. Finally, a co-ethnic community can vary by its class character (poor, working class, or professional or entrepreneurial) and presence/influence (non-existent, weak, or powerful and well established). These modes of incorporation interact with family structure and human capital to channel immigrant and later generations' mobility into one of three general directions: (1) the conventional, straight-line assimilation, upwardly mobile trajectory that many European immigrants followed during the nineteenth and early twentieth century; (2) assimilation into either a stagnant trajectory or a downwardly mobile trajectory associated with the urban poor, a condition stereotypically conflated with the experience of poor blacks; and (3) an upwardly mobile trajectory based on the maintenance of ties to a co-ethnic community with access to professional and entrepreneurial social and cultural capital. Because modes of incorporation impact immigrants' social relations and experiences in key institutions (e.g. labour markets, workplaces, neighbourhoods, schools, government services, etc.), they constrain opportunities to greater and lesser degrees, opportunities that individuals could relate to racialized groups' constrained opportunities. Socio-historical research confirmed that southern and eastern European immigrants, blacks and Mexicans, if not Hispanics as a whole, each encountered different opportunities in the early half of the twentieth century (Fox and Guglielmo 2012).

Perceptions of shared opportunities with whites

A mode of incorporation encompassing neutral government policy, neutral reception by society and its institutions, and a largely professional or entrepreneurial co-ethnic community would most likely foster PROPs associated with whites. Since beliefs about stratification and mobility have long revolved around the tenets of individualism and meritocracy (Kluegel and Smith 1986), perceptions of white opportunity would reflect the absence of structural constraints. An immigrant who sees his/her prospects, experiences and influence as both unfettered by institutions or another's actions is most likely to develop PROPs associated with whites. For this to occur, government policy towards immigrants would be neutral; either a hostile or favourable targeted policy would mark immigrants' experiences as non-normative, making their mobility less about individual effort and more about obstacles or special aid. Immigrants must also experience a largely non-prejudiced societal reception. A non-prejudiced societal reception facilitating close and intimate social relations with whites, in particular close friendships and marriage, might also contribute to perceptions of shared opportunities. A professional or entrepreneurial co-ethnic community could incubate PROPs associated with whites by providing examples of success and making obstacles seem surmountable. White political candidates might also target professional or entrepreneurial co-ethnic communities for votes and political contributions, creating a scenario for immigrants to feel as if they possess comparable influence over the political process as whites. Common to all these examples is the absence of targeted support or structural constraints, easily facilitating immigrants' socio-economic and political progress.

Perceptions of shared opportunities with blacks

A mode of incorporation primarily featuring prejudiced societal reaction and either a poor or a weak, working class co-ethnic community would most likely nurture PROPs associated with blacks. Portes and Rumbaut (2001, p. 47) argued:

> In America, race is a paramount criterion of social acceptance that can overwhelm the influence of class background, religion, or language. Regardless of their class origin or knowledge of English, nonwhite immigrants face greater obstacles in gaining access to the white middle-class mainstream and may receive lower returns for their education and work experience.

They referred to obstacles akin to 'structural' factors that stratification beliefs scholars documented as explanations given by whites, blacks and Hispanics for black/white inequality and poverty (Kluegel and Smith 1986; Hunt 2004, 2007).

Propinquity to high black concentrations in segregated poor neighbourhoods would further develop a sense of shared opportunity with blacks. The low income resulting from human capital disparities and occupational wage inequalities can cause immigrants to reside in low-income and/or racially segregated neighbourhoods (Portes 2007; Jargowsky 2009). Local schools in low-income neighbourhoods often lack sufficient resources to provide a high-quality education to immigrants or later generations (Darling-Hammond 2004; Hao and Pong 2008).

Other neighbourhood-based factors might also prove influential in promoting PROPs associated with blacks. Some immigrants may experience racial profiling or harassment at the hands of law enforcement officers patrolling their neighbourhoods. Immigrants may also find themselves utilizing government services, such as public transportation, affordable housing offices and so on, alongside African Americans. Latinos' policy interests at times overlap with African Americans, for example affirmative action and welfare (Pantoja, Ramirez and Segura 2001), and Latinos are courted to support black political candidates (Kaufmann 2003a). Finally, simple face-to-face social interactions, friendships, intimate relations and marriages between immigrants and blacks could be a factor in perceiving shared opportunity.

The presence of a poor co-ethnic community or a weak, working-class co-ethnic community would make it difficult for immigrants to surmount many of the aforementioned structural obstacles. The absence of a professional or entrepreneurial co-ethnic community would limit access to high-quality jobs and information, as well as gainfully employed role models. Immigrants in this context may face the social isolation that middle-class black out-migration produced for poor urban blacks (Wilson 1990). Taken together, these structural factors impose constraints on immigrants' opportunities similar to the constrained opportunities that blacks encounter based on race and class, and their interaction.

Perceptions of shared opportunities with Latinos

A mode of incorporation involving utilization of a tightly knit co-ethnic community with social capital, regardless of class or occupational character, to overcome obstacles posed by hostile government policy or nativist societal reception would most likely foster PROPs associated with Latinos. This mode of incorporation differs from the mode for perceived white opportunities in that immigrants rely on co-ethnic ties to overcome obstacles that are largely absent when societal reception is neutral. Furthermore, this mode of incorporation differs from that promoting identification with black opportunity because of a mobility trajectory (through a close-knit co-ethnic community with social capital) unavailable to blacks either living in social isolation in under-resourced neighbourhoods or social exclusion in middle-class areas. Society's hostility would also differ in character: founded upon nativism, questions of immigration legality (hostile government policy), or resentment regarding advantages for refugees (favourable government policy).

A variety of institutional contexts (labour market, neighbourhoods, schools, etc.) could also promote PROPs associated with Latinos. Established communities of national ancestry associated with high levels of unauthorized immigration (Jiménez 2008) can lead to presumptions of being undocumented and difficulty securing formal labour market jobs. Immigrants may utilize social networks to move into immigrant occupational niches (Waldinger 1994) or jobs requiring bilingual Spanish/non-Spanish proficiency (Linton and Jiménez 2009). Some immigrants may find themselves supplanting native whites and blacks as part of co-ethnic recruitment (Marrow 2009; Lopez-Sanders 2011). Attempts to unionize Latino workers as an ethnic group could also prove influential.

Neighbourhood segregation alongside other Latinos, particularly in established ethnic enclaves (Portes and Stepick 1994; Guarnizo, Sanchez and Roach 1999; Itzigsohn et al. 1999), provides additional contexts for identifying with Latino opportunities. Ethnic commercial enclaves peppered with signs and product labels in Spanish can provide employment. Neighbourhood schools may track students into Limited English Proficiency courses (Zhou et al. 2008) or require a Spanish translator to help immigrant parents interact with school personnel. Politicians may target enclaves for donations and votes, appealing to Latino political interests.

Finally, a nativist social reception also promotes identifying with Latino opportunities. Discomfort or hostility directed at immigrants' Spanish language use, accented English or adoption of other Latino-associated cultural markers (music, dress, religion, etc.) could play a role (Jiménez 2008; Marrow 2009), especially if those ethnic-distinctive markers are perceived to limit upward socio-economic mobility or steer immigrants towards friendships or marriage with other Latinos. All of these factors represent support or constraints based specifically on a Latino background, marking these opportunities as distinct from those associated with whites or blacks.

Political parties and racialized group interests

Studies have indicated that individuals view parties through a racialized lens, despite major US political parties' attempts to develop a diverse constituency. Carmines and Stimson (1989) document racial conservatism's ascendance among Republicans, marked by Goldwater's presidential nomination in 1964, and Democrats' adoption of racial liberalism. In the 1980s, Ronald Reagan's success in appealing to southern white voters, even across the traditional conservative/liberal divide, further consolidated the Republican Party's reputation as representing white interests (Black and Black 2002). In the post-civil rights era, partisan strategy continues to employ implicit racial messages to appeal to voters' racial predispositions (Mendelberg 2001).

While these historical events and campaign strategies contributed to native-born whites and blacks perceiving the major political parties through a racialized lens, immigrants also acquire these racialized partisan lenses through a number of similar dynamics, including historical events, shared policy interests and political campaigns, both local and national. During the 1960s, Cesar Chavez organized a union of farm workers, many of them Latino immigrants; his United Farm Workers was associated with both the civil rights movement and Democrats (Bruns 2011). In the aftermath of contentious immigrant policy and Mexican American ethnic studies debates, a Republican state representative in 2012 called for a holiday celebrating white people (Erwin 2012). Moreover, various public policies affecting immigrants readily fall along black/white and Democrat/Republican divides. Many Latinos benefit from welfare and affirmative action policies (Bobo 1998; Nicholson and Segura 2005; Bowler, Nicholson and Segura 2006), although Mexican immigrants had greater difficulty accessing welfare than European immigrants (Fox 2012). Blacks and Democrats typically support, and whites and Republicans typically although not monolithically oppose, both policies (Tolbert and Grummel 2003; Alvarez and García Bedolla 2004). Finally, elections featuring black Democratic candidates reaching out to Latinos underscored the association between Democrats and black interests (Muñoz and Henry 1986). Latino immigrants settling into co-ethnic communities that witnessed or learned about these occurrences might readily link Democrats to black interests and Republicans to white interests. Latino immigrants are more likely than native-born Latinos to perceive racism as a significant problem and are politically more informed in anxiety-provoking political contexts (Pantoja and Segura 2003).

Given the Republican Party's contemporary association with white interests, I hypothesize:

H1:   As identification with white opportunities increases, the likelihood of Latino immigrants identifying as Republican increases compared to 'Don't Know' or 'Don't Care' about party identification.

H2:   As identification with white opportunities increases, the likelihood of Latino immigrants identifying as Republican increases compared to Democrat identification.

In contrast, the national Democratic Party championed racial liberalism against Southern Democrats' segregationist interests in the heat of civil rights struggles (Carmines and Stimson 1989; Black and Black 2002). Democratic strategy continues to target and attract black voters in the post-civil rights era. I therefore hypothesize:

H3:   As identification with black opportunities increases, the likelihood of Latino immigrants identifying as Democrat increases compared to 'Don't Know' or 'Don't Care' about party identification.

H4:   As identification with black opportunities increases, the likelihood of Latino immigrants identifying as Republican decreases compared to Democrat identification.

Finally, to the extent that Latino immigrants share a 'minority group status' alongside blacks (Cain, Kiewiet and Uhlaner 1991), I predict that Republicans' contemporary association with white interests will shift many Latino immigrants to prefer Democrats. Latinos' beliefs that Democrats are better able than Republicans to address Latino concerns will facilitate such a shift (Nicholson and Segura 2005).

H5:   As identification with Latino opportunities increases, the likelihood of Latino immigrants identifying as Democrat increases compared to 'Don't Know' or 'Don't Care' about party identification.

H6:   As identification with Latino opportunities increases, the likelihood of Latino immigrants identifying as Republican decreases compared to Democrat identification.

Data

To test the PROPs mechanism, I utilize the 2006 Latino National Survey (LNS) (Fraga et al. 2006). The LNS spans a geographic coverage consisting of fifteen states housing 87.5 per cent of the US Latino population: Arizona, Arkansas, California, Colorado, Florida, Georgia, Illinois, Iowa, Nevada, New Jersey, New Mexico, New York, North Carolina, Texas, Washington, as well as the District of Columbia (encompassing DC Metro, parts of Maryland and Virginia). Data from 8,634 adult, Latino respondents were collected between November 2005 and August 2006 using computer-assisted telephone interviews (CATI) in the respondents' preferred language (English or Spanish). The survey design involved state-level geographic stratification to ensure that each state's sample matched that state's Latino demographic profile. To buttress representativeness of the sample, the data includes post-stratification survey weights, calculated using Geoscape's American Marketscape DataStream 2006, which provides detailed information on specific ancestry subgroups. I employ these weights in the models (see Table A1 in Appendix A for sample and population distribution comparisons) to address possible non-response bias (Groves 2006). I analyse the foreign-born portion of the sample ($N = 5,717$).

Dependent variable

The present study's dependent variable measures respondents' party identification: 'Generally speaking, do you usually consider yourself a Democrat, a Republican, an Independent, some other party, or what?' Responses were classified as Democrat, Republican, Independent, 'Don't Care' and 'Don't Know/Other Party'.

Figure 1 illustrates the percentages of Latino immigrants in the five categories as a function of number of years in the USA. Over half identify with either the 'Don't Care' or 'Don't Know/Other Party' categories during their first few years. By their fourth decade, less than a third still identify with these initial categories, while the remaining two-thirds identify as Democrat or Republican. With less than 20 per cent identifying as Democrat or Republican shortly after arrival, the data suggest a process of assimilation into partisan identities over time.

Independent variables

I utilize a normalized, standardized scale based on two survey items to measure PROPs associated with each reference group (whites, blacks and Latinos). Initial survey items consisted of a unipolar scale with four ordered response categories – nothing, little in common, some in common, and a lot in common – with another category for 'Don't Know' or not applicable. The first survey item taps perceptions of shared socio-economic opportunity:

> Thinking about issues like job opportunities, educational attainment or income, how much do Hispanics/Latinos have in common with other racial groups in the United States today? Would you say Hispanics/Latinos have a lot in common, some in common, little in common, or nothing at all in common with...: Whites? African-Americans?

When referring to other Latinos, the survey item is worded to address the respondent's national ancestry:

Figure 1 *Party identification among foreign-born Hispanics, by years in the USA*

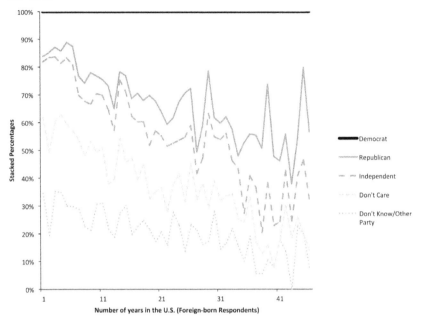

Source: Latino National Survey 2006.

Thinking about issues like job opportunities, education or income, how much do [respondent's national ancestry] have in common with other Latinos or Hispanics? Would you say [respondent's national ancestry] share a lot in common, some things in common, little in common, or nothing in common with other Latinos?

The second survey item measures perceptions of shared opportunities in the political domain:

Now I'd like you to think about the political situation of Hispanics/Latinos in society. Thinking about things like government services and employment, political power and representation, how much do Hispanics/Latinos have in common with other racial groups in the United States today? Would you say Hispanics/Latinos have a lot in common, some in common, little in common, or nothing at all in common with... Whites? African-Americans?

Again, with other Latinos as the reference group:

Now thinking about things like government services and employment, political power and representation, how much do [respondent's national ancestry] have in common with other Hispanics or Latinos? Would you say [respondent's national ancestry] share a lot in common, some things in common, little in common, or nothing in common with other Latinos?

To construct the PROPs scales, I first re-coded 'Don't Know' or not applicable responses as equivalent to the 'nothing in common' or lowest-response category.[2] I then standardized each of the two survey items, summed the standardized scores into a combined PROPs scale per reference group, and normalized the scales (scores ranging from 0 to 1). Cronbach α for the two items within each scale was 0.64 for white opportunities, 0.61 for black opportunities and 0.68 for Latino opportunities.

Control variables

The models controlled for some social background and demographic characteristics: age, education, income, racial identification and gender. To minimize missing data, I re-coded many of the variables into dummy categories with a separate variable to indicate missing. I created age categories for respondents aged 18–24, 25–34, 35–44, 45–54, 55–64, 65 plus and 'Refuse to state', with 18–24 serving as the reference. Education controls included some high school, high school graduation, some college, college graduation and postgraduate education; eighth grade or below served as the reference category. After analysing the initial results, I later collapsed some high school and high school graduate into one category. Three dummy-coded variables controlled income: between $25,000 and $65,000 household income in 2004; more than $65,000; and 'Refused to state'. Income less than $25,000 served as the reference. A dummy variable with 1 indicating white and 0 indicating non-white (reference category) controlled racial identification. A binary variable with 1 indicating female controlled for gender (male reference).

Models also controlled for political ideology, perceived black competition (Bobo 1999) and perceived linked fate (Dawson 1994). With conservative as the reference, I created four dummy variables for 'liberals', 'middle of the road', 'don't think of self in these terms,' and 'don't know'. I used four survey items measuring perceived black competition in access to jobs, quality schooling, government jobs and political representation (see Appendix B for survey language). Each of the four items used three categories: 'No competition at all', 'Weak competition' and 'Strong competition'. I averaged the four items to create a scale anchored at the low end by individuals who averaged 'No competition at all' on all four items, with the high end representing 'Strong competition' on all four items. Alpha reliability for perceived black competition was 0.79. To differentiate between PROPs and perceived linked fate, I also added two variables controlling for black- and Latino-linked fate. Each draws on one item ranging from 1 ('Nothing') to 4 ('A Lot'). I re-coded 'Don't Know/NA' responses for Latino-linked fate (7.8 per cent of responses) as 'Nothing'; black-linked fate required no re-coding. There was some correlation between the black PROPs scale and perceived black-linked fate (0.20) and the Latino PROPS scale and perceived Latino-linked fate (0.42), but no multi-collinearity issues arose.

Finally, I introduced controls based on prior research on Latino partisanship. The first set account for ethnicity/national origin (Alvarez and García Bedolla 2003; Dutwin et al. 2005; Uhlaner and Garcia 2005). Using three dummy variables, I control for years spent living in the USA (Cain, Kiewiet and Uhlaner 1991; Wong 2000; Uhlaner and Garcia 2005). A dummy variable controlled for union membership (Cain, Kiewiet and Uhlaner 1991; Nicholson and Segura 2005). While the split-ballot design did not allow for a full range of controls for policy attitudes (half the sample was asked about school vouchers and abortion), I control for attitude towards government intervention in health care (Alvarez and García Bedolla 2003). To the extent that English proficiency lowers access barriers to political participation (Wong 2000), I control for English versus Spanish media preference for political information (three-value scale with English media reliance anchoring one end and Spanish media reliance on the opposite end) and interview language preference (1 = Spanish, 0 = English). Wong (2000) also explored the media exposure's impact, a factor that I control using a four-point ordinal scale measuring whether the respondent reads a newspaper daily, most days, once or twice a week, or almost never. Finally, I control for trust in the government to do the right thing (Dutwin et al. 2005). Appendix B details some of these survey items.

Method

I employed the method used by Alvarez and García Bedolla (2003) and estimated multinomial logistic regression models using survey weights to predict the likelihood that Latino immigrants would self-identify in a partisan category such as Republican or Democrat compared to a reference category such as 'Don't Care' or 'Don't Know/Other Party'. I estimated a series of nested models, beginning with the key independent variables (PROPs) and subsequently adding clusters of controls. The first cluster of controls consisted of age, education and income. I then controlled for white identification, gender, political ideology and black group competition. The fourth model controlled national origin-based ethnicity, while the fifth model controlled years in the USA. The final, saturated model introduced the remaining controls from prior research. Only the final models are displayed to simplify presentation; intermediate models are discussed as needed (available upon request).

Results

Table 1 provides univariate descriptive statistics about the Latino immigrant sample. The plurality of respondents identify as Democrat, followed by those who 'Don't Know' their party identification, and those who 'Don't Care'. Republican identification is relatively small at 8 per cent. About 40–45 per cent of Latino immigrants perceive some or a lot of shared opportunities with either whites or blacks; 65–75 per cent perceive some or a lot of shared opportunities with Latinos. Separate χ^2 tests of partisan identification with each of the two items comprising the PROPs scales indicate that cell distributions are not random ($p < .001$, results available upon request).

Becoming Democrat

Table 2 presents the models comparing Democrat identification to those who (1) 'Don't Know' their party identity or identify as 'Other Party', or (2) 'Don't Care'. Initial models containing only the PROPs predictors (not shown, available upon request) provide support for Hypothesis H3: Latino immigrants who perceive a higher level of PROPs associated with blacks are more likely to identify as Democrat. This effect persists to the final model with 'Don't Know/Other Party' as the reference and to the penultimate model when 'Don't Care' is the reference. Once the latter model takes into account English language preference, PROPs associated with blacks loses its significant effect ($p > .05$). Also, controlling for older age, education beyond the eighth grade and length of stay decreases the magnitude of the effect of PROPs associated with blacks on Democrat identification.

The data also partially support the co-ethnic opportunity hypothesis (H5) predicting Democrat identification. Immigrants who perceive higher levels of shared opportunity with other Latinos are more likely to identify as Democrat compared to those who 'Don't Know' or identify as 'Other Party'. However, there is no co-ethnic shared opportunity effect differentiating Democrat from 'Don't Care' after controlling for factors beyond age, education, income and gender.

Compared to 'Don't Care' respondents, Democrat identification was surprisingly also associated with a high level of PROPs with whites. This result contradicts the earlier theoretical prediction connecting white opportunity identification solely to Republican identity. The next section tests this hypothesized Republican–white association.

Becoming Republican

Table 2 presents data that support Hypothesis H1's prediction of a positive connection between PROPs with whites and Republican

Table 1. *Weighted descriptives (5,717 Latino immigrants)*

	%	
Party identification		
Democrat	26.1	
Republican	8.2	
Independent	19.3	
Don't Care	21.7	
Don't Know/Other Party	24.8	
Perceptions of shared	By socio-economic type[a]	By political type[b]
opportunities with...	(%)	(%)
Whites (A Lot)	16.4	13.8
(Some)	26.8	26.8
(Little)	28.8	29.8
(Nothing)	17.3	17.4
(Don't Know, N/A)	10.7	12.1
Blacks (A Lot)	16.8	14.9
(Some)	29.3	27.7
(Little)	24.2	28.3
(Nothing)	17.7	15.9
(Don't Know, N/A)	12.1	13.2
Latinos (A Lot)	44.3	30.1
(Some)	31.3	34.2
(Little)	14.3	21.7
(Nothing)	4.3	6.5
(Don't Know, N/A)	5.7	7.4
Age (years)	%	
18–24	37.5	
25–34	18.9	
35–44	17.2	
45–54	10.9	
55–64	6.1	
65 +	4.5	
Refuse to state	5.0	
White	22.8	
Female	51.5	
Education		
Eighth grade or below	27.3	
Some high school and high school graduate	47.6	
Some college	15.4	
College graduate	5.7	
Postgraduate	3.9	
Income (household)		
Less than $25,000	40.0	
$25,000–$65,000	30.0	
More than $65,000	5.9	
Refuse to state	24.1	

Table 1. (*Continued*)

	%
Political Ideology	
Conservative	21.1
Liberal	12.0
Middle of the road	15.4
Don't know	20.4
Don't think of self in these terms	31.0
Years in USA	
Less than 10	40.2
10–19	27.5
20 +	24.7
Missing	7.5
Black competition $(M)^c$	7.42
	(0.044)
Linked fate $(M)^d$	
Blacks	2.79
	(0.015)
Latinos	3.03
	(0.015)
Ethnicity	
Mexican	71.5
Puerto Rican	1.0
Cuban	4.6
Dominican	4.3
Salvadoran	6.3
Hispanic	6.8
Central American	5.6
Controls from previous studies	
Union	7.8
Government intervention in health care	
Strongly oppose	2.8
Oppose	3.9
Not sure/Don't know	9.1
Support	28.7
Strongly support	55.6
English media reliance	
English	12.5
Spanish	61.9
Both equally	24.7
Other/Don't know	0.9
Frequency reading newspaper	
Daily	11.8
Most days	5.1
Once or twice a week	29.0
Almost never	54.1

Table 1. (*Continued*)

	%
Government trust	
Never	19.0
Some of the time	49.9
Most of the time	16.3
Spanish preference	81.1

Source: Latino National Survey 2006 (Fraga et al. 2006).
[a] Job opportunities, education or income
[b] Government services and employment, political power and representation
[c] Range = 4–12; linearized standard error in parentheses
[d] Range = 1–4; linearized standard error in parentheses

identity. The PROPs-associated-with-whites effect remains significant, despite introducing various controls. This effect persists even controlling for Cuban immigrants' historic Republican preference, confirmed as a strong effect. Also, while controlling for older age, education beyond the eighth grade and length of stay diminishes the effect of PROPs associated with blacks on Democrat identification, these variables have hardly any effect on the relationship between white opportunity identification and Republican identity. Although not theoretically predicted, a high level of PROPs associated with blacks is inversely related to Republican identity compared to those who 'Don't Care'.

Republican vs Democrat

If the data indicate that PROPs associated with whites influence Latino immigrants to identify as either Democrat or Republican, does the PROPs theory fail to differentiate between the two? Table 3 compares Republican identification to Democrat and presents results indicating a difference. Latino immigrant Republicans differ from their Democrat counterparts in the former's higher PROPs associated with whites, supporting Hypothesis H2.

Moreover, the data support hypothesis (H4) about PROPs associated with blacks. Recall, higher levels of PROPs associated with blacks positively influenced Latino immigrants' Democrat identification, while such perceptions were negatively related with the likelihood of Republican identification. This relationship is again apparent in Table 3; Latino immigrants are less likely to identify as Republican rather than Democrat when they have higher levels of PROPs associated with blacks.

Interestingly, the data do not support one of the co-ethnic hypotheses (H6). PROPs associated with other Latinos do not differentiate Republicans and Democrats. The absence of an effect may indicate

Table 2. *Multinomial Logistic Regression Predicting Party Identification (5,717 Latino Immigrants)*

	Don't Know/Other Party (Reference)			Don't Care (Reference)		
	Democrat	Republican	Independent	Democrat	Republican	Independent
Perceptions of racialized opportunities associated with:[a]						
Whites	−0.0305	0.892**	0.608**	0.405*	1.328***	1.044***
	(0.203)	(0.302)	(0.228)	(0.203)	(0.301)	(0.226)
Blacks	0.584**	−0.315	0.453*	0.252	−0.647*	0.121
	(0.212)	(0.318)	(0.237)	(0.206)	(0.312)	(0.229)
Latinos	0.507**	0.406	−0.143	0.246	0.145	−0.404*
	(0.192)	(0.291)	(0.211)	(0.196)	(0.296)	(0.213)
Age (years)[b]						
25–34	0.160	−0.371*	−0.166	0.180	−0.351	−0.147
	(0.149)	(0.224)	(0.150)	(0.151)	(0.227)	(0.151)
35–44	0.156	0.0265	−0.316*	0.284*	0.154	−0.188
	(0.157)	(0.225)	(0.163)	(0.162)	(0.229)	(0.168)
45–54	0.391*	0.0895	−0.386*	0.355*	0.0533	−0.422*
	(0.185)	(0.263)	(0.204)	(0.184)	(0.264)	(0.203)
55–64	0.389*	0.219	−0.542*	0.960***	0.791**	0.0289
	(0.216)	(0.297)	(0.239)	(0.234)	(0.311)	(0.255)
65+	1.381***	1.380***	−0.198	1.381***	1.381***	−0.198
	(0.260)	(0.324)	(0.311)	(0.265)	(0.329)	(0.318)
Refuse to state	0.391*	0.0450	−0.601**	0.480*	0.134	−0.512*
	(0.213)	(0.325)	(0.255)	(0.220)	(0.331)	(0.260)
Education[c]						
Some high school and high school graduate	0.507***	0.552**	−0.00156	0.446***	0.491**	−0.0630
	(0.124)	(0.182)	(0.143)	(0.125)	(0.184)	(0.143)
Some college	0.531**	0.579*	−0.134	0.281	0.329	−0.384*
	(0.184)	(0.257)	(0.207)	(0.177)	(0.253)	(0.199)

Table 2. (*Continued*)

	Don't Know/Other Party (Reference)			Don't Care (Reference)		
	Democrat	Republican	Independent	Democrat	Republican	Independent
College graduate	0.882***	0.842**	0.331	0.985***	0.946**	0.434
	(0.249)	(0.325)	(0.275)	(0.252)	(0.331)	(0.271)
Postgraduate	0.985***	0.521	0.411	0.762**	0.297	0.187
	(0.307)	(0.349)	(0.330)	(0.312)	(0.349)	(0.334)
Income (household)[d]						
$25,000–$65,000	0.0244	0.211	0.0245	-0.0276	0.159	-0.0274
	(0.124)	(0.183)	(0.136)	(0.130)	(0.187)	(0.143)
More than $65,000	0.0327	0.301	0.198	0.658*	0.927**	0.823**
	(0.254)	(0.322)	(0.275)	(0.287)	(0.354)	(0.314)
Refuse to state	-0.498***	-0.168	-0.375**	-0.287*	0.0436	-0.163
	(0.140)	(0.214)	(0.157)	(0.142)	(0.216)	(0.158)
White	-0.0585	0.0411	0.113	0.122	0.221	0.293*
	(0.121)	(0.164)	(0.135)	(0.128)	(0.170)	(0.141)
Female	-0.151	-0.0755	-0.329**	-0.137	-0.0616	-0.315**
	(0.106)	(0.148)	(0.116)	(0.108)	(0.150)	(0.118)
Political ideology[e]						
Liberal	0.867***	0.0870	0.823***	0.573**	-0.207	0.529**
	(0.206)	(0.286)	(0.221)	(0.200)	(0.282)	(0.216)
Middle of the road	0.250	0.157	0.514**	0.437*	0.344	0.701***
	(0.176)	(0.223)	(0.185)	(0.196)	(0.240)	(0.206)
Don't know	-1.598***	-2.060***	-1.519***	-1.299***	-1.761***	-1.220***
	(0.159)	(0.254)	(0.192)	(0.171)	(0.264)	(0.203)
Don't think of self in these terms	-0.0496	-0.907***	-0.160	-0.452***	-1.309***	-0.563***
	(0.138)	(0.188)	(0.157)	(0.141)	(0.191)	(0.160)

Table 2. (*Continued*)

	Don't Know/Other Party (Reference)			Don't Care (Reference)		
	Democrat	Republican	Independent	Democrat	Republican	Independent
Black Competition	0.307***	0.295**	0.284***	0.307***	0.295**	0.284***
	(0.0783)	(0.114)	(0.0872)	(0.0799)	(0.115)	(0.0883)
Linked fate: Blacks	0.00412	−0.174**	−0.0767	0.114*	−0.0641	0.0328
	(0.0526)	(0.0715)	(0.0566)	(0.0527)	(0.0716)	(0.0569)
Linked fate: Latinos	−0.0426	0.0398	0.0173	−0.0541	0.0283	0.00581
	(0.0558)	(0.0768)	(0.0608)	(0.0578)	(0.0783)	(0.0629)
Ethnicity[f]						
Cuban	−0.261	1.342***	0.174	−0.241	1.363***	0.195
	(0.268)	(0.245)	(0.261)	(0.267)	(0.248)	(0.262)
Dominican	0.470**	−0.566*	−0.146	0.479*	−0.557	−0.137
	(0.191)	(0.322)	(0.258)	(0.240)	(0.358)	(0.302)
Salvadoran	0.240	−0.159	−0.0376	0.152	−0.247	−0.126
	(0.199)	(0.296)	(0.231)	(0.203)	(0.301)	(0.239)
Hispanic	0.467**	0.0964	0.399*	0.102	−0.268	0.0345
	(0.193)	(0.272)	(0.224)	(0.202)	(0.278)	(0.231)
Central American	0.224	0.520*	0.136	0.0187	0.315	−0.0695
	(0.265)	(0.313)	(0.273)	(0.255)	(0.299)	(0.262)
Years in the USA						
10–19	0.437***	0.162	0.113	0.472***	0.196	0.147
	(0.141)	(0.222)	(0.145)	(0.142)	(0.223)	(0.146)
20+	0.993***	0.722***	0.502***	0.958***	0.687**	0.467**
	(0.149)	(0.231)	(0.162)	(0.154)	(0.235)	(0.169)
Missing	0.269	−0.222	0.0800	0.256	−0.235	0.0662
	(0.215)	(0.367)	(0.244)	(0.221)	(0.370)	(0.249)

Table 2. (*Continued*)

	Don't Know/Other Party (Reference)			Don't Care (Reference)		
	Democrat	Republican	Independent	Democrat	Republican	Independent
Controls from previous studies						
Union	0.447**	−0.535*	−0.148	0.504**	−0.477	−0.0903
	(0.190)	(0.280)	(0.222)	(0.214)	(0.301)	(0.247)
Government intervention in health care	0.150**	0.0595	0.147**	0.103*	0.0125	0.100
	(0.0520)	(0.0760)	(0.0603)	(0.0566)	(0.0799)	(0.0646)
Frequency reading newspaper	0.142**	0.185**	0.0419	0.159**	0.202**	0.0591
	(0.0548)	(0.0708)	(0.0604)	(0.0554)	(0.0711)	(0.0609)
English media reliance	0.226**	0.438***	0.134	0.200*	0.413***	0.109
	(0.0860)	(0.123)	(0.0933)	(0.0895)	(0.126)	(0.0982)
Spanish preference	0.330*	0.0830	0.454**	−0.785***	−1.032***	−0.662***
	(0.160)	(0.229)	(0.175)	(0.185)	(0.248)	(0.201)
Government trust	0.0217	0.273***	0.0489	0.0497	0.301***	0.0769
	(0.0544)	(0.0745)	(0.0593)	(0.0563)	(0.0765)	(0.0617)
Constant	−2.385***	−2.955***	−1.216**	−1.517***	−2.087***	−0.349
	(0.368)	(0.504)	(0.397)	(0.389)	(0.520)	(0.414)

* $p < .05$, ** $p < .01$, *** $p < .001$ (one-tailed).
Source: Latino National Survey 2006 (Fraga et al. 2006).
Omitted categories: [a] Normalized z-score (0–1)
[b] 18–24
[c] Eighth grade or below
[d] Less than $25,000
[e] Conservative
[f] Mexican, Puerto Rican

both parties' successes in ethnic opportunity-based appeals to the Latino community, although issue-based appeals, such as immigration reform proposals, may differ between the two parties.

Also noteworthy, government trust increases the likelihood of identifying with the Republican Party (see Tables 2 and 3). Latino immigrants who are more likely to trust the government to do what is right are more likely to identify as Republican, a counter-intuitive finding given the conventional Republican stance of limiting government influence in individuals' lives but consistent with the fact that a Republican was president at the time of data collection.

Becoming Independent

While Independent identification was not this study's central theoretical concern (Hajnal and Lee 2004), the results reveal that PROPS also relate to Independent identification. High levels of white-associated PROPs differentiate Independents from those who 'Don't Know' or 'Don't Care' (Table 2) and from Democrats (Table 3). Latino immigrants have two political identity options when they perceive shared opportunities with whites: Republican or Independent.

Discussion and conclusion

Segmented assimilation theorists described how distinct modes of incorporation in tandem with an immigrant's human capital and family structure can steer immigrants towards differentiated assimilation outcomes; this study suggests that partisan identity may be one of these outcomes. Just as a mode of incorporation structures immigrants' mobility into upward, downward or stagnant trajectories, immigrants are also learning about group-based opportunities. As they place themselves in relation to these opportunities, their assimilation becomes not only structural but social psychological as well. Immigrants also come to learn about a country's politics and the group interests that political parties are perceived to represent. Eventually, immigrants make connections between all of these ideas.

Racial stereotypes, prejudice and discrimination are among the key characteristics defining the context of reception and mode of incorporation that immigrants encounter in the USA. The structural presence (or absence) of bias can limit (or maintain) the quality of opportunities affecting immigrants' life chances. When immigrants encounter a prejudiced society, particularly manifested in the labour market, workplace, schools or neighbourhoods, they likely see their opportunities as constrained in ways similar to that of blacks. When immigrants encounter obstacles founded upon their immigrant status (questions about language proficiency, documentation, etc.) and they

Table 3. *Multinomial logistic regression predicting party identification (5,717 Latino immigrants)*

	Democrat (Reference)	
	Republican	Independent
Perceptions of racialized opportunities, associated with:[a]		
Whites	0.922***	0.639**
	(0.278)	(0.207)
Blacks	−0.899***	−0.130
	(0.287)	(0.206)
Latinos	−0.101	−0.650***
	(0.278)	(0.199)
Age (years)[b]		
25–34	−0.531**	−0.327*
	(0.224)	(0.150)
35–44	−0.130	−0.472**
	(0.222)	(0.164)
45–54	−0.302	−0.777***
	(0.251)	(0.191)
55–64	−0.169	−0.931***
	(0.281)	(0.225)
65 +	−0.000561	−1.579***
	(0.293)	(0.287)
Refuse to state	−0.346	−0.992***
	(0.321)	(0.259)
Education[c]		
Some high school and high school graduate	0.0450	−0.509***
	(0.177)	(0.135)
Some college	0.0482	−0.665***
	(0.235)	(0.184)
College graduate	−0.0396	−0.551**
	(0.284)	(0.230)
Postgraduate	−0.464	−0.574*
	(0.289)	(0.268)
Income (household)[d]		
$25,000–$65,000	0.187	0.000159
	(0.172)	(0.126)
More than $65,000	0.269	0.165
	(0.268)	(0.220)
Refuse to state	0.330	0.123
	(0.212)	(0.158)
White	0.0996	0.171
	(0.150)	(0.122)
Female	0.0755	−0.178*
	(0.138)	(0.107)
Political ideology[e]		
Liberal	−0.781***	−0.0450
	(0.239)	(0.168)
Middle of the road	−0.0930	0.264*
	(0.194)	(0.157)
Don't know	−0.462*	0.0787
	(0.260)	(0.200)
Don't think of self in these terms	−0.857***	−0.111
	(0.174)	(0.141)

Table 3. (*Continued*)

| | Democrat (Reference) | |
	Republican	Independent
Black competition	−0.0125	−0.0233
	(0.107)	(0.0825)
Linked fate: Blacks	−0.178**	−0.0808
	(0.0674)	(0.0540)
Latinos	0.0825	0.0600
	(0.0731)	(0.0597)
Ethnicity[f]		
Cuban	1.604***	0.435
	(0.228)	(0.278)
Dominican	−1.036***	−0.616**
	(0.312)	(0.248)
Salvadoran	−0.399	−0.278
	(0.276)	(0.208)
Hispanic	−0.370	−0.0674
	(0.239)	(0.188)
Central American	0.296	−0.0883
	(0.276)	(0.248)
Years in the USA[g]		
10–19	−0.276	−0.325*
	(0.220)	(0.145)
20 +	−0.271	−0.491***
	(0.224)	(0.156)
Missing	−0.491	−0.189
	(0.362)	(0.241)
Controls from previous studies		
Union	−0.982***	−0.595***
	(0.247)	(0.183)
Government intervention in health care	−0.0905	−0.00262
	(0.0720)	(0.0569)
Frequency reading newspaper	0.0430	−0.1000*
	(0.0612)	(0.0518)
English media reliance	0.212*	−0.0917
	(0.112)	(0.0845)
Spanish preference	−0.247	0.124
	(0.206)	(0.158)
Government trust	0.251***	0.0272
	(0.0699)	(0.0542)
Constant	−0.570	1.169***
	(0.481)	(0.377)

Source: Latino National Survey 2006 (Fraga et al. 2006).
Note: Standard errors in parentheses.
Omitted categories: [a] Normalized z-score (0–1)
[b] 18–24
[c] Eighth grade or below
[d] Less than $25,000
[e] Conservative
[f] Mexican, Puerto Rican
[g] Less than 10, * $p < .05$, ** $p < .01$, *** $p < .001$ (one-tailed).

utilize a co-ethnic community to overcome these barriers, they likely see their opportunities as closer to that of co-ethnics. Immigrants who do not experience any race- or nativity-based challenges or exceptions likely view their opportunities as similar to whites. Thus, immigrants can easily relate their structural mode of incorporation to their social psychological perceptions of the opportunities available to racialized groups.

This study reveals that perceptions of racialized opportunities are related to the partisan identities into which Latino immigrants assimilate. PROPs associated with whites are likely to draw Latino immigrants into the Republican fold, and to a lesser extent, the Democratic one as well. Higher levels of PROPs associated with blacks and Latinos increase the likelihood of Latino immigrants identifying as Democrat. While mode of incorporation may affect immigrants' life chances and initially shape identification with racialized opportunities, these perceptions exert a social psychological effect on partisan identity independent of immigrants' social structural location or other assimilation indicators (Cain, Kiewiet and Uhlaner 1991; Kaufmann 2003b). PROPs in effect take on semi-autonomous lives of their own.

These findings present additional avenues for future research. Future studies could more clearly specify the relationship between particular indicators of modes of incorporation and PROPs. Given the use of cross-sectional data and the likelihood of some endogeneity between PROPs and partisan identity, studies employing longitudinal data would be useful. Finally, studies could explore PROPs interactions (e.g. individuals identifying highly with white and black opportunities simultaneously, or with white, black and co-ethnic opportunities simultaneously, etc.) on various outcomes.

Notes

1.   I use the terms Hispanic and Latino interchangeably. The Latino National Survey uses ancestry (Latin American descent) to ground Hispanic or Latino identities, and recent research has discussed the racialization of Latinos (Cobas, Duany and Feagin 2009).
2.   The results discussed do not differ substantially when coding PROPs as dummy variables, preserving 'Don't Know' and 'Not Applicable' as separate attitudes (available upon request).

References

ALVAREZ, R. MICHAEL and GARCÍA BEDOLLA, LISA 2003 'The foundations of Latino voter partisanship: evidence from the 2000 election', *Journal of Politics*, vol. 65, no. 1, pp. 31–49
—— 2004 'The revolution against affirmative action in California: racism, economics, and Proposition 209', *State Politics & Policy Quarterly*, vol. 4, no. 1, pp. 1–17
BARRETO, MATT A., *et al.* 2008 '"Should they dance with the one who brung 'em?" Latinos and the 2008 presidential election', *PS: Political Science and Politics*, vol. 41, no. 4, pp. 753–60

BLACK, EARL and BLACK, MERLE 2002 *The Rise of Southern Republicans*, Cambridge, MA: The Belknap Press of Harvard University Press

BOBO, LAWRENCE D. 1998 'Race, interests, and beliefs about affirmative action', *American Behavioral Scientist*, vol. 41, no. 7, pp. 985–1003

—— 1999 'Prejudice as group position: microfoundations of a sociological approach to racism and race relations', *Journal of Social Issues*, vol. 55, no. 3, pp. 445–72

BOWLER, SHAUN, NICHOLSON, STEPHEN P. and SEGURA, GARY M. 2006 'Earthquakes and aftershocks: race, direct democracy, and partisan change', *American Journal of Political Science*, vol. 50, no. 1, pp. 146–59

BRUNS, ROGER 2011 *Cesar Chavez and the United Farm Workers Movement*, Santa Barbara, CA: ABC-CLIO

CAIN, BRUCE E., KIEWIET, D. RODERICK and UHLANER, CAROLE J. 1991 'The acquisition of partisanship by Latinos and Asian Americans', *American Journal of Political Science*, vol. 35, no. 2, pp. 390–422

CAMPBELL, ANGUS, *et al.* 1960 *The American Voter*, Chicago, IL: University of Chicago Press

CARMINES, EDWARD G. and STIMSON, JAMES A. 1989 *Issue Evolution: Race and the Transformation of American Politics*, Princeton, NJ: Princeton University Press

COBAS, JOSE A., DUANY, JORGE and FEAGIN, JOE R. (eds) 2009 *How the United States Racializes Latinos: White Hegemony and its Consequences*, Boulder, CO: Paradigm Publishers

DARLING-HAMMOND, LINDA 2004 'The color line in American education: race, resources, and student achievement', *Du Bois Review: Social Science Research on Race*, vol. 1, no. 2, pp. 213–46

DAWSON, MICHAEL C. 1994 *Behind the Mule: Race and Class in African-American Politics*, Princeton, NJ: Princeton University Press

DUTWIN, DAVID, *et al.* 2005 'Latinos and political party affiliation', *Hispanic Journal of Behavioral Sciences*, vol. 27, no. 2, pp. 135–60

ERWIN, ELIZABETH 2012 'AZ lawmaker suggests holiday for white people', *CBS 5 Arizona News*, 1 February. Available from: http://www.kpho.com/story/16656530/state-representative-suggests-holiday-for-white-people [Accessed 11 March 2013]

FOX, CYBELLE 2012 *Three Worlds of Relief: Race, Immigration, and the American Welfare State from the Progressive Era to the New Deal*, Princeton, NJ: Princeton University Press

FOX, CYBELLE and GUGLIELMO, THOMAS A. 2012 'Defining America's racial boundaries: blacks, Mexicans, and European immigrants, 1890–1945', *American Journal of Sociology*, vol. 118, no. 2, pp. 327–79

FRAGA, LUIS R., *et al.* 2006 'Latino National Survey (LNS), 2006'. ICPSR20862-v5 ed.: Inter-university Consortium for Political and Social Research (ICPSR)

GIMPEL, JAMES G. and KAUFMANN, KAREN 2001 *Impossible Dream or Distant Reality?: Republican Efforts to Attract Latino Voters*, Washington, DC: Center for Immigration Studies

GOMEZ, SERAFIN 2011 'Jeb Bush: The Political Math of Conservatives Needs to Include Latinos', *Fox News Latino*, 14 January. Available from: http://politics.blogs.foxnews.com/2011/01/14/jeb-bushthe-political-math-conservatives-needs-include-latinos-0

GONZALES, FELISA 2008 'Statistical Portrait of Hispanics in the United States, 2006', *Pew Hispanic Center*. Available from http://www.pewhispanic.org/2008/01/23/statistical-portrait-of-hispanics-in-the-united-states-2006/ [Accessed 22 March 2013]

GRIECO, ELIZABETH M. 2009 'Race and Hispanic Origin of the Foreign-Born Population in the United States: 2007', American Community Survey Reports, ACS-11, U.S. Census Bureau, Washington, DC

GROVES, ROBERT M. 2006 'Nonresponse rates and nonresponse bias in household surveys', *Public Opinion Quarterly*, vol. 70, no. 5, pp. 646–75

GUARNIZO, LUIS EDUARDO, SANCHEZ, ARTURO IGNACIO and ROACH, ELIZABETH M. 1999 'Mistrust, fragmented solidarity, and transnational migration:

Colombians in New York City and Los Angeles', *Ethnic and Racial Studies*, vol. 22, no. 2, pp. 367–96

HAJNAL, ZOLTAN and LEE, TAEKU 2004 *Latino Independents and Identity Formation under Uncertainty*, San Diego, CA: University of California, Center for Comparative Immigration Studies. Available from: http://www.escholarship.org/uc/item/93139050

HAO, LINGXIN and PONG, SUET-LING 2008 'The role of school in the upward mobility of disadvantaged immigrants' children', *The ANNALS of the American Academy of Political and Social Science*, vol. 620, no. 1, pp. 62–89

HUNT, MATTHEW O. 2004 'Race/ethnicity and beliefs about wealth and poverty', *Social Science Quarterly*, vol. 85, no. 3, pp. 827–53

——— 2007 "African-American, Hispanic, and white beliefs about black/white inequality, 1977–2004", *American Sociological Review*, vol. 72, no. 3, pp. 390–415

ITZIGSOHN, JOSE, *et al.* 1999 'Mapping Dominican transnationalism: narrow and broad transnational practices', *Ethnic and Racial Studies*, vol. 22, no. 2, pp. 316–39

JARGOWSKY, PAUL A. 2009 'Immigrants and neighbourhoods of concentrated poverty: assimilation or stagnation?', *Journal of Ethnic and Migration Studies*, vol. 35, no. 7, pp. 1129–51

JIMÉNEZ, TOMÁS R. 2008 'Mexican immigrant replenishment and the continuing significance of ethnicity and race', *American Journal of Sociology*, vol. 113, no. 6, pp. 1527–67

KAUFMANN, KAREN M. 2003a 'Black and Latino voters in Denver: responses to each other's political leadership', *Political Science Quarterly*, vol. 118, no. 1, pp. 107–26

——— 2003b 'Cracks in the rainbow: group commonality as a basis for Latino and African-American political coalitions', *Political Research Quarterly*, vol. 56, no. 2, pp. 199–210

KLUEGEL, JAMES R. and SMITH, ELIOT R. 1986 *Beliefs about Inequality: Americans' Views of What Is and What Ought to Be*, New York: Aldine De Gruyter

LEAL, DAVID L., *et al.* 2005 'The Latino vote in the 2004 election', *PS: Political Science and Politics*, vol. 38, no. 1, pp. 41–9

LEAL, DAVID L., *et al.* 2008 'Latinos, immigration, and the 2006 midterm elections', *PS: Political Science and Politics*, vol. 41, no. 2, pp. 309–17

LINTON, APRIL and JIMÉNEZ, TOMÁS R. 2009 'Contexts for bilingualism among US-born Latinos', *Ethnic and Racial Studies*, vol. 32, no. 6, pp. 967–95

LOPEZ-SANDERS, LAURA 2011 'The dynamics of ethnic labor replacement in new immigrant destinations', *Mini-Conference on Work, Power, and Inequality at the Southern Sociological Society 74th Annual Meeting*, April 8, Jacksonville, Florida

MARROW, HELEN B. 2009 'New immigrant destinations and the American colour line', *Ethnic and Racial Studies*, vol. 32, no. 6, pp. 1037–57

MENDELBERG, TALI 2001 *The Race Card: Campaign Strategy, Implicit Messages, and the Norm of Equality*, Princeton, NJ: Princeton University Press

MUÑOZ, CARLOS and HENRY, CHARLES 1986 'Rainbow coalitions in four big cities: San Antonio, Denver, Chicago and Philadelphia', *PS: Political Science and Politics*, vol. 19, no. 3, pp. 598–609

NICHOLSON, STEPHEN P. and SEGURA, GARY M. 2005 'Issue agendas and the politics of Latino partisan identification', in Gary M. Segura and Shaun Bowler (eds), *Diversity in Democracy: Minority Representation in the United States*, Charlottesville, VI: University of Virginia Press, pp. 51–71

PANTOJA, ADRIAN D., RAMIREZ, RICARDO and SEGURA, GARY M. 2001 'Citizens by choice, voters by necessity: patterns in political mobilization by naturalized Latinos', *Political Research Quarterly*, vol. 54, no. 4, pp. 729–50

PANTOJA, ADRIAN D. and SEGURA, GARY M. 2003 'Fear and loathing in California: contextual threat and political sophistication among Latino voters', *Political Behavior*, vol. 25, no. 3, pp. 265–86

PORTES, ALEJANDRO 2007 "The new Latin nation", *Du Bois Review: Social Science Research on Race*, vol. 4, no. 2, pp. 271–301

PORTES, ALEJANDRO, FERNÁNDEZ-KELLY, PATRICIA and HALLER, WILLIAM 2005 'Segmented assimilation on the ground: the new second generation in early adulthood', *Ethnic and Racial Studies*, vol. 28, no. 6, pp. 1000–40

────── 2009 'The adaptation of the immigrant second generation in America: a theoretical overview and recent evidence', *Journal of Ethnic and Migration Studies*, vol. 35, no. 7, pp. 1077–104

PORTES, ALEJANDRO and RUMBAUT, RUBÉN G. 2001 *Legacies: The Story of the Immigrant Second Generation*, 1st edn. Berkeley, CA: University of California Press

PORTES, ALEJANDRO and STEPICK, ALEX 1994 *City on the Edge: The Transformation of Miami*, Berkeley, CA: University of California Press

PORTES, ALEJANDRO and ZHOU, MIN 1993 'The new second generation: segmented assimilation and its variants', *The ANNALS of the American Academy of Political and Social Science*, vol. 530, pp. 74–96

STEPICK, ALEX and STEPICK, CAROL DUTTON 2010 'The complexities and confusions of segmented assimilation', *Ethnic and Racial Studies*, vol. 33, no. 7, pp. 1149–67

TOLBERT, CAROLINE J. and GRUMMEL, JOHN A. 2003 'Revisiting the racial threat hypothesis: white voter support for California's Proposition 209', *State Politics & Policy Quarterly*, vol. 3, no. 2, pp. 183–202

UHLANER, CAROLE J. and GARCIA, F. CHRIS 2005 'Learning which party fits: experience, ethnic identity, and the demographic foundations of Latino party identification', in Gary M. Segura and Shaun Bowler (eds), *Diversity in Democracy: Minority Representation in the United States*, Charlottesville, VA: University of Virginia Press, pp. 72–101

WALDINGER, ROGER 1994 'The making of an immigrant niche', *International Migration Review*, vol. 28, no. 1, pp. 3–30

WILSON, WILLIAM JULIUS 1990 *The Truly Disadvantaged: The Inner City, the Underclass, and Public Policy*, Chicago, IL: University of Chicago Press

WONG, JANELLE S. 2000 'The effects of age and political exposure on the development of party identification among Asian American and Latino immigrants in the United States', *Political Behavior*, vol. 22, no. 4, pp. 341–71

ZHOU, MIN 1997 'Segmented assimilation: issues, controversies, and recent research on the new second generation', *International Migration Review*, vol. 31, no. 4, pp. 975–1008

ZHOU, MIN, *et al.* 2008 'Success attained, deterred, and denied: divergent pathways to social mobility in Los Angeles's new second generation', *The ANNALS of the American Academy of Political and Social Science*, vol. 620, no. 1, pp. 37–61

Appendix A. *LNS weighted sample versus US Latino population distributions on key demographics*

	Total		Foreign born	
	ACS 2006 (%)	LNS 2006 (%)	ACS 2006 (%)	LNS 2006 (%)
Age (years)[a]				
24 and below	45.7	40.2	20.9	37.5
25–34	18.0	16.8	25.9	18.9
35–44	15.2	15.4	23.6	17.2
45–54	10.1	10.7	14.7	10.9
55–64	5.7	7.0	7.9	6.1
65 +	5.3	5.7	7.0	4.5
Refuse to state	n/a	4.1	n/a	5.0
Education[b]				
Eighth grade or below	23.8	19.5	34.0	27.0
Some high school	15.80	17.0	16.7	18.6
High school graduate	28.20	29.3	25.6	29.0
Some college	19.90	21.1	13.6	15.4
College graduate	12.30	13.1	10.1	9.6
Female	48.4	52.7	46.1	51.5
Ethnicity[c]				
Mexican	64.1	70.0	64.4	71.5
Cuban	3.4	3.8	5.4	4.6
Dominican	2.7	3.6	4.0	4.3
Puerto Rican	9.0	7.6	0.3	1.0
Salvadoran	3.1	4.8	5.4	6.3
Central American	4.7	4.0	7.7	5.6
Hispanic	6.9	6.2	3.2	6.8
South American	6.1	N/A	9.6	N/A

Source: American Community Survey 2006: Pew Hispanic Center tabulations (Gonzales 2008); Latino National Survey 2006 (Fraga et al. 2006).
[a] Latino National Survey age data reflects population 18 years and older
[b] American Community Survey education data reflects population 25 years and older
[c] National origin data for Hispanic foreign-born from American Community Survey 2007 (Grieco 2009)

Appendix B: Survey Items (selected)

Perceived Competition with African-Americans

Some have suggested that [Latinos/Hispanics] are in competition with African-Americans. After each of the next items, would you tell me if you believe there is strong competition, weak competition, or no competition at all with African-Americans? How about...

1. In getting jobs?
2. Having access to education and quality schools?
3. Getting jobs with the city or state government?
4. Having Hispanic/Latino representatives in elected office?

Perceived African-American Linked Fate

How much does [Latinos/Hispanics] 'doing well' depend on African-Americans also doing well? A lot, some, a little, or not at all?

Perceived Latino Linked Fate

How much does [ancestry] 'doing well' depend on how other [Latinos/Hispanics] are also doing well? A lot, some, a little, or not at all?

Government Intervention in Health Care

The current health-care system needs government intervention to improve access and reduce costs...
(Strongly oppose, Oppose, Support, Strongly Support)

Frequency Reading Newspaper

How often would you say you read a daily newspaper? Would it be daily, most days, only once or twice a week, or almost never?

Reliance on English Media

For information about public aairs and politics, would you say you rely more heavily on Spanish-language television, radio, and newspapers, or on English-language TV, radio, and newspapers?
(English More, Spanish More, Both Equally (Bilingual), Other/DK/NA)

Government Trust

How much of the time do you trust the government to do what is right – just about always, most of the time, some of the time or never?

Defining immigrant newcomers in new destinations: symbolic boundaries in Williamsburg, Virginia

Deenesh Sohoni and Jennifer Bickham Mendez

Abstract

This article examines media representations of immigration in Williamsburg, Virginia, a 'new immigrant destination' in the USA. Through a content analysis of coverage in Williamsburg's local newspaper, we explore how reporters, columnists and readers draw on nationally and internationally circulating discourses to produce public interpretations of immigration issues and construct symbolic boundaries between and among in-groups and 'others' in the community. 'National boundaries drawn locally' captures how media actors use nationally recognizable frames to interpret local issues and define the parameters of community and national belonging. 'Localized symbolic boundaries' take their meanings from place-based, cultural understandings, specific economic conditions and demographics in the local setting. Newspaper discussions in Williamsburg distinguish between 'deserving' foreign student workers (primarily from Eastern Europe and Asia) and 'undeserving', racialized, Latino 'others'. Our analysis advances theories of boundary construction and holds implications for the politics of belonging more generally in other immigrant-receiving contexts.

Introduction

In recent decades, global migration patterns have changed to incorporate new nation states, cities and localities as sites of immigrant origin and destination, generating new points of social and political tension. Immigrant-receiving countries contend with conflicts stemming from the growing demand for cheap labour combined with the perceived threat that newcomers pose to social and cultural cohesion and dwindling public resources (Castles and Miller 2009).

Attempts to reconcile these tensions are reflected in the heated political debates and the intensification of immigration control taking place in countries around the world (De Genova and Peutz 2010). Increased expressions of anti-immigrant sentiments resonate globally, embodying ways of imagining national identity that span across a range of nations (Brotherton and Kretsedemas 2008; Fassin 2011). Yet, despite their cross-national resonance, immigration controversies and tensions play out within communities, which possess their own specific histories and place-based identities.

In the USA, such tensions have increasingly registered locally in 'new immigrant destinations', as migration streams have shifted away from traditional, urban gateways to include small towns, rural areas and suburbs (Jones 2008). In many of these sites, local governments have proposed and successfully enacted, local immigration enforcement policies, justifying these measures as a response to the federal government's failure to address the immigration "problem" (Walker and Leitner 2011).

Through making issues 'public', and giving form to people's fears and anxieties, the media plays an important role in constructing the boundaries between 'mainstream' society and immigrant 'others' that underlie such policies (Hall 1996; Korteweg and Yurdakul 2009). In the USA, contestations around these boundaries reflect the contradictory position that immigrants occupy within the national imaginary and the ambiguities contained in public discourse surrounding immigration issues (van der Veer 1995).

While most previous research on immigration issues and the media in the USA has centred analysis on outlets with national audiences (Chavez 2001; Menjívar and Kil 2002; Ono and Sloop 2002) or those in major cities (Dunaway, Branton and Abrajano 2010; McConnell 2011), current immigration patterns have rendered smaller communities important sites for understanding public interpretations of and responses to immigration issues (Varsanyi 2010). The continued prevalence of newspapers as sources of news makes them critical for exploring these processes (Padín 2005).

Our study fills an important gap in the literature by examining coverage and public reactions in a media outlet directed at one such community – a new immigrant destination that occupies a prominent position within the national imaginary of the USA. Perhaps best known as the eighteenth-century capital of one of the first British colonies in the USA, historic Williamsburg, Virginia has undergone rapid growth and development, transforming it from a small, tourist and college town into an 'upscale destination' for retirees and professionals. These changes have coincided with the arrival of immigrants from Latin America and temporary foreign workers from Eastern Europe and Asia, drawn to the area by growing numbers of entry-level, service-sector jobs.

Through a content analysis of over 500 texts appearing in the *Virginia Gazette* – Williamsburg's local newspaper – we examine the discourses that journalists and local residents use to produce public interpretations of immigration issues. We advance understandings of symbolic boundary construction by identifying ways in which community-level imaginings draw upon nationally and internationally recognizable discourses. We identify two patterns. The first, 'national boundaries drawn locally', captures how media actors make use of nationally recognizable frames to interpret local issues and events, thereby constructing the parameters of both community and nation. The second, 'localized symbolic boundaries', produces distinctions between 'us' and 'them' in ways that draw meanings from locally specific economic conditions, demographics and cultural understandings. In Williamsburg, this latter pattern takes a distinctive shape, as journalists and readers distinguish between 'deserving' foreign student workers (primarily from Eastern Europe and Asia) and 'undeserving', racialized, Latino 'others'.

Immigration discourse: symbolic boundaries and social membership

Scholars have devoted significant attention to analysing media coverage of immigration issues and related legislation (e.g. Calavita 1996; Coutin and Chock 1997; Chavez 2001; Ono and Sloop 2002), as well as representations of Latinos in mainstream media outlets (Padín 2005; Chavez 2008; McConnell 2011). Others have focused on public officials' use of discourses in debates about immigration reform (Newton 2008) and by community residents and politicians in controversies over proposed local enforcement measures (Esbenshade et al. 2010).

Researchers note the power of the media to produce and disseminate discourses – sets of ideas, images and statements that construct ways of knowing and talking about a particular topic; and how media representations created by journalists shape knowledge about events, peoples and places in the world (Hall 1996). Media actors draw from surrounding discourses, employing culturally resonant tropes and metaphors to narrate events. But beyond this, they actively construct, adjudicate and contest meanings in order to make sense of and produce knowledge about conditions and occurrences in a particular time and place (Coutin and Chock 1997). Therefore, the media serves as a critical site of cultural and symbolic struggle where ideologies, identities, social meanings and beliefs about the world are negotiated and debated (Bourdieu 1991). Through the words and images used to cover events, the media also plays an important role in the construction of social categories of people, and in the creation of distinctions between those who should and should not be included in the national imagined community (Chavez 2001).

Lamont and Molnár's (2002) conceptualization of social and symbolic boundaries proves useful in understanding this process. They define symbolic boundaries as conceptual distinctions drawn by social actors to categorize people into groups, which emerge through struggles over the creation of collective definitions of reality. Once they are widely agreed upon, symbolic boundaries influence and shape social boundaries – 'objectified forms of social differences manifested in unequal access to and unequal distribution of resources (material and nonmaterial) and social opportunities' (Lamont and Molnár 2002, p. 168). Localized debates about immigration are important sites for the construction of symbolic boundaries. Understanding how journalists and readers who contribute to the *Virginia Gazette* define, contest and construct them has implications for recent immigrant-receiving contexts more generally.

Local journalists and newspaper audiences encounter ways of talking about and understanding immigration issues that resonate at the national level. Widely influential narratives framed in relation to national identity often underlie public policy (Newton 2008). In the USA, nationalist narratives that depict the country as a 'nation of immigrants', extolling the exemplary characteristics and epic struggles of past immigrants (usually those hailing from Europe), coexist with nativist discourses that paint immigrants as threatening alien 'others' who erode the national culture, steal jobs, exploit public services and commit crimes (De Genova 2005).

As a 'new immigrant destination', Williamsburg presents a useful site for studying boundary-making processes as they unfold in communities undergoing economic and demographic transitions (Massey 2008; Marrow 2011). Like other recent sites of immigrant reception, Williamsburg's incorporation into new migration streams coincided with a period of rapid growth and development. Thus, debates about immigration have emerged amid broader public discussions about issues related to these changes, such as the availability of affordable housing, the loss of 'small town life' and the construction of new schools and redistricting (Dawkins et al. 2007). At the same time, Williamsburg's symbolic position within the national imaginary and its identity as the 'birthplace' of the USA adds a particular flavour to the ways in which residents derive their understandings of immigration issues. Shedding light on this process – how the *national* community is imagined *locally* – is a central aim of our study (Anderson 1983).

Background: Williamsburg, Virginia

Located on the Virginia Peninsula with an estimated population of 136,000 (US Census Bureau 2009), Greater Williamsburg[1] is home to nationally important historic sites and has been a widely recognized tourist destination since the 1950s. Tourist attractions include Colonial Williamsburg, 'the world's largest living history museum' designed to recreate eighteenth-century life in colonial Virginia; Jamestown, the first permanent European settlement; and the revolutionary battle-fields at Yorktown. In the 1970s and 1980s, visitors' attractions expanded to include popular amusement and water parks, like Busch Gardens and Water Country USA, as well as major golf courses.

As was the case for many sites across the US South, in the 1990s and early 2000s Greater Williamsburg experienced significant growth and development, transforming it from a quaint, rural town to increasingly, a suburb without a city (Deeb-Sossa and Mendez 2008). The early 2000s brought a construction boom, and Williamsburg began to be marketed as an 'upscale' retirement destination, further spurring residential and commerical development. Between 2000 and 2007 the area's population increased by 15 per cent (nearly double the state average), largely driven by the influx of affluent retirees drawn to Williamsburg's historic appeal, natural beauty, lower taxes and 'quality of life' (US Census Bureau 2009). Residential and commercial development brought increasing numbers of jobs in the retail and hospitality industries as well as landscaping and grounds keeping, and construction (Dawkins et al. 2007). The plentiful low-wage jobs in these industries, particularly in the tourist season, acted as an important 'pull factor' for migrant labour.

In the 1990s, local theme parks began to recruit foreign students to fill summer jobs (Gilligan 1999). These young people, who typically hail from Eastern Europe, China and a few other Asian countries, enter the USA with J-1 Exchange Visitor visas, which allow them to work for up to three months and to travel for up to thirty days prior to the start of the programme. Hotels, grocery stores and restaurants also drew on this seasonal labour force, facilitated by contract agencies specializing in job placement, transportation and housing for student exchange workers.

The 1990s also brought a wave of immigration from Latin American countries – primarily from Mexico and Central America. Latino newcomers ranged from seasonal migrants (often with H2B visas[2]) to long-term settlers, and from those with undocumented status to those with US citizenship. While still a relatively small percentage of the total population (3.5 per cent), the local Hispanic population saw unprecedented growth between 1990 and 2007, nearly quadrupling in size from approximately 1,250 to just over 4,700 (Pew Hispanic Center 2008).[3] Health care providers, social services and schools began to report sharp increases in Spanish-speaking, Latino patients and clients as well as students eligible for Limited English Proficiency instruction (WCHF 2008; Rita Welsh Adult Literacy Center, personal communication, 12 January 2010). As this group of culturally distinct newcomers became increasingly visible locally and as immigration surged onto the national agenda, immigration issues became the subject of heated public debate in Williamsburg.

Data and methods

We base our study on a data set comprised of news articles, letters to the editors, op-ed pieces, columns and public commentary published in the *Virginia Gazette*, the oldest, non-daily newspaper in the USA. Serving the Greater Williamsburg area, the paper is published twice a week and enjoys a paid circulation of 16,500 (*Virginia Gazette* 2012).[4] One of its best-known sections is the 'Last Word', which features readers' anonymous contributions, grouped according to 'hottest local topics', ranging from major national and world events to local issues, like the possible threat posed to the community's songbird population by cat owners (cf. *Virginia Gazette* 2010).[5]

We conducted a content analysis of all texts referencing immigration published in the *Virginia Gazette* in 2006 and 2007 – two pivotal years in which coverage of immigration issues and community debates about the 'immigration problem' in Williamsburg reached their apex. These local debates were spurred by publicized controversies at the national, regional and state levels. For example, in the USA, 2006 was a landmark year for the immigrant rights movement – when over the course of twelve weeks an estimated 3.7–5 million people took to the streets in over 160 cities to rally for immigrant rights (Bloemraad, Voss and Lee 2011, p. 3).

Also during this period, a number of restrictive measures that garnered extensive media attention were introduced in Northern Virginia (Walker and Leitner 2011). For example, in 2007 Prince William County passed a resolution that denied certain public benefits to those unable to prove legal permanent residency and granted authority to local police to check immigration status if there was probable cause to suspect someone of lacking legal status (Wilson, Singer and DeRenzis 2010). This resolution represented an important precursor to current immigrant enforcement laws such as SB 1070 in Arizona. State and local elections in 2007 also became platforms for debating immigration issues. Furthermore, several local crimes received media coverage, which framed them as 'immigration issues' by highlighting the undocumented status of the suspected perpetrators.

We developed an initial coding guide using a set of identified themes shown to correspond with prevalent discourses about immigration within national- and local-level public discussions (Perea 1997; Chavez 2001; Sohoni 2006; Chavez 2008).[6] Using a sub-sample of media texts, we conducted a pilot study to refine our coding mechanism, adding and collapsing categories to incorporate themes that emerged from the data set. We then coded all 522 texts using six categories: (1) Culture; (2) Economy and Labour Market; (3) Government Responsibility; (4) Community Resources; (5) Crime/Border Enforcement; and (6) Multiple Arguments.[7]

Since many of the texts included multiple themes related to immigration, we assigned each text a primary code corresponding with an identified dominant theme and in some cases secondary codes for less prominent themes. Lengthy pieces that devoted substantial discussion to several themes (e.g. feature articles about the overall impact of immigration for the local area) were coded as Multiple Arguments. Each text was read and coded by two coders with inter-coder reliability ranging from 0.81 to 0.88.[8]

In addition to assigning thematic codes, we also classified texts by type (news article, opinion piece/column, op-ed, letter to the editor, Last Word entry), and by expressed attitudes regarding immigration issues. We classified texts as 'exclusionary' when they expressed anti-immigrant sentiments and/or support for rigorous immigration enforcement or restrictionist measures. We labelled entries 'inclusive' when they expressed sympathetic attitudes towards immigrants and/or opposition to restrictionist or strict enforcement measures. Because 'news discourse' is understood to present stories in an 'objective' manner (McElmurry 2009), we classified as 'balanced'[9] news articles and select feature columns and editorials that followed professional norms of 'objective' reporting by ostensibly telling 'both sides of the story' and representing both pro-immigrant and restrictionist/exclusionary positions.

As other scholars have noted, the categorization of discourses is a tricky business (Ono and Snoop 2002). While we recognize the risk of reifying the typologies that we develop and employ in this study, our analysis treats these classifications as heuristic devices, not as un-changing, objective phenomena. The advantage of combining a systematic content analysis with this analytical strategy lies in allowing us to probe the meanings that these discourses hold and the roles that they play in the construction of symbolic boundaries, while avoiding some of the pitfalls of discourse analyses that rely solely on subjective interpretations (cf. Adams and Roscigno 2005).

Findings

Figure 1 shows the frequency of references to immigration issues and the number of texts by expressed position within each coding category. Over half of the texts (51 per cent) expressed anti-immigrant or

Figure 1. *Coverage of immigration issues by category and attitude 2006–07*

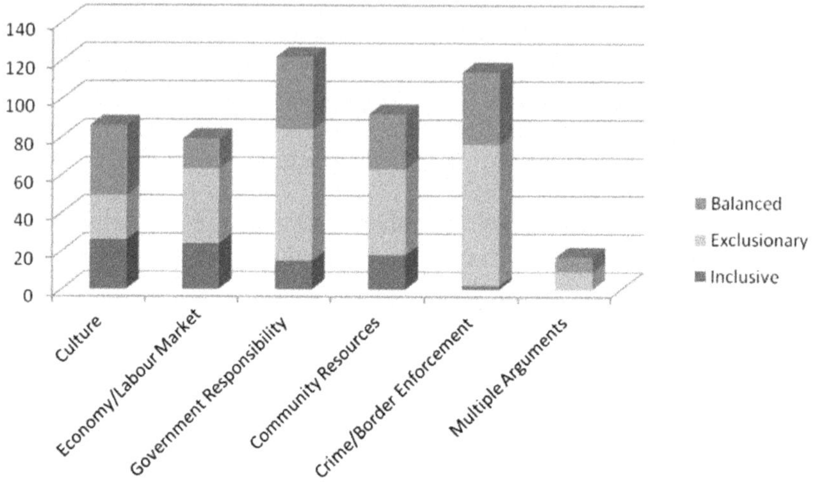

pro-enforcement sentiments, compared to only 17 per cent that expressed more inclusive attitudes towards the immigrant population. The remaining 33 per cent, which consisted mainly of feature articles or news items, were coded as 'balanced'.[10] In only one of the six coding categories did inclusive texts outnumber exclusionary ones – the category of Culture. The other five categories contained significantly greater numbers of exclusionary than inclusive texts (see Figure 1).

Debates about immigration published in the *Gazette* were often triggered by news coverage of local and regional events (e.g. a crime committed by an identified 'illegal' immigrant, a local election, or a proposed restrictionist measure). As seen in Figure 2, the *Gazette*'s coverage of immigration issues in 2006–07 varied greatly over time in response to these as well as national events, and spikes in public commentary followed 'up-ticks' in news coverage.

Newspaper content submitted by readers (342 letters to the editor or Last Word entries) was nearly double that of texts authored by journalists and regular columnists (177 news articles, columns and editorials).[11] It is in these texts authored by readers (often written in response to columns and editorials) that symbolic boundary construction is most evident. We identify two patterns of symbolic boundary construction revealed in discussions in the *Gazette*: (1) national boundaries drawn locally; and (2) localized symbolic boundaries.

National boundaries drawn locally

In the first pattern, media contributors 'download' largely intact narratives and discursive frameworks about immigration that resonate

Figure 2. *Media texts per issue by month, 2006–07*

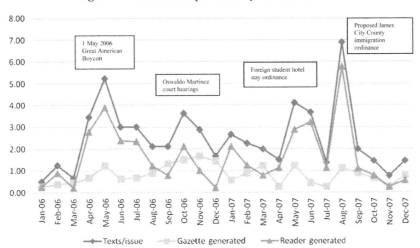

nationally, and often internationally, to generate understandings about local happenings. In these instances discussions about local issues become a forum for constructing symbolic boundaries that delineate national belonging, and community-level boundaries map entirely onto national ones. For example, a reader's letter to the editor employs 'multiple' discourses to interpret local immigration issues and to construct a 'we' that defines community and national membership:

> I moved here from another area of the country where illegal immigrants were also not considered a problem – initially. That changed within a very few years. The school scores drastically declined. Homes became filled with multiple families/individuals who created noise issues. Unkempt houses caused neighboring homes to lose their value. Drugs, crime, gangs and graffiti increased dramatically.... If the illegal immigration issue is allowed to continue, we will in fact become a Third World country like those that the illegal immigrants are trying to leave. If illegal immigration is left unchecked in greater Williamsburg... our way of life will be destroyed (Munn 15 August 2007).[12]

Local constructions of national symbolic boundaries use pre-existing discourses to frame local conditions or events. Since our coding categories are derived from themes that correspond with these discourses, we use them to organize our analysis of this pattern of boundary making in order to demonstrate how these frames were employed.

Culture. Cultural debates in the pages of the *Gazette* largely mirrored contestations and ambivalence regarding the role of immigration in nationalist constructions of 'American' identity (Chavez 2001; Honig 2001). Reflective of this ambivalence, there were nearly equal numbers of inclusive (twenty-six) and exclusionary (twenty-three) texts that made reference to immigrants and cultural issues. Readers and columnists debated if immigrants were culturally threatening or reinvigorated the cultural life of the community and nation through their embodiment of the 'American' entrepreneurial spirit. Mirroring themes in the national media, nativist depictions of Latino immigrants as 'unassimible' were prevalent (Chavez 2008). Texts in this category also made frequent reference to the USA as a land of immigrants, of immigrants' pursuit of the American dream, and other assimilation narratives central to US nationalism (De Genova 2005).

Some comments referred to the area's role in the formation of the nation, by invoking Williamsburg's colonial history (Last Word 6 May 2006, 10 May 2006). For example, a letter to the editor reflects the prevalent theme of Mexican immigrants as an invading force seeking to 'reconquer' the nation by describing them as a 'colonizing' threat to current 'natives' (Chavez 2008):

> Immigrants leave their old country fully intending to switch allegiance to the new, including history, culture and language. Colonizers...intend to replicate as much of the old country in the new as they can, just as did the English who came to Jamestown in 1607. (V. Watkins 8 April 2006)

However, most cultural debates about immigration coalesced around language. In a 2006 Last Word (26 April 2006) comment a reader criticizes those who 'lament the presence of hard-working Hispanic, Asian and other immigrants' and blame them for not speaking English, 'when in reality they function in two languages'. Other readers cite specific cases of encountering 'foreign' languages in Williamsburg (usually Spanish) as evidence of a threat to the cultural fabric of both the nation and community. For example, a 2006 issue printed an image of the American flag with the words 'Welcome to America, Now Speak English' next to a letter decrying the use of Spanish in the Williamsburg post office as a dangerous sign 'of a creeping loss of language and culture' (E. Watkins 3 May 2006).

Other Last Word discussions criticized local organizations for providing interpretation services and resources in Spanish, arguing that these provisions enabled immigrants to avoid assimilation (Last Word 22 April 2006). Some expressed adamant disapproval of the *Gazette*'s addition of a weekly column in Spanish (with English translation) (Last Word 19 April 2006, 16 August 2006; 23 August

2006; 22 December 2007), while others labelled these claims 'xeno-phobic', questioning why people were 'yowling about one measly page in the newspaper given over to our Latino community' (Last Word 26 December 2007).

Economy and labour market. Debates about immigrant workers in Williamsburg's tourist, retail and hospitality industries also featured familiar and contending national discourses – this time used to interpret local labour market conditions. For example, the tropes of immigrants 'stealing' jobs from Americans and depressing wages for the native born (Last Word 5 April 2006, 20 January 2007, 19 May 2007, 8 September 2007), versus that of immigrants as hard workers who provide for their families, performing jobs that the native born are unwilling to do (Last Word 18 February 2006, 22 August 2007, 25 August 2007) were prevalent. While there were a large number of inclusive texts that stressed the vital role of immigrants in the economy (twenty-four), these were outnumbered by texts that depicted im-migrants as detrimental to the economy or as a threat to American labourers (thirty-nine). Notably, contributors to the *Gazette* who stressed immigrants' work ethic and positive contributions frequently referred specifically to foreign student workers, differentiating them from Hispanic immigrant labourers. We return to this point in a later section.

Another reoccurring frame assigned blame for the immigration 'problem' to corporations that hire immigrants at lower pay because they are only worried about 'their bottom line' (Meyer 3 May 2006) – and local employers who 'pay workers under the table' and 'never hire American workers because they are not worth $8 an hour' (Last Word 22 November 2006). This latter commentator makes a nationalist call to the Williamsburg community:

> If you need a local contractor, make sure that you ask plenty of questions first. Otherwise, you may be supporting a business that should be investigated for its hiring practices. It's time for American workers to stand up for American workers.

Government responsibility. Anti-corporate frames were often discur-sively linked to complaints about the failure of the federal government to control immigration, reflecting the filtering down of a populist framework for anti-immigrant positions promulgated at the national level by conservative media pundits. Both arguments support pro-enforcement positions, but in different ways. Whereas contributors who expressed anti-corporate sentiments often depicted immigrants as victims of 'big business' (e.g. Last Word 5 April 2006), texts that criticized government officials were far more likely to blame immigrants (exclusionary texts outnumbered inclusive ones by over four to one in this category). The perceived failures of politicians and the government to 'do something' about immigration led some contributors to call for various legal reforms, including local ones (Last Word 13 May 2006, 15 July 2006).

One reader responded to a proposed county ordinance to limit eligibility for local services to those who can provide proof of authorized immigration status:

> Personally, I like the fact that James City County might be willing to take a look at this national problem ... Since the federal government can't or won't deal with the illegal immigration problem, then let a whole bunch of counties, cities and states try their hand at it. (Warren 4 August 2007)

Another reader applauded the actions of a group of residents who repaired a section of a county road in their neighbourhood:

> Cheers to the Jolly Pond Road citizens. Isn't it amazing how quickly and cheaply things can be done when the government is not involved? Makes you wonder how fast a wall could be put in place on the Mexican border if the government would just get out of the way and let the citizens build it. (Last Word 21 July 2007)

Local elections provided a platform for public commentary linking the local 'immigration problem' to failures to regulate immigration at the national level. For instance, a restrictionist ordinance proposed by a local politician during his campaign for re-election sparked a heated debate about national and local immigration enforcement, as did the campaign materials of an incumbent Republican candidate for state office. In the latter case, a campaign mailing featured an image of two brown-skinned men climbing over a barbed-wire fence. The caption read: 'Brenda Pogge will fight to give officers the tools they need to fight illegal immigrants and the crime they bring.' (Republican Party of Virginia 2007). One of the *Gazette*'s regular columnists reprinted the image and endorsed Pogge's candidacy: 'Here's some good news for those fed up with our open border policies ... Brenda Pogge ... is tough enough to make the crackdown on illegals the centerpiece of her campaign. That should be enough reason to elect her' (Johnson 19 September 2007).

Community resources. Local debates about immigrants' entitlement to public services were largely dominated by restrictionist positions with exclusionary texts outnumbering inclusive ones by over two to one

(45:18). Last Word contributors frequently invoked the nativist construction of immigrants as a 'tax burden' and drain on social services (Calavita 1996):

> If area residents are paying attention to the news in any format, they have to know that people here illegally are costing the citizens hugely.... Considering we have many unfunded expenses locally... why is it fair or reasonable for our hard-earned dollars to go to non-citizens? We have an obligation to care for our own people first... Williamsburg cannot be the receiver for the uneducated, sick people who somehow end up here from other countries. (Last Word 7 February 2007)

Specifically, commentators stressed the cost of immigrants' illegitimate access to 'free' health care, food stamps and in-state college tuition (Last Word 22 February 2006, 12 April 2006, 15 April 2006), as well as their drain on law enforcement and overcrowding of local jails (Last Word 22 February 2006, 1 April 2006). Like the Last Word entry cited above, contributors emphasized immigrants' presumed illegality to argue that they were undeserving of services designated for 'American taxpayers' and 'not entitled to any services or privileges... except a one-way trip back to where they came from' (Wilderman 8 August 2007).

Crime/border enforcement. Reflective of the prevalence of criminaliza-tion of immigration at the national (Harrison and Lloyd 2011) and indeed, international level (Fassin 2011), the discourse of criminality appeared frequently across the thematic categories in our data set. With the exception of Culture, Crime/Border Enforcement was the most frequent secondary code for every category of texts in our data set. In the public discussions in the *Gazette* criminality served as a 'master frame' (Benford and Snow 2000) that enabled proponents of restrictionist positions to connect a variety of issues and claims in formulating anti-immigrant positions (Chavez 2008).

The category Crime/Border Enforcement also contained the greatest ratio of exclusionary to inclusive entries (67:2), reflecting a relatively uncontested fusing of criminalization with immigration (Esbenshade et al. 2010). Writing in support of a proposal to earmark local police funding 'to crack down on and deport illegal lawbreakers', a letter to the editor makes these links explicitly: 'Illegal equals lawbreaker, which equals alien, non-entitled squatter-scavenger' (Dowling 29 August 2007). *Gazette* readers also associated immigrants with social security and identity theft, tax evasion, gang activities, drug dealing, terrorism and even littering (Last Word 6 May 2006, 14 March 2007; Munn 15 August 2007).

The linking of undocumented immigration status with criminal activity frequently occurred in conjunction with news coverage of local cases, such as the arrest and prosecution of Oswaldo Martínez, a deaf and mute Salvadoran man who was charged with the rape and murder of Brittany Binger, a teenage girl:

> How much have we paid for Oswaldo Martinez who is accused of raping and murdering Brittany Binger? Look around and you find illegal aliens are committing more crimes, more rapes and more murders because they don't see us enforcing our laws. More Americans die each year at the hands of illegal immigrants than are dying in war. Our politicians stand back and do nothing... It's time the politicians and judges be held... responsible for allowing Americans to be terrorized in their own country. (Last Word 22 August 2007)[13]

Regional cases also sparked coverage in the *Virginia Gazette* with columnists and readers alike citing these events to support alarmist and exclusionary positions about immigration. For example, the 2007 case of a drunk driver who caused the deaths of two teenage girls in the nearby city of Virginia Beach received national attention as well as considerable public comment in the *Gazette* when it was featured on the politically conservative *Fox News*. Political commentator Bill O'Reilly zeroed in on the immigrant driver's undocumented status and linked the crime to lenient immigration enforcement (i.e. 'sanctuary cities'), which he argued attracted illegal immigrants and criminal activity (Last Word 7 April 2007).[14]

While a few Last Word contributors lambasted O'Reilly for using the tragedy to further his own political agenda (Last Word 11 April 2007, 14 April 2007), others saw this case as holding implications for Williamsburg:

> Williamsburg is already a sanctuary for illegal aliens. If you don't believe that check out the parking lot of [name of a local apartment complex]. There are vehicles there with no city stickers because they have out-of-state plates. There are several immigrants who live in that apartment complex, and I'm sure they're not all here legally. (Last Word 18 April 2007)

Commentators in the *Virginia Gazette* also frequently employed constructions of immigrants as criminals to strengthen the urgency of their calls for local and federal government enforcement of immigration – regardless of cost. In a letter to the editor, one reader cites the increased need for such measures in light of recently passed local enforcement ordinances in other parts of Virginia:

The illegals in Loudoun and Prince George's (sic) counties are going to need a place to go to very soon. Do you think they might get word that James City is looking the other way? Please pay attention, elected officials: Cost is not the main issue when it comes to illegal aliens. The principal [sic] of right and wrong is the primary concern. The illegals are wrong for breaking our laws... This is plain and simple. (Jonkovic 11 August 2007)

Localized symbolic boundaries: 'good' and 'bad' immigrants

The second pattern of symbolic boundary construction that we found had a particular local flavour and appeared across the five coding categories. Rather than involving a straightforward application of an intact discursive framework about immigration, local boundaries were constructed in ways that were rendered intelligible within specific local debates by incorporating place-specific, cultural understandings and identities. In Greater Williamsburg, these constructions emerged in local debates about the merits and potential threats posed by different groups of newcomers to the area. For instance, a Last Word comment compares recent immigrants to Greeks who in the 1950s 'became a mainstay of our hospitality industry' and notes that 'they are us'. The reader goes on to differentiate between recent immigrants and native-born transplants from other states: 'I admire the courage and ambition of our foreign immigrants and detest domestic, pompous people who came here to avoid real estate taxes up North and bemoan others who came from much further away...' (Last Word 26 April 2006).

The construction of localized symbolic boundaries was by far most prevalent in public commentary that distinguished between young people from Eastern Europe and Asia who work in the area during the tourist season (often referred to as 'foreign workers' or 'exchange visitors') and a group labelled illegal/Hispanic/Mexican 'immigrants' – or as one editorialist candidly acknowledges: 'What we have in greater Williamsburg are "good" immigrants and "bad" immigrants' (O'Donovan 21 February 2007). Media representations in the *Gazette* were far more likely to depict this first group in a positive light, often stressing 'foreign workers'' contribution to the community and even characterizing them as potential victims of crimes in need of protection. When we compare entries from our data set that refer to these two groups, exclusionary texts that reference 'illegal immigrants', 'Hispanics' or 'Mexicans' outnumber inclusive ones by four to one. In contrast, of the texts referencing 'foreign workers' or 'exchange visitors', *inclusive* texts outnumber exclusionary ones by 1.6 to 1.

Local debates about housing and labour market participation served as the primary arena for the construction of localized symbolic boundaries. Contributors to the *Gazette* praise 'foreign workers' for their strong work ethic, which they associate with true 'American-ness'. Others approvingly note that working in the USA would expose these young, temporary workers to American values of hard work and entrepreneurialism, which they could later bring back to their home countries (Last Word 12 July 2006, 7 March 2007, 1 August 2007).

News coverage described opponents of a proposed ordinance that would grant hotels permits to house temporary workers as 'invok[ing] the specter of "1,700 Hispanic men descending" on the city' (Vaughan 15 November 2006) and later objecting to the measure's use of the term 'guest workers', which was regarded as 'code for illegal immigrants from Mexico' (Vaughan 6 January 2007). A news article reporting on a town hall meeting clarifies that the permits would be designated for housing for student workers who 'in fact, ... come primarily from Asia and Eastern Europe, with few Hispanics' (Vaughan 15 November 2006).

While the differences between young student workers and 'Hispanic' immigrants are accentuated in these debates, differences between legitimate members of the community (citizens) and young foreign workers are minimized. The same news article quotes the Vice President of the Greater Williamsburg Chamber & Tourism Alliance who uses class and age-based definitions to clearly distinguish 'exchange visitors' from undesirable 'migrant workers':

> They are not migrant workers ... They are college students, often from families that are quite well off. We want them to have an excellent experience here, which they can go back and share with their families, many of whom have the disposable income to travel. They aren't any different from your kids or my kids. (Vaughan 15 November 2006)

In contrast, 'illegal [Hispanic or Mexican] immigrants' are depicted as a distinct and threatening group. The potential for this group to settle more permanently in Williamsburg seemed to represent the greatest perceived danger. In a letter to the editor, one Williamsburg resident contrasts the undesirability of illegal 'full-time residents' with the necessary labour of foreign exchange visitors. For this reader, making housing available to the former group '...means extra vehicles, girlfriends, children, and often "business activities" considered un-desirable that legitimate foreign workers do not bring to our commu-nity during their seasonal work.' The letter continues: 'We don't fear legitimate foreign workers. We fear illegitimate, illegal immigrants' (Bond 6 January 2007). Here, constructions of 'deserving' immigrants are also tied to social reproduction. Youthful, 'legitimate' workers are temporary visitors who will not raise families and who are not expected to integrate as fully fledged, adult members of the community.

The construction of 'exchange visitors' as both desirable and legitimate diverges from nationalist, assimilation myths depicted by Honig (2001) that describe immigrants as a source of 'national re-enchantment' (p. 74). Media accounts in the *Gazette* depict this group as embodying 'American' characteristics, but not as settlers who will contribute to the nation's 'melting pot'. Instead, this group's official status as 'visitors' likens them to foreign exchange students or even prospective tourists. Debates about foreign workers emphasize their youthfulness, legal designation as *temporary* workers and lack of ties to the area – characterizations that correspond with their attractiveness to employers, as a tractable and eager workforce with few social reproductive needs. Meanwhile, even as the deportability of undocumented, Hispanic immigrants foments their vulnerability as a workforce, media accounts in the *Gazette* characterize them as threatening, mirroring the mass media's cultivation of a 'moral panic' that justifies the policing of social borders.

Conclusion

Prior research on media representations of immigration issues has identified a set of nationally and internationally resonant discourses. Our analysis foregrounds the importance of local media outlets as sites of cultural struggle by revealing how these and more locally derived interpretative frames are deployed to construct symbolic boundaries. Our analysis suggests two prominent ways in which public discussions draw distinctions between and among in-groups and 'others' – either by adopting available interpretative frameworks so as to simultaneously define the boundaries of community and national belonging, or through a process that takes on meaning in the local setting.

We find that in newspaper discussions in the *Virginia Gazette*, contributors draw 'national boundaries locally' by adopting ambivalent nationalist narratives about the incorporation of immigrants into US culture and society as well as anti-corporate and anti-government discourses that frame immigrants as a cost to American workers and taxpayers. In addition, local media actors use the 'master frame' of criminality to link diverse issues and discourses in constructing anti-immigrant positions. The conflation of 'immigrant' with the racialized category of 'Hispanic/Mexican illegal' bolsters alarmist claims and fuels arguments about the responsibility of federal and local governments for the enforcement of various types of borders, including social ones.

Furthermore, we demonstrate how within specific local debates media actors construct 'localized symbolic boundaries' to produce distinctions between community members and various 'others', which take their meaning from place-based cultural understandings and specific characteristics of the locality. As contributors to the *Gazette* distinguish between groups of newcomers as threatening criminals or welcomed guests, they create locally constructed boundaries between 'us' and 'them' that diverge from national definitions of belonging. By differentiating between *legitimate* 'foreign workers' and the conflated category of 'illegal/ Hispanic/Mexican' immigrants, media representations reinforce the national narrative of the 'Latino threat' (Chavez 2008), homogenizing members of this group and cementing their status as the 'other'.

Yet, even in sympathetic portrayals of newcomers, boundary-making processes construct both groups as outsiders. As in the case of national news magazines, contributors to the *Virginia Gazette* assume a readership that is 'implicitly constructed as culturally and racially singular' (Chavez 2001, p. 294). In these newspaper discussions, immigrants are objects of public discourse, but not subjects who participate in the public sphere to give voice to and interpret their own realities.

Beyond this local case, the ways that these boundaries are constructed hold implications for the politics of belonging more generally – particularly in recent immigrant-receiving sites. Clearly, local demographics and socio-economic conditions will vary – a group of newcomers defined as 'desirable' at a particular time and place may be interpreted as a danger to the majority community in another context. As tensions around immigration continue unabated, communities promise to become increasingly important sites for forging and contesting symbolic and social boundaries. If we can understand the ways in which interpretative frameworks are adopted, applied and reconfigured in particular local settings, perhaps we can imagine ways to counter these representations and render more nuanced understandings of immigration issues that could set the stage for constructing a more inclusive society.

Acknowledgements

An earlier version of this paper was presented at the 2009 Annual Meetings of the Latin American Studies Association in Rio de Janeiro, Brazil. We thank Beth Currans, Kay Jenkins, Tanya Golash-Boza, Eileen Diaz McConnell, Monica Varsanyi and the anonymous reviewers at ERS for their helpful comments on previous drafts of this article. Lori Beacham and Maura Ooi provided valuable research assistance on this project.

Notes

1.   Greater Williamsburg includes the city of Williamsburg, James City County and Upper York County.

2. H2B visas provide temporary work permits for seasonal, non-agricultural employment.

3. There exist no reliable data on foreign-born versus US-born Latino/as in Greater Williamsburg, and census data almost certainly under-report the presence of undocumented immigrants. However, a 2008 University of Virginia study reported that 40 per cent of Hispanic residents in Virginia were foreign born (Cai 2008, p. 2).

4. Since not every section of the newspaper is published online, the authors and their research assistants reviewed every printed issue of the *Gazette* to identify texts that contained keywords such as immigrant(s), immigration, 'illegals', 'aliens', foreigners, foreign workers, Mexicans and Hispanics.

5. With the exception of personal attacks, libel or comments deemed racist or bigoted, an estimated 80 per cent of contributions to the Last Word are printed (Rusty Carver, personal email communication, 20 March 2008).

6. Coding categories were drawn from the existing literature as well as from the extensive ethnographic research conducted by the second author in Williamsburg.

7. Twelve texts did not fit into these categories and were coded as 'miscellaneous'.

8. Each text was coded by one of the authors and by one of two research assistants. In cases where coders differed, the author who had not served as an original coder served as the arbitrator.

9. Despite our use of the designation 'balanced', we recognize that such representations can be employed to support anti-immigrant positions.

10. Amounts do not equal 100 percent due to rounding error.

11. Our data included three political advertisements, which we included in the analysis but not in tallies of texts authored by readers versus newspaper staff.

12. Citations of texts from our data set are provided parenthetically.

13. Coverage by the *Gazette* on the proceedings in these cases (such as Martinez's competency to stand trial) was frequently followed by extensive reader-generated commentary.

14. This case became the subject of an infamous debate between network news analysts Geraldo Rivera and Bill O'Reilly (http://www.youtube.com/watch?v=FhwwbNA3hjg).

References

ADAMS, JOSH and ROSCIGNO, VINCENT J. 2005 'White supremacists, oppositional culture and the World Wide Web', *Social Forces*, vol. 84, no. 2, pp. 759–78

ANDERSON, BENEDICT 1983 *Imagined Communities: Reflections on the Origin and Spread of Nationalism*, New York: Verso

BENFORD, ROBERT and SNOW, DAVID 2000 'Framing processes and social movements: an overview and assessment', *Annual Review of Sociology*, vol. 26, pp. 611–39

BLOEMRAAD, IRENE, VOSS, KIM and LEE, TAEKU 2011 'The protests of 2006', in Irene Bloemraad and Kim Voss (eds), *Rallying for Immigrant Rights: The Fight for Inclusion in 21st Century America*, Berkeley, CA: University of California Press, pp. 3–43

BOURDIEU, PIERRE 1991 *Language and Symbolic Power*, Cambridge, MA: Harvard University Press

BROTHERTON, DAVID C. and KRETSEDEMAS, PHILIP (eds) 2008 *Keeping Out the Other: A Critical Introduction to Immigration Enforcement Today*, New York: Columbia University Press

CAI, QIAN 2008 *'Hispanic Immigrants and Citizens In Virginia'*, Numbers Count Analysis Of Virginia Population, Charlottesville, VA: Demographics & Workforce Section Weldon Cooper Center, University of Virginia

CALAVITA, KITTY 1996 'The new politics of immigration: "balanced-budget conservatism" and the symbolism of Proposition 187', *Social Problems*, vol. 43, no. 3, pp. 284–305

CASTLES, STEPHEN and MILLER, MARK J. 2009 *The Age of Migration: International Population Movements in the Modern World*, 4th edn, New York: The Guilford Press

CHAVEZ, LEO 2001 *Covering Immigration: Popular Images and the Politics of the Nation*, Berkeley, CA: University of California Press

—— 2008 *The Latino Threat: Constructing Immigrants, Citizens, and the Nation*, Stanford, CA: Stanford University Press

COUTIN, SUSAN BIBLER and CHOCK, PHYLLUS PEASE 1997 '"Your friend, the illegal": definition and paradox in newspaper accounts of US immigration reform', *Identities*, vol. 2, nos. 1–2, pp. 123–48

DAWKINS, CASEY J. C. *et al.* 2007 'Housing needs assessment: James City County and Williamsburg', Blacksburg, VA: Virginia Center for Housing Research Virginia Tech. Available from: http://www.jccegov.com/pdf/bospdfs/bospdfs2007/121107readfile/item3.pdf [Accessed 10 August 2012]

DEEB-SOSSA, NATALIA and MENDEZ, JENNIFER BICKHAM 2008 'Enforcing borders in the *Nuevo* South: gender and migration in Williamsburg, VA and the Research Triangle, NC', *Gender and Society*, vol. 22, no. 5, pp. 613–38

DE GENOVA, NICHOLAS 2005 *Working the Boundaries: Race, Space and 'Illegality' in Mexican Chicago*, Durham, NC: Duke University Press

DE GENOVA, NICHOLAS and PEUTZ, NATHALIE (eds) 2010 *The Deportation Regime: Sovereignty, Space, and the Freedom of Movement*, Durham, NC: Duke University Press

DUNAWAY, JOHANNA, BRANTON, REGINA P. and ABRAJANO, MARISA A. 2010 'Agenda setting, public opinion, and the issue of immigration reform', *Social Science Quarterly*, vol. 91, no. 2, pp. 359–78

ESBENSHADE, JILL, WRIGHT, BENJAMIN, CORTOPASSI, PAUL, REED, ARTHUR and FLORES, JERRY 2010 'The "law and order" foundation of local ordinances: a four locale study of Hazleton, Pennsylvania; Escondido, California; Farmers Branch, Texas; and Prince William County, Virginia', in Monica W. Varsanyi (ed.), *Taking Local Control: Immigration Policy and Activism in U.S. Cities and States*, Stanford, CA: Stanford University Press, pp. 255–74

FASSIN, DIDIER 2011 'Policing borders, producing boundaries: the governmentality of immigration in dark times', *Annual Review of Anthropology*, vol. 40, pp. 213–26

GILLIGAN, GREGORY J. 1999 'Theme parks desperate for workers recruit foreign students', *The Washington Times*, 1 March

HALL, STUART 1996 'The question of cultural identity', in Stuart Hall, *et al.* (eds), *Modernity: An Introduction to Modern Societies*, Cambridge, MA: Blackwell Publishers, pp. 595–634

HARRISON, JILL LINDSEY and LLOYD, SARAH E. 2011 'Illegality at work: deportability and the productive new era of immigration enforcement', *Antipode*, vol. 44, no. 2, pp. 365–85

HONIG, BONNIE 2001 *Democracy and the Foreigner*, Princeton, NJ: Princeton University Press

JONES, RICHARD C. (ed.) 2008 *Immigrants outside Megalopolis: Ethnic Transformation in the Heartland*, Lantham, MD: Lexington Books

KORTEWEG, ANNA and YURDAKUL, GÖKÇE 2009 'Islam, gender, and immigrant integration: boundary drawing in discourses on honour killing in the Netherlands and Germany', *Ethnic and Racial Studies*, vol. 32, no. 2, pp. 218–38

LAMONT, MICHÈLE and MOLNÁR, VIRÁG 2002 'The study of boundaries in the social sciences', *Annual Review of Sociology*, vol. 28, pp. 167–95

MCCONNELL, EILEEN DIAZ 2011 'An "incredible number of Latinos and Asians:" media representations of racial and ethnic population change in Atlanta, Georgia', *Latino Studies*, vol. 9, no. 2/3, pp. 177–97

MCELMURRY, SARA E. 2009 'Elvira Arellano no Rosa Parks: creation of "us" versus "them" in an opinion column', *Hispanic Journal of Behavioral Sciences*, vol. 31, no. 2, pp. 182–203

MARROW, HELEN 2011 *New Destination Dreaming: Immigration, Race, and Legal Status in the Rural American South*, Stanford, CA: Stanford University

MASSEY, DOUGLAS 2008 (ed.) *New Faces in New Places: The Changing Geography of American Immigration*, New York: Russell Sage Foundation

MENJÍVAR, CECILIA and KIL, SANG H. 2002 'For their own good: benevolent rhetoric and exclusionary language in public officials' discourse on immigrant-related issues', *Social Justice*, vol. 29, nos. 1–2, pp. 160–76

NEWTON, LINA 2008 *Illegal, Alien, or Immigrant: The Politics of Immigration Reform*, New York: New York University Press

ONO, KENT A. and SLOOP, JOHN M. 2002 *Shifting Borders: Rhetoric, Immigration, and California's Proposition 187*, Philadelphia, PA: Temple University Press

PADÍN, JOSÉ A. 2005 'The normative mulattoes: the press, Latinos and the racial climate on the moving immigration frontier', *Sociological Perspectives*, vol. 48, no. 1, pp. 49–75

PEREA, JUAN F. (ed.) 1997 *Immigrants Out! The New Nativism and the Anti-Immigrant Impulse in the United States*, New York: New York University Press

PEW HISPANIC CENTER 2008 'Latino settlement in the new century'. Available from: http://pewhispanic.org/files/reports/96.pdf [Accessed 10 August 2012]

REPUBLICAN PARTY OF VIRGINIA 2007 'Brenda Pogge for House of Delegates', Campaign Flyer.

SOHONI, DEENESH S. 2006 'The immigrant problem: modern day nativism on the web', *Current Sociology*, vol. 54, no. 6, pp. 827–50

US CENSUS BUREAU 2009 'Table 1: Annual estimates of the population for counties of Virginia: April 1, 2000 to July 1, 2007'. US Census Bureau.

VAN DER VEER, PETER 1995 *Nation and Migration: The Politics of Space in the South Asian Diaspora*, Philadelphia, PA: University of Pennsylvania

VARSANYI, MONICA W. (ed.) 2010 *Taking Local Control: Immigration Policy and Activism in US Cities and States*, Stanford, CA: Stanford University Press

VIRGINIA GAZETTE 2012 'About us'. Available from: http://www.vagazette.com/services/va-services_gazhistory,0,5332906.story?page=1 [Accessed 10 August 2012]

—— 2010 '25 years of Last Word', *Virginia Gazette*, 2 June

WALKER, KYLE and LEITNER, HELGA 2011 'The variegated landscape of local immigration policies in the United States', *Urban Geography*, vol. 32, no. 2, pp. 156–78

WCHF (WILLIAMSBURG COMMUNITY HEALTH FOUNDATION) 2008 *Service Area Needs Assessment*, Chester, VA: WCHF

WILSON, JILL H., SINGER, AUDREY and DERENZIS, BROOKE 2010 'Growing pains: local responses to recent immigration to Washington, DC', in Monica W. Varsanyi (ed.), *Taking Local Control: Immigration Policy and Activism in US Cities and States*, Stanford, CA: Stanford University Press, pp. 193–215

Skin tone, biracial stratification and tri-racial stratification among sperm donors

Carol S. Walther

Abstract

Conception through donor insemination is an attractive option for many couples and single women in the USA, being a relatively simple and inexpensive way of having a baby by a biological birth. Sperm banks provide online catalogues in which sperm donors can be selected according to their physical and social characteristics. One sperm bank's catalogue was analysed based on the pregnancy of selected donors. Three hypotheses were tested related to colourism, biracial stratification and tri-racialism. Specifically, the selection of donors did not reflect: (1) any general preference for a lighter skin tone; (2) a black–white polarity; or (3) any trend towards tri-racialism. Donors who could be identified as Jewish or Muslim were more likely to be selected. Donors whose major was law were less likely to be selected.

Introduction

In the USA, sperm donors usually donate to a sperm bank once a week, undergo expensive testing and are paid for their donation, if their donation meets sperm count requirements. Typically people select and purchase semen from a sperm bank and then use artificial insemination. Most US sperm banks provide an online catalogue for potential customers to examine the sperm donors. In many European countries, sperm donors are not paid for their donation.

Researchers have examined the biological, social and psychological components of artificial insemination through the use of donor sperm. Previous literature has focused on four threads: (1) sperm donors as a threat to hetero-patriarchal families (Hertz 2008); (2) the commodification of bodies (Almeling 2006, 2007, 2009, 2011); (3) women's reproduction and relationship to offspring (Martin 1992); and (4) the altruistic motivations of donors (Bowen et al. 2010). These various threads often focus on comparisons between women and men, rather than differences between men.

In addition to the four main areas of research, some studies on sperm selection have been based on self-assigned racial characteristics (Chabot and Ames 2004; Almeling 2007; Quiroga 2007; Ryan, Moras and Shapiro 2010; Whittaker and Speier 2010; Almeling 2011). Race is important in the marketing of sperm because parents often select sperm in an attempt to 'match' racial characteristics of one or both parents to maintain family resemblance (Quiroga 2007; Mason 2008; Nordqvist 2010). Race was often discussed among interracial couples or people of colour, but not among white families (Ryan, Moras and Shapiro 2010).

Outside the USA, researchers have focused on resource-poor countries and reproductive technologies (Whittaker and Speier 2010). Additionally, other researchers have documented an increase in the access of reproductive technologies in China (Handwerker 2002), Ecuador (Roberts 2006), Egypt (Inhorn 2003), India (Gupta 2006), Iran (Tremayne 2006), Mali (Horbst 2006) and Vietnam (Pashigian 2009).

In this study, I examine whether colourism, biracial stratification status or tri-racial stratification status impacts the selection of sperm donors. Utilizing a sperm bank catalogue that contains information such as donor profiles and essays written by the donors and the staff, I analyse men's physical and social characteristics ($N = 282$). In this study, I test three different perspectives. First, I examine whether lighter-skinned men experience a higher probability of being selected for a pregnancy (colourism). Second, I examine Yancey's (2003) perspective that racial poles of black and non-black stratification increase the probability of being selected for a pregnancy. Third, I examine Bonilla-Silva's (2001) tri-racialism thesis, which suggests that US society has three tiers of stratification: white, honorary white and collective black. I find little support for any of these three perspectives. However, Alemling's (2011) research that suggests racial and religious minority sperm donors are selected more often than white sperm donors is supported. These findings confound the intersectionality perspective that predicts that white men's semen would be more likely to be selected than racial minority men's semen.

This research contributes to the literature in three ways. First, while most studies about sperm donation have used interviews and observations to examine individuals selecting sperm (Chabot and Ames 2004; Almeling 2007; Quiroga 2007; Ryan, Moras and Shapiro

2010; Almeling 2011), this research examines the selection of sperm quantitatively. Second, very few researchers have examined sperm donor selection together with US race and ethnic relationships (Chabot and Ames 2004; Quiroga 2007; Ryan, Moras and Shapiro 2010). Past research has examined kin selection and masculinity among people selecting sperm qualitatively; this study allows for the testing of three theoretical perspectives that should influence the selection of semen. Third, most studies have not examined the three perspectives of colourism, biracial stratification and tri-racialism together in one study. US race relations may be related to reproductive technology experiences more as an intersection between race, religion and social class than the three perspectives, colourism, biracial stratification or tri-racialism, would suggest.

The USA was selected for this study because of the unique sperm banks in this country. First, US sperm banks voluntarily follow guidelines on how many children should be conceived from one sperm donor; the sperm bank industry is not regulated in this regard as it is in western Europe. Second, some countries (Canada, for example) often do not pay donors for their sperm as is done predominately in US sperm banks. Third, countries such as Sweden release more complete information about the donors to the customers, whereas in the USA donors typically remain anonymous until the child's 18th birthday (Sydsjö et al. 2011). Fourth, the USA may have a different racial hierarchy than other countries.

This research does not examine the customers of sperm donors per se. The study does not have qualitative analyses of women who have selected and utilized sperm banks. I do examine the profiles of the sperm donors to see if white men have a higher probability of being selected than other men. In other words, I am not examining how or why people choose specific sperm, but the possible relationship between skin tone, biracial stratification and tri-racialism.

Selection of sperm donors

Conception through donor insemination is an attractive option for many couples and single women, because it is the most simple and inexpensive method of alternative conception. Heterosexual couples, in which the man is infertile due to previous vasectomies, chemotherapy or other conditions, were once the majority of donor insemination users. For women who may not have male partners, donor insemination is a viable and readily obtainable option. Donor insemination is now widely used by many lesbian couples and single women as well.

Typically, families are indicated by shared physical characteristics (Mason 2008). Many researchers have examined aspects of kinship in the selection of sperm donors (Becker, Butler and Nachtigall 2005;

136

Nordqvist 2010; Ryan, Moras and Shapiro 2010). With families constructed via sperm donations, families may select donors who share similar physical characteristics to the non-biological partner, possibly ensuring family resemblances (Quiroga 2007; Nordqvist 2010). For example, heterosexual couples often match sperm donors who closely match the infertile male partner. Because of wanting kin to have a family resemblance to the non-biological parent, many consumers choose sperm that is racially and ethnically the same as the non-biological parent. Additionally, people are encouraged by sperm bank staff members and doctors to select a sperm donor who is racially or ethnically similar to themselves (Almeling 2007; Quiroga 2007; Nordqvist 2010; Thompson 2009). Quiroga (2007, p. 144) argues that the use of same-race sperm donors privileges 'white kinship and fears about race mixing' with few white couples choosing a non-white donor. Nordqvist (2010) finds that UK lesbian couples specifically discuss having a sperm donor who physically resembles the parents in eye colour, hair colour and skin tone, which effectively reifies racial categorization.

Other research has examined the selection of sperm donors based on racial categorization (Chabot and Ames 2004; Quiroga 2007; Nordqvist 2010; Ryan, Moras and Shapiro 2010). For instance, Ryan, Moras and Shapiro (2010) found that although rarely discussed explicitly, race and ethnicity largely informed lesbian couples' decisions of donors. They argued that gay and lesbian families reflect institutional scripts of families infused with racial biases and suggest that the lack of discourse about race within white, lesbian families serves to normalize a narrative of whiteness. White participants who were partnered with white women sought out white donors so that their children would be identifiable as their own, implying white donors were favourable. These participants sought donors who were similar to their partners in appearance and physical traits, such as hair colour, eye colour and skin tone. Similarly, white participants who were partnered with women of colour actively sought out donors who matched their partner's ethnicity and physical traits so that the child conceived would physically reflect both mothers.

Because a donor's race plays such a major role in the decision-making process of sperm selection, researchers have examined the availability of donors of colour. Donor pools in the USA are made up of predominately white, college-aged men; some sperm banks have no African American donors to choose from while other banks have very few African American donors and other donors of colour. Often, sperm banks recruit students from the nation's highest-ranked colleges and universities (Epstein 2010).

There are at least two reasons for the shortage of donors of colour (Whittaker and Speier 2010). First, sperm banks have a rigorous screening process that includes social and psychological testing, testing of semen and a commitment of at least six months of coming to the clinic before the donor is available for customers. Only about one fifth of all applicants are accepted. Second, most banks require the donors to be highly educated; the minimum level of education a potential donor must possess is a bachelor's degree. Literature suggests that education is a proxy for human and cultural capitals (Almeling 2011). Twenty-four per cent of adult white men in the USA graduate from college, compared to only 12 per cent of adult black men. Furthermore, adult Latino men graduate at even lower rates than adult black men in the USA, while Asian men graduate at similar rates to adult white men. Therefore, due to the educational requirement, the pool of potential black and Latino donors decrease significantly in contrast to white and Asian donors.

Economies of colour

Many researchers have documented inter-group and intra-group discrimination related to skin tone and the conceptual discourse on colourism (Hunter 2005; Bonilla-Silva 2009). Glenn (2008, p. 281) defines colourism as the 'preference for and privileging of lighter skin and discrimination against those with darker skin . . .'. The practices of colourism tend to favour lighter skin individuals over darker skin individuals (Hall 2005). Colourism practices and beliefs operate within and across racial and ethnic groupings (Bonilla-Silva 2009).

Several studies have highlighted that skin colour functions as 'epidermic capital', providing lighter-skinned people economic privileges and advantages (Keith and Herring 1991; Espino and Franz 2002; Herring, Keith and Horton 2004; Morales 2008; Keith 2009). Other researchers have found that darker-skinned individuals are viewed as less intelligent, less trustworthy and less attractive (Herring, Keith and Horton 2004; Maddox 2004; Hunter 2005). Being physically attractive signifies that individuals are more intelligent, kind, confident, interesting, sexy, assertive, poised, modest and successful, as well as more feminine for women. Some researchers found that darker-skinned minorities are more likely to grow up in poverty, more likely to abuse drugs and less likely to marry (Hochschild and Weaver 2007). Extensive evidence suggests that light-skinned individuals have higher emotional well-being and higher self-esteem (Thompson and Keith 2001). Additionally, darker-skinned blacks experienced more discrimination than their co-ethnics with lighter skin (Klonoff and Landrine 2000). Harvey and colleagues (2005) suggest that skin tone is a form of social stigma whereby dark skin tone is stigmatized in certain contexts.

Because of a focus on whiteness, race scholars have often pointed out that colourism is a source of internal dynamics within families of colour (Hall 2005; Burton et al. 2010), sometimes with intra-group racism as a result (Keith et al. 2010). Colourism is considered by some scholars to be highly influential on individuals' and families life-course outcomes, privileging lighter-skinned individuals within a family with more resources and power transmitted across generations. This is especially true for white families (Hill 2000; Wade and Bielitz 2005; Twine and Gallagher 2008; Grossman and Charmaraman 2009). Harris (2009, p. 5) writes: 'Skin color...carries fantasies about personal identity and family unity as well as the confirmation, or disruption, of racial orders.'

As aforementioned, men with lighter skin tones are perceived as having higher material resources such as socio-economic status and education. This would suggest that individuals using the sperm bank would select donors who have lighter skin tones. Thus, I hypothesize that lighter-skinned men will be more likely to be chosen for a pregnancy than darker-skinned men.

Biracial stratification system and tri-racialism system

One perspective on shifting demographics in the USA is that the racialized system remains biracial, that is, US society will only have two dominant categories: black and non-black (Warren and Twine 1997; Gans 1999; Fields 2001; Yancey 2003; Lee and Bean 2004). The shift in demographics is due to the growth of Hispanic and Latino populations, which have grown four times more than the total US population (Landale and Oropesa 2007). Asian American, African American and Pacific Islander populations have grown much less than the Hispanic and Latino populations, but more than whites, American Indians and Alaska Natives (Passel and Cohn 2008). Many demographers project that by 2050, the white population in the USA will have decreased, with many states having majority minority populations (Landale and Oropesa 2007; Johnson and Lichter 2010). Intermarriage has increased among whites and Asian Americans and whites and Latinos, which increases biracial and multiracial children (Bean and Stevens 2003). With these demographic shifts, what will be the US racial system? Yancey (2003) and Lee and Bean (2004) find support for a biracial system, while Bonilla-Silva (2001, 2003, 2009) finds support for tri-racialism.

Yancey (2003) suggests that a biracial stratification system will have a black and non-black divide, with the black category remaining at the bottom of the US racial hierarchy. Yancey (2003) argues that many groups that we view as white today were distinct white ethnic groups historically (Jacobson 1999). Ethnic groups such as Asians and Latinos would be incorporated into non-black categories via assimilation (Lee and Bean 2004). Furthermore, through different forms of assimilation (structural, cultural and identification), Yancey (2003) finds support that Asian and Latinos will become defined as white. Additionally, Lee and Bean (2004) argue that through assimilation, Asian and Latinos assimilate to the white dominant population at higher rates than blacks. Yancey (2003) suggests that blacks are considered the out-group and are thus alienated from and less successful in assimilating to the white dominant population.

However, instead of having a two-tiered system of black and non-black as Yancey (2003) and others suggest, Bonilla-Silva (2004, p. 121) proposes that the US racial stratification is becoming a tri-racial system with whites, honorary whites and collective blacks (Bonilla-Silva and Dietrich 2009). Bonilla-Silva and his colleagues' divisions are based on skin tone, education, culture, citizenship and language (Bonilla-Silva 2009; Bonilla-Silva and Dietrich 2009). The 'white' category is composed of light-skinned people such as English, Germans, Italians and Irish. The 'honorary white' category is composed of light-skinned Japanese, Chinese and Koreans. The 'collective black' category contains US-born blacks, African immigrants and dark-skinned Latinos (Bonilla-Silva and Glover 2004). Bonilla-Silva and Dietrich (2009) find income, education and occupational stratification among whites, honorary whites and collective blacks. Additionally, they find support for more marriages occurring between whites and honorary whites than between whites and members of the collective blacks.

Forman, Goar and Lewis (2002) find only partial support of a tri-racialism system. For example, they analyse attitudes of government support for racial minorities and conclude that Latinos are more likely to endorse government assistance and help for blacks than non-Hispanic whites. Furthermore, they find a similar pattern when examining attitudes towards increased government assistance for legal immigrants and refugees. However, when they examine inter-group differences among Latinos in attitudes towards racialized issues, they find mixed results.

Additionally, because of the US's racial system, men who are non-black should also be chosen more often from the sperm bank than black donors. Thus, I hypothesize that non-black men will be more likely to be chosen for a pregnancy than all other groups of men. Moreover, Bonilla-Silva's (2001, 2004, 2009) tri-racial hierarchy would suggest that men who are in the white and honorary white categories should be chosen more often than men who are in the collective black category. Therefore, I hypothesize that white and honorary white men will be more likely to be chosen for a pregnancy than men who are collective black.

Methods and data

The data for analyses derive from the online donor profiles at one sperm bank. The cryobank website offers those interested in purchasing sperm access to complete donor profiles including medical and family history, educational background, donor essays, photos of donors as children and short essays. All of the donor profiles in the catalogue were collected from September 2010 to December 2010.

The method of data collection can be broken down into several steps. First, various cryobanks and sperm banks in the USA were explored. Upon close examination, I focus primarily on one sperm bank because its donor pool is one of the largest and most ethnically diverse in the country. Furthermore, the sperm bank offers medical history, donor profiles, educational background and personal information about each donor. Second, information was gathered about each donor including donor type, height, weight, hair colour, hair texture, eye colour, skin tone, ancestry, ethnic origin, religion, education level, area of study, occupation and whether or not a pregnancy has occurred with each donor's sperm.[1]

Table 1 contains the demographic characteristics of the sperm donors. The demographic variables include social characteristics such as body mass index (BMI), social class (occupational prestige index and education majors), religious category and education major. Sperm banks tend to only have men who are at least 5' 8" tall and not overweight (Almeling 2011). However, religious and racial minority men's semen is often included in the sperm bank database to diversify the selection of sperm (Almeling 2011). A physical characteristic control variable that was utilized in this paper is *BMI*, which was calculated using the height and weight of each donor. The mean BMI was 24.63 with a range of 18.46–38.24.

Additionally, to check whether people were selecting sperm based upon characteristics of higher social class, I measured social class with Hauser and Warren's (1997) male socio-economic index to calculate the *occupational prestige score* and *education majors* of the donors. The mean occupational prestige score was 41.24 with a range of 12.15–74.72. Men who are majoring in higher-income majors in the USA, such as science and business, have higher social class than those donors who major in art, humanities and social science. Among the men in this study, 23 per cent majored in business and 21 per cent majored in science. Furthermore, social science majors were 14 per cent with art and humanities majors at lower percentages.

Some religious faith traditions, such as Jewish, Muslim and Catholic, suggest that donations transgress religious culture and laws. For example, Culley and Hudson (2009) found that Muslim women expressed concern about gamete donation as being religiously

Table 1 *Descriptive statistics of sperm donors, 2010*

	M	SD	Range
Pregnancies	0.22	0.42	0–1
BMI	24.63	3.28	18.46–38.24
Social class			
Occupational prestige scores	41.24	10.08	12.15–74.72
Major			
Social science	0.14	0.34	0–1
Law	0.02	0.15	0–1
Art	0.14	0.35	0–1
Business	0.23	0.42	0–1
Engineering	0.14	0.35	0–1
Science	0.21	0.41	0–1
Humanities	0.12	0.32	0–1
Religious categories			
Atheists/agnostic	0.04	0.19	0–1
Other religions	0.10	0.30	0–1
Conservative Christian	0.24	0.43	0–1
Catholic	0.29	0.45	0–1
Liberal Christian	0.14	0.35	0–1
None	0.20	0.20	0–1
Skin tone			
Dark	0.06	0.24	0–1
Olive	0.43	0.50	0–1
Medium	0.43	0.50	0–1
Fair	0.34	0.46	0–1
Ethnicity			
European	0.64	0.48	0–1
Latino	0.07	0.25	0–1
Asian	0.14	0.35	0–1
Middle Eastern	0.02	0.13	0–1
Black	0.02	0.15	0–1
Tri-racial stratification system			
Whites	0.72	0.45	0–1
Honorary whites	0.10	0.30	0–1
Collective blacks	0.18	0.43	0–1

unacceptable. I measure religion by the variable *religious category* that the sperm donors notated on their long form. Among these sperm donors, 29 per cent stated that they were Catholic while 20 per cent stated that they did not have any religious category (none). Jewish and Muslim donors accounted for 10 per cent of the sperm donors.

The independent variables are: (1) skin tone for colourism; (2) non-black for a biracial stratification system; and (3) white and honorary white for a tri-racial stratification system. The first independent variable was *skin tone*. Skin tone was measured by the staff at the sperm bank and is often noted by various US sperm banks. There were five skin tone categories: very fair, fair, medium, olive and dark. Staff who classified men who were very fair skin tone donors was only 1 per cent of the sample. Because the donors with a very fair skin tone comprised only 1 per cent and were a very small sample, they were combined with those of fair skin tone. Donors of fair skin tone accounted for 34 per cent of the catalogue. Men with medium and olive skin tones made up 43 per cent. Dark-skinned men were 6 per cent of the sperm donors available. The skin tones of the donors were closely tied to the affiliations listed as 'ancestry' in the database. In this database, dark skin tone is tied with the label of black; olive is paired with Mediterranean, Southeast Asian or Latin American countries; fair skin tone is linked to western European countries such as Norway or Sweden.

The second independent variable was *black* and *non-black*. The variable, black, was constructed using all sperm donors who marked black or African American ancestry on their profile form. Because Yancey (2003) argues that Latino and Asian populations will become white, the non-black variable was defined as all other ancestries of the donors, such as white, Japanese, Korean and Latino. Ninety-six per cent of the sperm donors were non-black and four per cent were black.

The third independent variable relates to tri-racialism, measured as *white, honorary white* and *collective black*. Referring to Bonilla-Silva and colleagues' (2004) description of white, honorary white and collective black, 72 per cent of the men were white, 10 per cent were honorary white and 18 per cent were collective black.

Because there are no data available on how often a sperm donor is chosen or by whom the donor is chosen, the dependent variable is fathering a *pregnancy*. These data only have information regarding whether the sperm donor had fathered a pregnancy. The data do not provide a count of how many pregnancies occurred. For example, one sperm donor may have fathered multiple pregnancies while other sperm donors may have had only one pregnancy. The sperm bank indicates which donors have been purchased the most and are perceived as popular by displaying on their website slogans such as: 'Popular Donor # is now available.' However, this does not indicate the number of pregnancies for any of the sperm donors. Additionally, data are not provided on how many vials of sperm an individual purchases before a pregnancy occurs. On average, three treatments usually results in a pregnancy (Palermo et al. 1999). In the current sample, seventy-eight per cent of the donors have fathered a pregnancy.

To compare and contrast colourism, biracial stratification and tri-racial stratification, I utilized a binominal logistic regression. A binominal logistic regression is used for model estimation because the dependent variable is a dichotomous response, scored as 1 for having fathered a pregnancy and 0 for having not fathered a pregnancy. The odds ratios (ORs) reported estimate the odds of an event. In this study, the odds of an event occurring are an increase or decrease in the odds of a sperm donor being selected, relative to the men who are not selected. An OR of 1.00 is not statistically significant. An OR greater than 1.00 means that the sperm donor has a higher probability of being selected when compared to men who were not selected, while an OR less than 1.00 means that the men who have lighter skin tone were less likely to have been selected when compared to men who were not selected (Agresti and Finlay 1997).

Limitations

Limitations of this study include: (1) only examining one US sperm bank catalogue; (2) a dependent variable of pregnancy; (3) racial composition of the sperm donors; and (4) more white sperm donors in the models than other racial minority men. The first limitation to the study is that only one sperm bank's catalogue was examined. This sperm bank's catalogue was chosen because it is one of the largest sperm banks in the USA. Additionally, the sperm bank staff actively recruit men of colour for donation. Other sperm banks have relatively few men of colour who donate. Therefore of US sperm banks, this one is the most diverse racially, ethnically and religiously.

A second limitation to this study is that sperm selection can only be determined based upon pregnancy. The sperm bank website suggests that the sperm of white males is selected more often than that of men of colour, but specific percentages of sperm selection cannot be determined, neither can the number of resulting pregnancies from one donor's sperm. As such, I do not purport to analyse which men were more appealing to customers. Instead, I examine racial categorization based on skin tone, a biracial stratified system or tri-racialism to explain the selection of sperm donors.

A third limitation is the fixed, catalogue survey data that is used in this study. The donors are asked to write their race and ethnicity on a long form, which is then incorporated into the catalogue. Many individuals change their race and ethnicity over their lifespan (Rockquemore and Delgado 2009), but because I am using fixed data at the point when the men filled out their long forms for the sperm bank, I cannot empirically study the blurring of racial categorization.

A fourth limitation to the study is the racial composition of the sperm donors. Because more white than non-white men are in the models, the resulting coefficients of may have larger standard errors. With larger standard errors, variables in this study may not be statistically significant, but still remain theoretically significant. Therefore, with a larger sample of sperm donors, one could expect some variables to become statistically significant. While this remains a limitation of this study, one needs to be cautious in interpreting the binominal logistic coefficients and I have erred on the side of variables not being statistically significant.

Results

As described in Table 2, none of my hypotheses was supported. The first hypothesis predicted that lighter-skinned men will be more likely to have a pregnancy than darker-skinned men. Table 2, Model 1 displays the results for colourism. Dark-skinned donors are the reference category. Olive-, medium- and fair-skinned men were less likely to have fathered a pregnancy than darker-skinned donors. Olive-skinned men were less likely to have fathered a pregnancy by 58 per cent when compared to darker-skinned donors (OR $= 0.41$, $p > .05$). Medium-skinned men were less likely to have fathered a pregnancy by 28 per cent (OR $= 0.72$, $p > .05$) and fair-skinned men were less likely to have fathered a pregnancy by 24 per cent (OR $= 0.76$, $p > .05$) when compared to darker-skinned donors. The general pattern does not support the first hypothesis and none of these results were statistically significant. However, it does support Almeling (2011) who found that racial minority men were sought out by sperm banks and customers at higher rates than white sperm donors, suggesting that sperm donors of colour are privileged higher in the market than white men.

Model 2 in Table 2 demonstrates the results for the second perspective that US race relations will become a biracial system (Yancey 2003). The second hypothesis predicted that non-black men will be more likely to have fathered a pregnancy than all other groups of men. Black sperm donors are the reference category. Non-black men decrease their odds of having fathered a pregnancy by 66 per cent (OR $= .34$, $p > .05$). This result is in the opposite direction of prediction. However, it is not statistically significant. This model does not support the second hypothesis, but it does support Almeling's (2011) findings.

Model 3 in Table 2 displays the results for a tri-racial system with collective blacks as the reference category. The third hypothesis suggests that white and honorary white men will be more likely to have fathered a pregnancy than men who are categorized as collective black. The white category of sperm donors is more likely to have fathered a pregnancy by 56 per cent (OR $= 1.56$, $p > .05$) when compared to men in the collective black category. Furthermore, honorary white men are more likely to have fathered a pregnancy by 28 per cent (OR $= 1.28$, $p > .05$) when compared to men in the collective black category. These findings support the third hypothesis in direction, but the results are not statistically significant.

Table 2 *Binominal logistic regression of sperm donors, 2010*

	Model 1 coefficient OR (SE)	Model 2 coefficient OR (SE)	Model 3 Coefficient OR (SE)
BMI	0.04	0.04	0.05
	1.04	1.04	1.05
	(0.05)	(0.05)	(0.05)
Occupational prestige scores	−0.01	−0.02	−0.01
	0.99	0.98	0.99
	(0.02)	(0.02)	(0.02)
Social science	−0.71	−0.75	−0.68
	0.49	0.47	0.51
	(0.64)	(0.64)	(0.64)
Law	−2.90***	−2.80***	−2.84***
	0.06	0.06	0.06
	(0.98)	(0.98)	(0.98)
Art	−0.89	−0.89	−0.87
	0.41	0.41	0.42
	(0.61)	(0.61)	(0.61)
Business	−0.16	−0.21	−0.16
	0.86	0.81	0.85
	(0.61)	(0.60)	(0.61)
Engineering	−0.10	−0.10	−0.10
	0.90	0.90	0.90
	(0.66)	(0.66)	(0.66)
Science	−0.65	−0.70	−0.69
	0.52	0.50	0.50
	(0.59)	(0.58)	(0.58)
Atheists/agnostic	−1.26	−1.16	−1.35
	0.28	0.31	0.26
	(0.73)	(0.72)	(0.73)
Other religions	0.37	0.42	0.46
	1.45	1.53	1.59
	(0.66)	(0.65)	(0.66)
Conservative Christian	−0.14	−0.04	−0.09
	0.87	0.96	0.92
	(0.48)	(0.47)	(0.47)
Catholic	−0.34	−0.29	−0.39
	0.71	0.75	0.68
	(0.46)	(0.45)	(0.46)
Liberal Christian	−0.26	−0.06	−0.27
	0.77	0.94	0.76
	(0.56)	(0.55)	(0.56)
Olive	−0.88		
	0.41		
	(0.73)		
Medium	−0.33		
	0.72		
	(0.69)		

Table 2 (*Continued*)

	Model 1 coefficient OR (SE)	Model 2 coefficient OR (SE)	Model 3 Coefficient OR (SE)
Fair	−0.28 0.76 (0.70)		
Non-black		−1.07 0.34 (1.09)	
White			0.45 1.56 0.35
Honorary white			0.24 1.28 0.53
Constant	1.91***	2.76***	1.00***
Log likelihood	−139.51	−140.19	−139.99
LR χ^2	20.56	19.20	19.61
Prob $> \chi^2$	0.20	0.16	0.19
Pseudo R^2	0.07	0.06	0.07
N	282	282	282

*** $p < .01$

Examining the variables of physical characteristics, social class and religious affiliation, only men who are majoring in law are less likely to be selected as a sperm donor. The physical characteristic variable, BMI, is not statistically significant, but a one-point increase in BMI increases the probability of being selected as a sperm donor. Occupational prestige scores decrease the probability of the sperm donor having a pregnancy. The only variable that remains consistently statistically significant in all three models is the education majors of the sperm donors. In each model, men who were majoring in law were less likely to be selected as donors than men who were majoring in humanities. This result is a mixed finding relating to social class, as it was predicted that men who had higher-earning majors would be selected more often. Sperm donors who were categorized with other religious faiths, such as Jewish or Muslim, were more likely to have fathered a pregnancy when compared to men who were categorized with no faith tradition. Atheists/agnostics, conservative Christians, Catholics and liberal Christians were less likely to have fathered a pregnancy than those men who had no religious category. This supports previous findings that individuals who select sperm based on religious faith are more likely to purposely choose sperm donors who practise Jewish or Muslim faith traditions (Almeling 2007; Culley and Hudson 2009).

Discussion and conclusion

Rockquemore and Brunsma (2004) suggest that skin tone and other physical characteristics are not value-neutral body differences, but carry symbolic, racialized meanings. In this research, identification as lighter-skinned men decreases the probability of being selected as a donor when compared to darker-skinned donors. This finding is inconsistent with previous research that suggests economic and social psychological advantages for individuals who have lighter skin tones. Gullickson (2005) questions the persistence of a light-skin advantage. He suggests that the changes engendered by the civil rights movement increasingly brought African Americans into contact with white gatekeepers for whom skin tone variations were less salient. I find little support for the studies that suggest that people are choosing lighter-skinned men as sperm donors. However, I find more support for Almeling's (2011) finding that women privilege racial-minority men in the selection of sperm more than white men, which challenges the intersectionality perspective.

The intersectionality perspective asserts that race, class, gender and ethnicity are intertwined and that stratification occurs at the intersections of these identities in different social contexts (Collins 2008). Choo and Ferree (2010, p. 131) argue that there are three aspects of intersectionality: (1) inclusion (intersecting identities); (2) analytical interactions (multi-level analysis of inter-categorical and intra-caterogrical intersections); and (3) institutional primacy (systemic intersectionality). Utilizing Collins' (2008) matrix of domination in this study, in which hegemonic identities are privileged over non-hegemonic identities, white men's sperm should be selected more often than the sperm of racial-minority men. However, I found support that darker-skinned men were more likely to have fathered a pregnancy than lighter-skinned men. This finding suggests an inversion of the matrix of domination in this specific context.

When examining whether sperm donors are selected based on biracial systems or tri-racialism, I find little support for either. Yancey (2003) argues that the USA will become a biracial system with non-black groups assimilating to the white dominant society. Yancey thus suggests that individuals who are selecting sperm donors should choose sperm donors who are non-black. However, I find that non-black sperm donors are less likely to have fathered a pregnancy. Furthermore, Bonilla-Silva (2001) suggests that the US racial system is tri-racialism. There is a positive relationship between white and honorary white sperm donors having fathered a pregnancy; however, the results are not statistically supported. In conclusion, I find little support for the three perspectives of colourism, biracial system or tri-racialism. Because of the larger number of white sperm donors compared to the number of non-white sperm donors in these models, the binomial logistic regression coefficients have large standard errors. A larger sample of sperm donors may result in statistically significant results.

Additionally, mixed results are noted related to religious category, physical and social class characteristics. Men who have higher occupational prestige scores and men who are majoring in law are less likely to have had a pregnancy. Individuals are selecting sperm donors who are of Jewish or Muslim faith categories, but are less likely to select sperm donors from other faith categories.

These results suggest that future research should examine other types of sperm banks and the intersection of race and ethnicity upon the selection of sperm donors. First, cross-national settings should be examined to see if there are differences in how sperm donors are cataloged. Second, other US sperm bank catalogues (sperm banks that are for profit and non-profit; sperm banks that have heterosexual and homosexual men's sperm) should be examined for sperm donors' racial and ethnic descriptions.

Note

1.   A donor type of 'open' means that once a child has reached the age of 18, he/she may make contact with the donor up to two times, either by phone, email or letter. The child and donor can agree to meet in person or to not be contacted again. A donor type of 'anonymous' means that the child may not contact the donor and the child has little legal recourse to determine the sperm donor.

References

AGRESTI, ALAN and FINLAY, BARBARA 1997 *Statistical Methods in the Social Sciences*, 3rd edn, Upper Saddle River, NJ: Prentice Hall

ALMELING, RENE 2006 "Why do you want to be a donor?': gender and the production of altruism in egg and sperm donation', *New Genetics and Society*, vol. 25, no. 2, pp. 143–57

——— 2007 'Selling genes, selling gender: egg agencies, sperm banks, and the medical market in genetic material', *American Sociological Review*, vol. 72, no. 3, pp. 319–40

——— 2009 'Gender and the value of bodily goods: commodification in egg and sperm donation', *Law and Contemporary Problems*, vol. 72, no. 3, pp. 37–58

——— 2011 *Sex Cells: The Medical Market for Eggs and Sperm*, Berkley, CA: University of California Press

BEAN, FRANK and STEVENS, GILLIAN 2003 *America's Newcomers and the Dynamics of Diversity*, New York: Russell Sage Foundation

BECKER, GAY, BUTLER, ANNELIESE and NACHTIGALL, ROBERT D. 2005 'Resemblance talk: a challenge for parents whose children were conceived with donor gametes in the US', *Social Science and Medicine*, vol. 61, no. 6, pp. 1300–9

BONILLA-SILVA, EDUARDO 2001 *White Supremacy and Racism in the Post-Civil Rights Era*, London: Lynne Rienner
—— 2004 'From biracial to tri-racial: towards a new system of racial stratification in the USA', *Ethnic and Racial Studies*, vol. 27, no. 6, pp. 931–50
—— 2009 'Are the Americas "sick with racism" or is it a problem at the poles? A reply to Christina A. Sue', *Ethnic and Racial Studies*, vol. 32, no. 6, pp. 1071–82
BONILLA-SILVA, EDUARDO and DIETRICH, DAVID R. 2009 'The Latin American-ization of US race relations: a new pigmentocracy', in Evelyn Nakano Glenn (ed.), *Shades of Difference: Why Skin Color Matters*, Stanford, CA: Stanford University Press, pp. 40–60
BONILLA-SILVA, EDUARDO and GLOVER, KAREN 2004 'We are all Americans! The Latin Americanization of race relations in the USA', in Amanda E. Lewis and Maria Krysan (eds), *The Changing Terrain of Race and Ethnicity: Theory, Methods, and Public Policy*, New York: Russell Sage Foundation, pp. 149–83
BOWEN, JAMES M. *et al.* 2010 *Altruistic Sperm Donation in Canada: An Iterative Population-Based Analysis* [Report No. TEMMP-X022-2010.REP], Submitted to Assisted Human Reproduction Canada (AHRC), Hamilton, ON: Programs for Assessment of Technology in Health (PATH) Research Institute
BURTON, LINDA M., *et al.* 2010 'Critical race, theories, colourism, and the decade's research on families of color', *Journal of Marriage and Family*, vol. 72, no. 3, pp. 440–59
CHABOT, JENNIFER M. and AMES, BARBARA D. 2004 '"It wasn't 'let's get pregnant and go do it"': decision making in lesbian couples planning motherhood via donor insemination', *Family Relations*, vol. 53, no. 4, pp. 348–56
CHOO, HAE YEON and FERREE, MYRA MARX 2010 'Practicing intersectionality in sociological research: a critical analysis of inclusions, interactions, and institutions in the study of inequalities', *Sociological Theory*, vol. 28, no. 2, pp. 129–49
COLLINS, PATRICIA H. 2008 *Black Feminist Thought: Knowledge, Consciousness, and the Politics of Empowerment*, New York: Routledge
CULLEY, LORRAINE and HUDSON, NICKY 2009 'Constructing relatedness: ethnicity, gender and third party assisted conception in the UK', *Current Sociology*, vol. 57, no. 2, pp. 249–67
EPSTEIN, RANDI HUTTER 2010 *Get Me Out: A History of Childbirth from the Garden of Eden to the Sperm Bank*, New York: W. W. Norton & Company
ESPINO, RODOLFO and FRANZ, MICHAEL M. 2002 'Latino phenotypic discrimina-tion revisited: the impact of skin color on occupational status', *Social Science Quarterly*, vol. 83, no. 2, pp. 612–23
FIELDS, BARBARA J. 2001 'Whiteness, racism, and identity', *International Labor and Working-Class History*, vol. 60, pp. 48–56
FORMAN, TYRONE A., GOAR, CARLA and LEWIS, AMANDA E. 2002 'Neither black nor white? An empirical test of the Latin Americanization thesis', *Race & Society*, vol. 5, no. 1, pp. 65–84
GANS, HERBERT 1999 'The possibility of a new racial hierarchy in the twenty-first century United States', in Michelle Lamont (ed.), *The Cultural Territories of Race*, Chicago, IL: University of Chicago Press, pp. 371–90
GLENN, EVELYN NAKANO 2008 'Yearning for lightness: transnational circuits in the marketing and consumption of skin lighteners', *Gender & Society*, vol. 22, no. 3, pp. 281–302
GROSSMAN, JENNIFER M. and CHARMARAMAN, LINDA 2009 'Race, context, and privilege: white adolescents' explanations of racial-ethnic centrality', *Journal of Youth and Adolescence*, vol. 38, no. 2, pp. 139–52
GULLICKSON, AARON 2005 'The significance of skin color declines: a re-analysis of skin tone differentials in post-Civil Rights America', vol. 84, no. 1, pp. 157–80
GUPTA, JYOTSNA A. 2006 'Towards transnational feminisms: some reflections and concerns in relation to the globalization of reproductive technologies', *European Journal of Women's Studies*, vol. 13, no. 1, pp. 23–38

HALL, RONALD E. 2005 'From the psychology of race to the issue of skin color for people of African descent', *Journal of Applied Social Psychology*, vol. 35, no. 9, pp. 1958–67

HANDWERKER, LISA 2002 'The politics of making modern babies in China: reproductive technologies and the "new" eugenics', in Marcia C. Inhoran and F. Van Balen. Berkley (eds), *Infertility around the Globe: New Thinking on Childlessness, Gender, and Reproductive Technologies*, Berkley, CA: University of California Press, pp. 298–314

HARRIS, ANGELA P. 2009 'Introduction: economies of color', in Evelyn Nakano Glenn (ed.), *Shades of Difference: Why Skin Color Matters*, Stanford, CA: Stanford University Press, pp. 1–6

HARVEY, RICHARD D., *et al.* 2005 'The intragroup stigmatization of skin tone among black American', *Journal of Black Psychology*, vol. 31, no. 3, pp. 237–53

HAUSER, ROBERT M. and WARREN, JOHN ROBERT 1997 'Socioeconomic indexes of occupational status: a review, update, and critique', in Adrian Raftery (ed.), *Sociological Methodology*, Cambridge: Blackwell Publishers, pp. 177–298

HERRING, CEDRIC, KEITH, VERNA and HORTON, DERRICK (eds) 2004 *Skin Deep: How Race and Complexion Matter in the 'Color-Blind' Era*, Chicago, IL: IRRPP

HERTZ, ROSANA 2008 *Single by Choice, Mothers by Choice: How Women are Choosing Parenthood without Marriage and Creating the New American Family*, New York: Oxford University Press

HILL, MARK E. 2000 'Color differences in the socioeconomic status of African American men: results of a longitudinal study', *Social Forces*, vol. 78, no. 4, pp. 1437–60

HOCHSCHILD, JENNIFER L. and WEAVER, VESLA 2007 'The skin color paradox and the American racial order', *Social Forces*, vol. 86, no. 2, pp. 643–70

HORBST, VIOLA 2006 'Infertility and in-vitro fertilization in Bamako, Mali: women's experience, avenues for solution and social contexts impacting on gynecological consultations', *Curare*, vol. 28, no. 1, pp. 35–46

HUNTER, MARGARET L. 2005 *Race, Gender, and the Politics of Skin Tone*, New York: Routledge

INHORN, MARCIA C. 2003 'Global infertility and the globalization of new reproductive technologies: illustrations from Egypt', *Social Science Medicine*, vol. 56, no. 9, pp. 1837–51

JACOBSON, MATTHEW FRYE 1999 *Whiteness of a Different Color: European Immigrants and the Alchemy of Race*, Cambridge, MA: Harvard University Press

JOHNSON, KENNETH M. and LICHTER, DANIEL T. 2010 'Growing diversity among America's children and youth: spatial and temporal dimensions', *Population and Development Review*, vol. 36, no. 1, pp. 151–76

KEITH, VERNA 2009 'A colorstruck world: skin tone, achievement, and self-esteem among African American women', in Evelyn Nakano Glenn (ed.), *Shades of Difference: Why Skin Color Matters*, Stanford, CA: Stanford University Press, pp. 25–39

KEITH, VERNA, *et al.* 2010 'Discriminatory experiences and depressive symptoms among African American women: do skin tone and mastery matter? *Sex Roles*, vol. 62, nos. 1–2, pp. 48–59

KEITH, VERNA and HERRING, CEDRIC 1991 'Skin tone and stratification in the black community', *American Journal of Sociology*, vol. 97, no. 3, pp. 760–78

KLONOFF, ELIZABETH A. and LANDRINE, HOPE 2000 'Revising and improving the African American acculturation scale', *Journal of Black Psychology*, vol. 26, no. 2, pp. 235–61

LANDALE, NANCY S. and OROPESA, R. S. 2007 'Hispanic families: stability and change', *Annual Review of Sociology*, vol. 33, pp. 381–405

LEE, JENNIFER and BEAN, FRANK 2004 'Reinventing the color line: immigration and America's new race/ethnic divide', *Social Forces*, vol. 86, no. 2, pp. 561–86

MADDOX, KEITH B. 2004 'Perspectives on racial phenotypicality bias', *Journal of Personality and Social Psychology*, vol. 8, no. 4, pp. 383–401

MARTIN, EMILY 1992 *The Woman in the Body: A Cultural Analysis of Reproduction*, Boston, MA: Beacon

MASON, JENNIFER 2008 'Tangible affinities and the real life fascination of kinship', *Sociology*, vol. 42, no. 1, pp. 29–45

MORALES, MARIA CRISTINA 2008 'The ethnic niche as an economic pathway for the dark skinned: labor market incorporation of Latina/o workers', *Hispanic Journal of Behavioral Sciences*, vol. 30, no. 3, pp. 280–98

NORDQVIST, PETRA 2010 'Out of sight, out of mind: family resemblances in lesbian donor conception', *Sociology*, vol. 44, no. 6, pp. 1128–44

PALERMO, GIANPIER D., *et al.* 1999 'Fertilization and pregnancy outcome with intracytoplasmic sperm injection for azoospermic men', *Human Reproduction*, vol. 14, no. 3, pp. 741–8

PASHIGIAN, MELISSA 2009 'Inappropriate relations: the ban on surrogacy with in vitro fertilization and the limits of state renovation in contemporary Vietnam', in Daphna Birenbaum-Carmeli and Marcia C. Inhorn (eds), *Assisting Reproduction, Testing Genes: Global Encounters with New Biotechnologies*, New York: Berghahn Books, pp. 164–188

PASSEL, JEFFREY and COHN, D'VERA 2008 *U.S. Population Projections: 2005–2050*, Washington, DC: Pew Research Center

QUIROGA, SELINE 2007 'Blood is thicker than water: policing donor insemination and the reproduction of whiteness', *Hypatia*, vol. 22, no. 2, pp. 143–61

ROBERTS, ELIZABETH F. S. 2006 'God's laboratory: religious rationalities and modernity in Ecuadorian in vitro fertilization', *Culture Medical Psychiataist*, vol. 30, no. 4, pp. 507–36

ROCKQUEMORE, KERRY ANN and BRUNSMA, DAVID L. 2004 'Beyond black? The reflexivity of appearances in racial identification among black/white biracials', in Cedric Herring, Verna M. Keith and Hayward Derrick Horton (eds), *Skin Deep: How Race and Complexion Matter in the 'Color-Blind' Era*, Chicago, IL: IRRPP, pp. 99–127

ROCKQUEMORE, KERRY ANN and DELGADO, DANIEL 2009 'Racing to theory or re-theorizing race: understanding the struggle to build valid multiracial identity theories', *Journal of Social Issues*, vol. 65, no. 1, pp. 13–34

RYAN, MAURA, MORAS, AMANDA and SHAPIRO, EVE 2010 'Race matters in lesbian donor insemination: whiteness and heteronormativity as co-constituted narratives', Paper presented at the annual meeting of the American Sociological Association Annual Meeting, Hilton Atlanta and Atlanta Marriott Marquis, Atlanta, GA

SYDSJÖ, G., *et al.* 2011 'Who becomes a sperm donor: personality characteristics in a national sample of identifiable donors', *International Journal of Obstetrics and Gynecology*, vol. 119, no. 1, pp. 33–9

THOMPSON, CHARIS 2009 'Skin tone and the persistence of biological race in egg donation for assisted reproduction', in Evelyn Nakano Glenn (ed.), *Shades of Difference: Why Skin Color Matters*, Stanford, CA: Stanford University Press, pp. 131–47

THOMPSON, MAXINE S. and KEITH, VERNA M. 2001 'The blacker the berry: gender, skin tone, self-esteem, and self-efficacy', *Gender & Society*, vol. 15, no. 3, p. 336

TREMAYNE, SORAYA 2006 'Not all Muslims are luddites', *Anthropology Today*, vol. 22, no. 3, pp. 1–2

TWINE, FRANCE WINDDANCE and GALLAGHER, CHARLES 2008 'The future of whiteness: a map of the "third wave"', *Ethnic and Racial Studies*, vol. 31, no. 1, pp. 4–24

WADE, T. JOEL and BIELITZ, SARA 2005 'The differential effect of skin color on attractiveness, personality, evaluations, and perceived life success of African Americans', *Journal of Black Psychology*, vol. 31, no. 3, pp. 215–36

WARREN, JONATHAN and TWINE, FRANCE WINDDANCE 1997 'White Americans, the new minority? Non-blacks and the ever-expanding boundaries of whiteness', *Journal of Black Studies*, vol. 28, no. 2, pp. 200–18

WHITTAKER, ANDREA and SPEIER, AMY 2010 'Cycling overseas: care, commodification, and stratification in cross-border reproductive travel', *Medical Anthropology*, vol. 29, no. 4, pp. 363–83

YANCEY, GEORGE 2003 *Who is White? Latinos, Asians, and the New Black/Nonblack Divide*, Boulder, CO: Lynne Rienner

Body area dissatisfaction in white, black and Latina female college students in the USA: an examination of racially salient appearance areas and ethnic identity

Cortney S. Warren

Abstract

Dissatisfaction with one's physical appearance is rampant among women living in western cultures. However, little research has examined dissatisfaction with body areas that may be more salient to racial-minority groups (e.g., hair, eyes, skin colour). This study examined dissatisfaction with racially salient appearance areas and ethnic identity in self-identified black ($n = 76$), white ($n = 104$) and Latina ($n = 106$) female college students in the southern USA. Results revealed that Latina women reported significantly more dissatisfaction with their eyes and nose than white and black women. Additionally, white and Latina women reported significantly more dissatisfaction with their facial features, lips, lower body and overall body than black women. Stronger ethnic identity predicted lower levels of body dissatisfaction on most appearance areas for all women. These results suggest that social scientists should consider racially salient appearance areas in the measurement and conceptualization of body dissatisfaction in ethnically diverse women.

Introduction

Defined as the negative appraisal of one's physical appearance and accompanying discontent, *body dissatisfaction* is rampant in the USA to the degree that a moderate amount is considered normative in women (Rodin, Silberstein and Striegel-Moore 1984; Thompson et al. 1999). In a community sample of 3,452 women in the USA, for example, Garner (1997) found that 56 percent expressed dissatisfaction with their overall appearance; 89 per cent wanted to lose weight; and 15 per cent would give up five years of their life to attain their desired weight. Similarly, in a sample of over 800 adult women, almost 50 per cent expressed dissatisfaction with their weight, lower torso and upper torso (Cash and Henry 1995). Although body dissatisfaction is commonplace for women of all ages, rates are particularly high among female college students: research suggests that as many as 80 per cent report some body dissatisfaction and over 10 per cent report clinically elevated levels indicative of more severe pathology (e.g. Heatherton et al. 1995).

Accurately measuring body dissatisfaction is important because it is one of the strongest empirically supported risk factors for eating disorder development (Stice 2002). However, to date, most existing research does not conceptually or methodologically examine how race and living in a culture with a history of racism may influence dissatisfaction with specific body areas. Although likely under-studied because of the socially sensitive nature of the topic, this is problematic because cultural values and ideals of appearance vary substantially between ethnic and racial groups (e.g. Altabe 1998; Chamorro and Flores-Ortiz 2000; Rubin, Fitts and Becker 2003), strongly influence body dissatisfaction (Wildes, Emery and Simons 2001; Becker 2004; Grabe and Hyde 2006), and may affect the appearance areas with which individuals are most dissatisfied because of racist historical beliefs and practices (Hunter 2005; Smedley and Smedley 2005). Furthermore, intra-group factors related to culture that may be protective against body dissatisfaction (e.g. ethnic identity) are under-studied. Consequently, this study examined dissatisfaction with racially salient appearance areas and ethnic identity in self-identified white, black and Latina female college students living in the USA.

Western culture, beauty and body dissatisfaction

Culture dramatically influences beauty ideals and values of appearance (Thompson et al. 1999). Although it is evolutionarily desirable to be attractive to the opposite sex for mate selection and procreation across cultures (Buss and Shackelford 2008), the ideal appearance and its relative importance as a determinant of female value varies across cultures (Nasser 1997; Becker 2004). In western cultural contexts (which include the majority culture of the USA, Australia and most of Western Europe), paramount value is placed on physical appearance as a determinant of social standing and personal worth for women (Thompson et al. 1999; Buss and Shackelford 2008). Specifically, the ideal woman is depicted in mainstream US media as youthful with a very thin body, long legs, light eyes, white skin and blonde hair, who is preoccupied with sex, beauty and weight loss (Spitzer, Henderson and Zivian 1999; Sypeck, Gray and Aherns 2004; Davalos, Davalos and Layton 2007).

Additionally, western cultures value individualism, independence, rational thinking, competition and self-reliance (Katz 1985; Crandall et al. 2001). In the context of physical appearance, these values promote the belief that individuals should be in control of and are responsible for attaining an attractive appearance (Brumberg 1997; Crandall et al. 2001). Theoretically, when a woman is not deemed attractive by social standards (e.g. overweight), she is not only failing to meet cultural ideals of appearance but also failing in her moral character. Consequently, women living in western cultural contexts that place a high value on beauty and view those who do not meet the ideal as characterologically flawed learn that attaining and maintaining the ideal appearance is a lifelong project to ensure security, intimacy, success and life satisfaction (Brumberg 1997; Thompson et al. 1999). Although appearance-related pressure exists for both sexes, research suggests that the consequences of being unattractive disproportionately affect women because physical appearance is more strongly tied to the female gender role (APA 2007).

Measurement of body dissatisfaction: the importance of race and ethnicity

Given the high value placed on physical appearance as a determinant of female value and the rampant body dissatisfaction reported by most women living in the USA and other western cultures, it is essential to adequately conceptualize and measure it. One way researchers commonly measure body dissatisfaction is by examining dissatisfaction with specific *body areas*, such as the breasts, hips, stomach and legs. Psychometrically supported measures of body area dissatisfaction include the Body Dissatisfaction subscale of the Eating Disorder Inventory (Garner, Olmstead and Polivy 1983), Body Satisfaction Scale (Slade et al. 1990), Body Area Satisfaction Scale of the Multidimensional Body Self-Relations Questionnaire (MBSRQ-BASS; Brown, Cash and Mikulka 1990; Cash 2000) and the Physical Appearance State and Trait Anxiety Scale (Reed et al. 1991).

Despite the utility and importance of existing measures of body area dissatisfaction, most were written, conceptualized and normed using samples of young white, European American women. Consequently, they may fail to capture ethnic and racial differences with regard to the primary body areas of concern. Although often used interchangeably, the term *race* generally refers to the socially constructed characterization of individuals based on visible traits such as skin colour, hair texture and stature (Helms 1990; APA 2003; Byrd and Solomon 2005). Conversely, *ethnicity* is defined as a sense of belonging to or acceptance of the norms, mores and practices of one's cultural or subcultural group (Phinney 1996; APA 2003).

Although often highly correlated, ethnicity and race are conceptually distinct constructs that may concurrently but uniquely influence body area dissatisfaction in women. First, ethnicity may influence body area dissatisfaction because values and ideals of appearance vary substantially among cultural groups. In mainstream white American culture, for example, a woman's social value is based primarily on her ability to attain the ideal (thin) physical appearance (Rodin, Silberstein and Striegel-Moore 1984; Brumberg 1997). Conversely, traditional Hispanic/Latino culture idealizes a larger, curvy physique (Chamorro and Flores-Ortiz 2000; Warren et al. 2005) and values interdependent, close family relationships (*familismo*), communality, collectivism, deterministic thinking (*fatalismo*) and being a friendly, sociable person (*personalismo*) over other personal features (Santiago-Rivera, Arredondo and Gallardo-Cooper 2002). Similarly, African American culture traditionally idealizes a larger figure (e.g. larger buttocks and body weight) and a woman's overall attractiveness is based on having good style and the right attitude rather than on solely meeting a physical standard (Poran 2002; Rubin, Fitts and Becker 2003; Poran 2006). These substantive differences in the values and ideals of appearance between ethnic groups may influence the body areas on which women experience dissatisfaction.

Second, race may significantly influence body area dissatisfaction when living in a racist cultural context in which being white affords one unearned privileges whereas being non-white accrues undeserved disadvantages (Helms 1990; Feagin 2000; Smedley and Smedley 2005). Historically, race was used to legally justify slavery, discrimination and segregation in the USA, with preference given to slaves with lighter skin (Hunter 2005; Goff et al. 2008). Prejudice and discrimination experienced because of one's race may make women particularly aware of racial and ethnic aspects of their appearance (Hunter 2005; Frederick et al. 2007). For example, in part because of the historical justification of maltreatment based on race, racially salient appearance areas such as hair texture and skin colour are topics of considerable attention and meaning in the black/African American community (Banks 2000; Coard, Breland and Raskin 2001; Hunter 2005; Poran 2006). Furthermore, visible racial and ethnic minorities are rarely displayed in mainstream US fashion or beauty-oriented media (Spitzer, Henderson and Zivian 1999). When they are represented as the ideal, the handful of well-known racial-minority models generally reflect white, European American appearance ideals: they have thin, tall bodies, long straight hair (i.e. not naturally 'ethnic') and small facial features (Banks 2000). Taken together, a racist historical background and a dearth of models of colour in mainstream media may make racially salient appearance features particularly important to body area dissatisfaction in racial-minority women in the USA.

Racially salient appearance areas

To date, a large body of research has examined ethnic differences in body dissatisfaction, which generally suggests that African American women are more satisfied with their appearance than white, European American and Hispanic/Latina women (for meta-analyses, see Wildes, Emery and Simons 2001; Roberts et al. 2006). These studies are usually conducted by administering questionnaires to women who self-identify as belonging to a given ethnic or racial group and testing for group differences. However, given that western culture equates phenotypically white traits with beauty and provides preferential treatment to women who most closely approximate the socially prescribed appearance ideals, much existing research may fail to methodologically and conceptually capture dissatisfaction with appearance areas most relevant to race. In this paper, *racially salient appearance areas* are defined as aspects of physical appearance important in determining one's classification as a member of a given racial group. Features commonly identified in psychological, anthropological and sociological literature as being particularly racially salient include skin colour, eye colour, hair texture and length, facial features (e.g. flatness of face, nose shape, eye depth) and body shape (such as buttock prominence; e.g. Helms 1990; Hughes and Hertel 1990; Banks 2000; Hunter 2005; Frederick et al. 2007; Fergus 2009). This definition does not imply that such areas or features are relevant or important to all ethnic and racial-minority individuals, nor does it suggest that all racial minorities have certain phenotypic features. Instead, the purpose of identifying racially salient appearance areas is to investigate body features that may be more salient to one's overall experience of body dissatisfaction for racial minorities because of the sociocultural environment of the USA.

Only a handful of studies have attempted to examine racially salient appearance areas in their conceptualization and measurement of body dissatisfaction, most of which have examined the influence of skin colour on beauty ideals in black women. Overall, research suggests that race is highly important to body image for women in the USA (e.g. Hill 2002; Rubin, Fitts and Becker 2003; Poran 2006; Dixson et al. 2010; Stephens and Fernández 2012). For example, in a study examining the relationship between skin colour and body image in black women in the USA, Bond and Cash (1992) found that 53 per cent of black participants would change their skin colour if possible, with the large majority desiring lighter skin. Similarly, in a study examining skin colour preferences and attractiveness, Hill (2002) found that black women rated fairer skin as more attractive than darker skin. Finally, in a study examining skin colour satisfaction and overall appearance satisfaction, Falconer and Neville (2000) found that black women who were less satisfied with their skin colour were also less satisfied with their overall appearance.

Ethnic identity

Within racial and ethnic groups, *ethnic identity* may influence the strength of body area dissatisfaction. Defined as a subjective sense of belonging to and identifying with an ethnic group (Phinney 1996), research suggests that a stronger ethnic identity is associated with a variety of positive psychological outcomes, particularly for ethnic minority women (e.g. self-esteem, decreased psychological symptoms; e.g. Martinez and Dukes 1997; Turnage 2004; Rogers Wood and Petrie 2010). Based on theories of racial and ethnic identity formation (Helms 1990; Phinney 1996), one could hypothesize that women who feel more strongly attached to a cultural group that places less value on appearance as a determinant of worth and/or has a more realistic, flexible appearance ideal would be less likely to experience body dissatisfaction with racially salient appearance features. As such, a strong ethnic identity may be associated with less body dissatisfaction, particularly for minority groups.

Existing research investigating the relationship of ethnic identity and body dissatisfaction is limited, with the large majority examining this relationship in African American women. However, overall, a stronger ethnic identity in the form of identifying with and having positive feelings about one's ethnic group is associated with less maladaptive eating behaviours, less body dissatisfaction and lower drive for thinness (Turnage 2004; Henrickson, Crowther and Harrington 2010; Stojek, Fischer and Collins 2010). In a sample of 322 African American female college students, a stronger ethnic identity was associated with decreased internalization of US societal ideals of appearance and beauty (Rogers Wood and Petrie 2010). Similarly, in a study of 105 African American adolescent females, the relationships between global self-esteem, appearance evaluation and ethnic identity were significant and positive (Turnage 2004). Finally, in a sample of eighty-seven African American women, stronger ethnic identity predicted healthier body image (Schooler et al. 2004).

Current study

The most recent APA (2007) guidelines for psychological practice with girls and women mandate that psychologists understand the unique effects of socialization and life experiences of women across diverse cultural groups; the impact of bias and discrimination on mental health status; and use appropriate, unbiased assessments. Consistent with these guidelines, it is critical that assessment measures adequately consider appearance areas that may be particularly relevant for women of different racial and ethnic groups (Poran 2006). Furthermore, although western cultural values and ideals of appearance have long been etiologically tied to eating pathology (Thompson et al. 1999), relatively little research has examined the influence of racially salient appearance features. Consequently, building on previous research, the overarching goal of this study was to examine dissatisfaction with racially salient body areas in a sample of white, black and Latina female college students and to test the relationship between body dissatisfaction and ethnic identity. Given the sociocultural climate of the USA, I hypothesized that black women would report less general body dissatisfaction than white and Latina women, but that considerable variability would emerge with regard to satisfaction with racially salient areas. I also predicted that stronger ethnic identity would be associated with less body dissatisfaction for all women.

Methods

Participants

Two-hundred and eighty seven (287) females recruited from undergraduate psychology classes at a large public university in Texas (USA) participated in the current study. All participants received research credit in exchange for participation and self-identified as belonging to one of three racial groups: black ($n = 76$), white ($n = 104$) and Latina ($n = 106$). The mean age of participants was 18.99 (SD $= 1.96$), which did not differ significantly by group. Body mass index (BMI: weight in kg/height in m^2), a measure of adiposity, differed significantly by racial group ($F(2,\ 281) = 7.28,\ p < .01$). Specifically, black women had a significantly higher BMI ($M = 25.25$, SD $= 5.36$) than white ($M = 22.67$, SD $= 3.20$) and Latina women ($M = 23.69$, SD $= 4.81$), who did not differ significantly.

Measures

General body area dissatisfaction. Two commonly used measures of general body area dissatisfaction were used in the study. The Weight subscale of the Physical Appearance State and Trait Anxiety Scale (PASTAS-W; Reed et al. 1991) measured the degree of anxious, uncomfortable emotions participants felt with regard to eight weight-related body areas, such as the thighs, hips and legs. Participants rated the frequency with which they feel 'anxious, tense, or nervous' on a five-point scale from 'never' to 'always', with higher scores indicative of more dissatisfaction. In the current sample, the overall coefficient α was 0.90 (white = 0.89, black = 0.89, Latina = 0.88).

Additionally, the nine-item Body Areas Satisfaction Scale of the Multidimensional Body-Self Relations Questionnaire (MBSRQ-BASS; Brown, Cash and Mikulka 1990; Cash 2000) measured satisfaction with ten body parts, including height, weight, hair, face, muscle tone, lower torso and upper torso. Items are rated on a five-point scale from 'very dissatisfied' to 'very satisfied', with higher scores indicating more body satisfaction (i.e. less body dissatisfaction). Psychometric properties of the MBSRQ-BASS are strong: α was 0.82 in a community sample of Latina/Hispanic, black and white participants (Cash and Henry 1995) and one-week test-retest reliability has been found to be 0.94 (Cash 2000). In the current sample, overall coefficient α was 0.81 (white = 0.77, black = 0.84, Latina = 0.81).

Racially salient body area dissatisfaction. The Satisfaction with Racially Salient Appearance Features (SAT-R) was designed for the purposes of this study to measure dissatisfaction with racially salient appearance features. Using basic principles of questionnaire development (Rattray and Jones 2007) and drawing from existing literature (e.g. Hughes and Hertel 1990; Bond and Cash 1992; Banks 2000; Hill 2002; Byrd and Solomon 2005; Poran 2006), eight a priori categories of appearance features and body areas were identified to be of racial importance to Latina and black women: (1) skin (colour of skin, colour of inside of hands and feet, existence of freckles); (2) nose (shape, width, 'flatness'); (3) facial structure (face width, face shape, forehead distance, depth of facial features); (4) eyes (colour, distance between eyes, eyelids (epicanthic or 'double' fold)); (5) hair (length of hair on head, texture (e.g. course, fine), colour, shape [e.g. curly, straight), 'style-ability' (e.g. how easy it is to style hair as desired), visibility of facial hair, body hair); (6) lips (colour, fullness/ prominence); (7) lower body (buttocks, hips, legs); and (8) body (body proportions, frame size). From these features, thirty-five items were generated that were rated on a five-point scale from 'very dissatisfied' to 'very satisfied'. Items from each subscale were summed, yielding eight subscale scores for each participant (i.e. Facial Structure, Eyes, Hair, Lips, Skin, Nose, Lower Body, Body). Higher scores indicated more satisfaction (i.e. less body dissatisfaction) with the racially salient appearance area.[1]

Ethnic identity. The five-item Affirmation and Belonging subscale of the Multigroup Ethnic Identity Measure (MEIM; Phinney 1992) tested a sense of positive ethnic attitudes and a sense of belonging. Items are scored on a four-point Likert-type scale from 'strongly disagree' to 'strongly agree', with higher scores indicative of stronger ethnic identity. Internal consistency across a sample of Latina/ Hispanic, Asian American, European American and African American students yielded overall α of 0.90 (Phinney 1992). In the current sample, coefficient α was 0.83 (white $= 0.79$, black $= 0.77$, Latina $= 0.88$).

Results

Psychometric evaluation of the SAT-R

Prior to using the SAT-R, it was psychometrically evaluated to support its use. Of the original thirty-five items, three were removed due to poor psychometric values.[2] As displayed in Table 1, internal consistency values of the remaining thirty-two items by subscale ranged from $\alpha = 0.64$ (Skin) to $\alpha = 0.94$ (Nose).[3] Confirmatory factor analysis (CFA) using maximum likelihood tested the a priori eight-factor model, which suggested strong goodness of fit indices.[4] Finally, concurrent validity of the SAT-R was supported by examining correlations between each subscale of the SAT-R and other body measures of body dissatisfaction, all of which were statistically significant at $p < .01$ (SAT-R and PASTAS-W ranged from $r = 0.17$ to 0.68; SAT-R and MBSRQ-BASS ranged from $r = 0.40$ to 0.79).

General and racially salient body area dissatisfaction by ethnicity

General body area dissatisfaction was tested using univariate analyses of variance (ANOVAs) specifying scores on the PASTAS-W and MBSRQ-BASS as dependent variables (respectively), BMI as a covariate, and racial group as the independent variable. BMI was added as a covariate to all analyses because BMI: (1) significantly differed by race in the current sample; and (2) is highly correlated with body dissatisfaction (e.g. Warren et al. 2005). As presented in Table 2, on general measures of body dissatisfaction (i.e. PASTAS-W and MBSRQ-BASS), univariate ANOVAs indicated significant differences by racial group after controlling for BMI. Post-hoc tests with Bonferroni adjustments indicated that Latina and white women reported significantly more overall body dissatisfaction (MBSRQ-

Table 1. *Items, item-total correlations and α values for the SAT-R by subscale*

SAT-R subscale Subscale item	Item-total correlations
Face	
1. Cheek bone definition	.68
2. Face shape (e.g. round, heart-shaped, oval)	.58
3. Depth of facial features (i.e. flatness or indentation)	.64
Subscale α	*.84*
Eyes	
4. Eye size	.68
5. Distance between eyes	.67
6. Eye colour	.36
7. Eyelids (i.e. double-fold, depth of lids)	.58
Subscale α	*.77*
Hair	
8. Hair length	.45
9. Hair colour (of hair on head)	.46
10. Hair texture (i.e. coarse, fine)	.73
11. Hair 'style-ability', grooming or manageability (i.e. the way you can wear your hair, ability to colour/ perm hair)	.54
12. Hair shape (i.e. curly, straight)	.69
13. Hair thickness	.61
Subscale α	*.81*
Lips	
14. Lip colour	.66
15. Lip fullness	.66
Subscale α	*.79*
Skin	
16. Skin colour	.35
17. Color of inside of hands and feet	.44
18. Hair on body (e.g. legs, torso, arms)	.35
19. Nipple colour	.51
Subscale α	*.64*
Nose	
20. Nose width	.87
21. Nose height/length	.89
22. Nose shape	.88
Subscale α	*.94*
Lower body	
23. Leg length	.50
24. Hip size	.63
25. Leg shape	.64
26. Thigh muscle size	.56
27. Buttock size	.64
28. Buttock shape/prominence (e.g. flatness, fullness)	.56
Subscale α	*.82*

Table 1. (*Continued*)

SAT-R subscale Subscale item	Item-total correlations
Overall body	
29. Weight	.74
30. Body fatness	.75
31. Body proportions	.60
32. Frame size	.68
Subscale α	*.85*

Note: SAT-R = Satisfaction with Racially Salient Appearance Features

BASS) and negative emotion around weight-related body parts (PASTAS-W) than black women. The size of these effects was medium to large (as indicated by partial η^2 values).

With regard to racially salient body areas, a MANCOVA using all eight subscale scores of the SAT-R indicated significant differences by group (Pillai's Trace (16, 382) = 0.26, $F = 3.50$, $p < .01$, $\eta_p^2 = 0.13$; Wilk's Lambda (16, 380) = 0.76, $F = 3.57$, $p < .01$, $\eta_p^2 = 0.13$). Follow-up univariate ANOVAs testing each subscale by racial group indicated that groups differed significantly on seven of the eight subscales of the

Table 2. *Means (SDs) and Omnibus Tests of body area dissatisfaction by racial group controlling for BMI*

	White	Black	Latina	F	p	η_p^2
PASTAS-W	23.24 (7.08)$_a$	19.61 (8.01)$_b$	24.68 (7.34)$_a$	17.22	<.01	0.12
MBSRQ-BASS	3.21 (0.63)$_a$	3.54 (0.79)$_b$	3.07 (0.69)$_a$	15.27	<.01	0.10
SAT-R TOTAL	114.95 (19.40)$_a$	126.55 (20.75)$_b$	110.94 (20.68)$_a$	11.16	<.01	0.11
Face	11.10 (2.75)$_a$	12.38 (2.61)$_b$	10.43 (3.10)$_a$	8.68	<.01	0.07
Eyes	16.72 (2.87)$_{ab}$	17.61 (2.72)$_a$	16.24 (3.43)$_b$	3.86	.02	0.03
Hair	23.62 (4.39)	22.87 (5.89)	22.70 (5.23)	.84	ns	0.01
Lips	7.90 (1.64)$_a$	8.80 (1.68)$_b$	7.89 (1.83)$_a$	6.02	<.01	0.04
Skin	14.61 (3.03)$_a$	15.92 (2.69)$_b$	15.04 (2.91)$_{ab}$	3.88	.02	0.03
Nose	10.57 (3.08)$_{ab}$	11.62 (3.15)$_a$	10.05 (3.51)$_b$	4.54	.01	0.03
Lower body	17.63 (5.41)$_a$	21.46 (5.50)$_b$	18.23 (5.47)$_a$	16.31	<.01	0.11
Overall body	11.83 (4.09)$_a$	13.38 (4.64)$_b$	11.16 (4.00)$_a$	16.88	<.01	0.11

Note: PASTAS-W = Weight subscale of the PASTAS; MBSRQ-BASS = Satisfaction with Body Parts subscale of the MBSRQ; SAT-R = Satisfaction with Racially Salient Appearance Features total and subscale scores.
Means in the same row that do not share subscripts differ at $p < .05$. On the PASTAS-W, higher scores indicate more body dissatisfaction whereas on the MBSRQ-BASS and SAT-R, higher scores indicate more body satisfaction (i.e. less dissatisfaction).

SAT-R. As displayed in Table 2, examination of mean differences on subscale scores indicated that Latina and white women reported significantly more dissatisfaction than black women with regard to their facial features, lips, lower body and overall body. Additionally, Latina women reported significantly more dissatisfaction with their eyes and nose than black women (with neither black nor Latina women differing significantly from white women). Surprisingly, white women were significantly more dissatisfied with their skin than black women and no racial differences emerged with regards to hair. Finally, an ANOVA testing all items of the SAT-R together (i.e. SAT-R TOTAL) indicated a significant effect for ethnicity, with post-hoc tests with Bonferroni adjustments indicating that Latina and white women reported significantly more overall body dissatisfaction with racially salient appearance areas than black women.

Influence of ethnic identity

A multivariate analysis of covariance (MANCOVA) specifying SAT-R subscale scores from all eight racially salient appearance subscales as dependent variables, BMI as a covariate, and racial group, ethnic identity and the racial group*ethnic identity interaction as independent variables, a statistically significant main effect for ethnic identity (Wilk's Lambda (8, 176) $= 0.62$, $F = 2.36$, $p = .02$, $\eta_p^2 = 0.10$) and a non-statistically significant interaction. Follow up analyses examining standardized regression weights for ethnic identity predicting each SAT-R subscale indicated statistically significant main effects on five of the eight subscales (see Table 3). Specifically, a stronger ethnic identity predicted more satisfaction (i.e. less dissatisfaction) with the following appearance areas for women of all ethnic groups:

Table 3. *Ethnic identity predicting satisfaction with racially salient appearance features*

SAT-R subscale	df	F	P	η_p^2
Face	1	8.08	<.01	0.04
Hair	1	5.85	.02	0.03
Skin	1	15.70	<.01	0.08
Eyes	1	8.01	<.01	0.04
Lips	1	5.90	.02	0.03
Overall body	1	3.51	.06	0.02
Nose	1	2.78	.10	0.02
Lower body	1	2.65	.11	0.01

Note: This table reflects ethnic identity predicting satisfaction with racially salient appearance features (SAT-R) by subscale.

face ($\beta = 0.29$, $t = 4.08$, $p < .01$), skin ($\beta = 0.26$, $t = 3.83$, $p < .01$), nose ($\beta = 0.15$, $t = 2.46$, $p = .01$), eyes ($\beta = 0.20$, $t = 3.17$, $p < .01$), lips ($\beta = 0.24$, $t = 3.85$, $p < .01$), lower body ($\beta = 0.16$, $t = 2.66$, $p = .01$) and overall body ($\beta = 0.17$, $t = 3.09$, $p < .01$).

Discussion

This study investigating dissatisfaction with racially salient appearance areas and ethnic identity in white, black and Latina female college students yielded important information that has implications for body image assessment, conceptualization and research. As predicted and consistent with existing research using non-racially specific measures of body image (e.g. Wildes, Emery and Simons 2001), Latina and white women reported significantly more overall body area dissatisfaction than black women. However, when examining racially salient appearance features, more specific information about areas of dissatisfaction emerged: (1) Latina and white participants reported significantly more dissatisfaction with their facial features, lips, lower body and overall body than black women; and (2) Latina participants reported significantly more dissatisfaction with their eyes and nose than white or black women. Taken together, Latina women reported the most dissatisfaction with racially salient appearance features. Furthermore, consistent with previous research suggesting that ethnic identity is associated with positive body- and eating-related outcomes (Schooler et al. 2004; Stojek, Fischer and Collins 2010), stronger ethnic identity was associated with more positive feelings about racially salient appearance features for women of all ethnic groups in this sample.

Although most study findings were consistent with hypotheses and previous research, two findings regarding specific racially salient body areas were surprising and warrant mention. First, white women reported significantly more dissatisfaction with their skin than black women. Although contrary to hypotheses, similar findings have been found by some other researchers (e.g. Altabe 1998). For example, in a recent study examining Latina female college students who racially identified as white, pale skin was viewed as unattractive compared to 'tan' skin (Stephens and Fernández 2012). Furthermore, having the ideal, tan skin colour was associated with being more desirable in peer and dating contexts; more sexually appealing to men; and symbolic of one's Hispanic identity in social contexts (Stephens and Fernández 2012). One explanation for these findings revolves around trends in fashion media: at present, being tan and having a warm glow to one's skin is presented as ideal in the media. Consequently, it may be that white women are responding to a desire to have tan skin as opposed to a general darker complexion, which should be examined empirically in future research. A second explanation is that being extreme in any direction (i.e. having very pale or very dark skin) is less desirable than being medium coloured. For example, in a study of African American male and female college students, Coard, Breland and Raskin (2001) found that participants preferred a medium skin tone over a lighter or darker skin tone. More research investigating the relationship between skin colour and body dissatisfaction in female college students is warranted.

Second, in contrast to hypotheses, no significant differences emerged between groups with regards to hair. Although non-significant differences are generally undesirable in the social sciences, the fact that black women did not report more satisfaction with their hair than white or Latina participants when they reported more satisfaction with every other appearance area is noteworthy. Socio-logical and psychological literature consistently documents the importance of hair in the black community (e.g. Banks 2000). For example, having 'good hair' is a frequently discussed topic among black women and hair care generally consumes a large amount of time and energy. In a qualitative analysis of 185 female college students who ethnically self-identified as African American, Asian American, Caucasian American and Hispanic American, Altabe (1998) found that ethnic minority groups wanted longer hair. Future research should continue to investigate the relationship between hair (e.g. length, texture, colour) and body dissatisfaction in female college students of different racial groups.

Limitations

There are various limitations that should be considered when examining these results. The advantages of conducting this research with female college students include that eating pathology and body image concerns are rampant in this population (Heatherton et al. 1995) and that the sample is relatively demographically homogenous (e.g. with regard to education, age). However, the homogeneity in the sample likely limits the generalizability of study findings to other populations (e.g. older women, clinical samples). Additionally, the SAT-R aimed to measure racially salient appearance areas theorized to be most important to black, Latina and white women in the USA, which may limit the utility and validity of this measure for use with other ethnic and racial groups (e.g. Asian American women). Furthermore, ethnic groups are highly heterogeneous (Phinney 1996); consequently, items on the SAT-R may not comprehensively capture the interplay between body area dissatisfaction and race. Finally, the SAT-R did not test the direction of dissatisfaction on racially salient areas (e.g. when participants indicated dissatisfaction with their hair length, it was not asked how they would like their hair to be different (e.g. longer, shorter). Consequently, directionality is presumed but should be further investigated.

It is also important to note that although most research attributes the preference for phenotypically white appearance features in the USA to the Southern slave system and a history of racism, some theorists argue that skin colour preference is related to the evolutionary process of sexual selection (see the work of Peter Frost; e.g. Frost 2005). For example, there is some evidence that men prefer women with lighter skin in many regions of the world and that women and children tend to have lighter skin than men (see Jablonski 2004; Frost 2005). For example, in a study examining men and women living in the USA and New Zealand, men expressed a preference for women with lighter skin (Dixson et al. 2010). Although this study conceptualizes racially salient body area dissatisfaction from a sociocultural perspective, future research could examine the possible interactions between social consequences of race in a racist culture and basic evolutionary aspects of mate selection related to race.

Conclusion

Despite the above limitations, the extent to which physical and psychological health disparities are shaped by race and ethnicity is of growing research interest to social scientists (Hall 2005; Araújo and Borrell 2006). Given that paramount value is placed on physical appearance as a central determinant of social value for women and that the ideal appearance is white, thin and young in mainstream western culture (Thompson et al. 1999), researchers should be particularly concerned with body dissatisfaction in women: (1) immigrating to the USA from non-western cultural contexts; and (2) living in non-western cultures who are exposed to western ideals (e.g. through the media). For example, considerable evidence suggests that exposure to and internalization (or personal acceptance) of mainstream western media ideals is associated with body dissatisfaction in women living in the USA and abroad (Nasser 1997; Becker 2004; Warren et al. 2005). For example, in a qualitative study examining body image in adolescent girls in Fiji, Becker (2004) found that weight and shape preoccupation, purging behaviour to control weight, and body dissatisfaction increased from being relatively non-existent to being relatively common over a three-year period following the introduction of television to the country. As such, when racial-minority women are exposed to western ideals, they can be in a double-bind whereby the ideals promoted are impossible to attain both because they are impossible for all women and because the ideals are white. As this occurs, dissatisfaction with racially salient features like height, hair and facial structure may be particularly important.

Acknowledgements

This project was funded, in part, by a dissertation grant from the American Psychological Association, Minority Fellowship Program: Grant 1 T06 SM56564-01.

Notes

1. Items were written to be very specific. For example, instead of asking one's degree of satisfaction with their 'eyes', items asked about aspects of the eye that are believed to be related to race (e.g. eye shape, whether the eye has a double or epicanthic fold, eye colour, distance between eyes). The aim was to create items that maintained the eight basic categories of appearance features (represented as subscales) with at least two items in each subscale. During a research training seminar of the American Psychological Association Minority Fellowship Program, a prominent eating disorder researcher and three doctoral-level graduate students who study cross-cultural aspects of body image in racially and ethnically diverse women critiqued, reviewed and edited the items.

2. Kaiser's (1974) measure of sampling adequacy (MSA) determined whether the data were appropriate for factor analysis. MSA values at or above 0.80–0.90 are considered sufficient for analysis, whereas those ranging from 0.50–0.60 are poor, and any values under 0.50 are considered unacceptable (Kaiser 1974). Items with poor individual MSA values were sequentially removed from the scale. This was done by identifying the item with the lowest individual MSA below 0.75, removing it from the scale, and repeating the process until all individual-item MSAs were above 0.75. After removing three items due to poor MSA values, the total MSA of the scale was 0.87.

3. Although undesirable to have any subscale α below 0.70 (i.e. the Skin subscale fell below this threshold), given the salience of skin colour to race, the subscale was retained. Consequently, all eight subscales were retained as theoretically derived. Consequently, all eight subscales were retained as theoretically derived. Future researchers could use items with the SAT-R with only two subscales: one 'face' and one 'body'. When separated into two subscales, α values improved: the sixteen-item Body subscale (which included all hair, skin, body areas and buttocks items) had a subscale α of 0.84 and the twelve-item Face subscale (which included all nose, facial structure, eyes and lips items) yielded an α of 0.88.

4. Multiple fit indices tested model fit, including the Satorra-Bentler $\chi 2$ (SB; Satorra and Bentler 2001), Goodness-of-Fit Index (GFI; Jöreskog and Sörbom 1993), Normed Fit Index (NFI; Bentler and Bonett 1980), Comparative Fit Index (CFI; Bentler 1990), Non-Normed Fit Index or Tucker-Lewis Index (NNFI; Marsh, Balla and McDonald 1988), Standardized Root Mean Square Residual (SRMR; Jöreskog and Sörbom 1993) and Root Mean Square Error of Approximation (RMSEA; Browne and Cudeck 1993). According to Hu and Bentler (1999), values of the GFI, NFI, CFI and NNFI range from 0 to 1.0, with values 0.95 or greater indicating a close fit and 0.90 an acceptable fit. Conversely, values of the RMSEA range from 0 to 1.0 and values close to 0.05 indicate a close fit, 0.08 an adequate fit, and 0.10 or greater a poor fit of the data to the model. For the SRMR, values also range from 0 to 1.0, with values close to 0.06 indicating a close fit. Overall, goodness of fit indices were very strong $(SB\chi^2$ (df = 436) = 972.74, NFI = 0.93, NNFI = 0.96, CFI = 0.96, GFI = 0.80, RMSEA = 0.06). Standardized inter-factor correlations ranged from 0.32 (Hair and Face subscales) to 0.71 (Skin and Body subscales).

References

APA (AMERICAN PSYCHOLOGICAL ASSOCIATION) 2003 'Guidelines on multicultural education, training, research, practice, and organizational change for psychologists', *American Psychologist*, vol. 58, no. 5, pp. 377–402

—— 2007 'Guidelines for psychological practice with girls and women', *American Psychologist*, vol. 62, no. 9, pp. 949–79

ALTABE, MADELINE 1998 'Ethnicity and body image: quantitative and qualitative analysis', *International Journal of Eating Disorders*, vol. 23, no. 2, pp. 153–9

ARAÚJO, BEVERLY Y. and BORRELL, LUISA N. 2006 'Understanding the link between discrimination, mental health outcomes, and life chances among Latinos', *Hispanic Journal of Behavioral Sciences*, vol. 28, no. 2, pp. 245–66

BANKS, INGRID 2000 *Hair Matters: Beauty, Power, and Black Women's Consciousness*, New York: New York University Press

BECKER, ANNE E. 2004 'Television, disordered eating, and young women in Fiji: negotiating body image and identity during rapid social change', *Culture, Medicine, and Psychiatry*, vol. 28, no. 4, pp. 533–59

BENTLER, PETER M. 1990 'Comparative fit indexes in structural models', *Psychological Bulletin*, vol. 107, no. 2, pp. 238–46

BENTLER, PETER M. and BONETT, DOUGLAS G. 1980 'Significance tests and goodness of fit in the analysis of covariance structures', *Psychological Bulletin*, vol. 88, no. 3, pp. 591–606

BOND, SELENA and CASH, THOMAS F. 1992 'Black beauty: skin color and body image among African-American college women', *Journal of Applied Social Psychology*, vol. 22, no. 11, pp. 874–88

BROWN, TIMOTHY A., CASH, THOMAS F. and MIKULKA, PETER J. 1990 'Attitudinal body-image assessment: factor analysis of the Body-Self Relations Questionnaire', *Journal of Personality Assessment*, vol. 55, nos. 1–2, pp. 135–44

BROWNE, MICHAEL W. and CUDECK, ROBERT 1993 'Alternative ways of assessing model fit', in Kenneth A. Bollen and J. Scott Long (eds), *Testing Structural Equation Models*, Newbury Park, CA: SAGE, pp. 136–62

BRUMBERG, JOAN J. 1997 *The Body Project: An Intimate History of American Girls*, New York: Random House

BUSS, DAVID M. and SHACKELFORD, TODD K. 2008 'Attractive women want it all: good genes, economic investment, parenting proclivities, and emotional commitment', *Evolutionary Psychology*, vol. 6, no. 1, pp. 134–46

BYRD, AYANA and SOLOMON, AKIBA 2005 *Naked: Black Women Bare all about their Skin, Hair, Hips, Lips, and other Parts*, New York: Penguin Group

CASH, THOMAS F. 2000 *MBSRQ User's Manual*, Unpublished manuscript provided by the Author, Old Dominion University

CASH, THOMAS F. and HENRY, PATRICIA E. 1995 'Women's body images: the results of a national survey in the USA', *Sex Roles*, vol. 33, nos. 1–2, pp. 19–28

CHAMORRO, REBECA and FLORES-ORTIZ, YVETTE 2000 'Acculturation and disordered eating patterns among Mexican American women', *International Journal of Eating Disorders*, vol. 28, no. 1, pp. 125–9

COARD, STEPHANIE I., BRELAND, ALFIEE M. and RASKIN, PATRICIA 2001 'Perceptions of and preferences for skin color, black racial identity, and self-esteem among African Americans', *Journal of Applied Social Psychology*, vol. 31, no. 11, pp. 2256–74

CRANDALL, CHRISTIAN S. *et al.* 2001 'An attribution-value model of prejudice: anti-fat attitudes in six nations', *Personality and Social Psychology Bulletin*, vol. 27, no. 1, pp. 30–7

DAVALOS, DEANA B., DAVALOS, RUTH A. and LAYTON, HEIDI S. 2007 'Content analysis of magazine headlines: changes over three decades?', *Feminism & Psychology*, vol. 17, no. 2, pp. 250–8

DIXSON, BARNABY J. *et al.* 2010 'Human physique and sexual attractiveness in men and women: a New Zealand–US comparative study', *Archives of Sexual Behavior*, vol. 39, no. 3, pp. 798–806

FALCONER, JAMES W. and NEVILLE, HELEN A. 2000 'An examination of body mass, African self-consciousness, and skin color satisfaction', *Psychology of Women Quarterly*, vol. 24, no. 3, pp. 236–43

FEAGIN, JOE R. 2000 *Racist America: Roots, Current Realities, and Future Reparations*, New York: Routledge

FERGUS, EDWARD 2009 'Understanding Latino students' schooling experiences: the relevance of skin color among Mexican and Puerto Rican high school students', *Teachers College Record*, vol. 111, no. 2, pp. 339–75

FREDERICK, DAVID A. *et al.* 2007 'The UCLA Body Project I: gender and ethnic differences in self-objectification and body satisfaction among 2,206 undergraduates', *Sex Roles*, vol. 57, nos. 5–6, pp. 317–27

FROST, PETER 2005 *Fair Women, Dark Men: The Forgotten Roots of Color Prejudice*, Christchurch: Cybereditions Corporation

GARNER, DAVID M. 1997 'The 1997 body image survey results', *Psychology Today*, vol. 30, pp. 30–41

GARNER, DAVID M., OLMSTEAD, MARION P. and POLIVY, JANET 1983 'Development and validation of a multidimensional eating disorder inventory for anorexia nervosa and bulimia', *International Journal of Eating Disorders*, vol. 2, no. 2, pp. 15–34

GOFF, PHILIP A. *et al.* 2008 'Not yet human: implicit knowledge, historical dehumanization, and contemporary consequences', *Journal of Personality and Social Psychology*, vol. 94, no. 2, pp. 292–306

GRABE, SHELLEY and HYDE, JANET S. 2006 'Ethnicity and body dissatisfaction among women in the United States: a meta-analysis', *Psychological Bulletin*, vol. 132, no. 4, pp. 622–40

HALL, RONALD E. 2005 'From the psychology of race to the issue of skin color for people of African descent', *Journal of Applied Social Psychology*, vol. 35, no. 9, pp. 1958–67

HEATHERTON, TODD F. *et al.* 1995 'Body weight, dieting, and eating disorder symptoms among college students, 1982–1992', *American Journal of Psychiatry*, vol. 152, no. 11, pp. 1623–9

HELMS, JANET E. 1990 *Black and White Racial Identity: Theory, Research, and Practice*, New York: Greenwood Press

HENRICKSON, HEATHER C., CROWTHER, JANIS H. and HARRINGTON, ELLEN F. 2010 'Ethnic identity and maladaptive eating: expectancies about eating and thinness in African American women', *Cultural Diversity and Ethnic Minority Psychology*, vol. 16, no. 1, pp. 87–93

HILL, MARK E. 2002 'Skin color and the perception of attractiveness among African-Americans: does gender make a difference?', *Social Psychology Quarterly*, vol. 65, no. 1, pp. 77–91

HU, LI-TZE and BENTLER, PETER M. 1999 'Cutoff criteria for fit indexes in covariance structure analysis: conventional criteria versus new alternatives', *Structural Equation Modeling*, vol. 6, no. 1, pp. 1–55

HUGHES, MICHAEL and HERTEL, BRADLEY R. 1990 'The significance of color remains: a study of life chances, mate selection, and ethnic consciousness among black Americans', *Social Forces*, vol. 68, no. 4, pp. 1105–20

HUNTER, MARGARET L. 2005 *Race, Gender, and the Politics of Skin Tone*, New York: Routledge

JABLONSKI, NINA G. 2004 'The evolution of human skin and skin color', *Annual Review of Anthropology*, vol. 33, pp. 585–623

JÖRESKOG, KARL G. and SÖRBOM, DAG 1993 *LISREL 8 User's Reference Guide*, Chicago, IL: Scientific Software, International

KAISER, HENRY F. 1974 'An index of factorial simplicity', *Psychometrika*, vol. 39, no. 1, pp. 31–6

KATZ, JUDITH 1985 'The sociopolitical nature of counseling', *The Counseling Psychologist*, vol. 13, no. 4, pp. 615–24

MARSH, HERBERT W., BALLA, JOHN R. and MCDONALD, RODERICK P. 1988 'Goodness-of-fit indices in confirmatory factor analysis: the effect of sample size', *Psychological Bulletin*, vol. 103, no. 3, pp. 391–410

MARTINEZ, RUBÉN O. and DUKES, RICHARD L. 1997 'The effects of ethnic identity, ethnicity, and gender on adolescent well-being', *Journal of Youth and Adolescence*, vol. 26, no. 5, pp. 503–16

NASSER, MERVAT 1997 *Culture and Weight Consciousness*, New York: Routledge

PHINNEY, JEAN S. 1992 'The Multigroup Ethnic Identity Measure: a new scale for use with diverse groups', *Journal of Adolescent Research*, vol. 7, no. 2, pp. 156–76

–––––– 1996 'When we talk about American ethnic groups, what do we mean?', *American Psychologist*, vol. 51, no. 9, pp. 918–27

PORAN, MAYA A. 2002 'Denying diversity: perceptions of beauty and social comparison processes among Latina, black, and white women', *Sex Roles*, vol. 47, nos. 1–2, pp. 65–81

–––––– 2006 'The politics of protection: body image, social pressures, and the misrepresentation of young black women', *Sex Roles*, vol. 55, nos. 11–12, pp. 739–55

RATTRAY, JANICE and JONES, MARTYN C. 2007 'Essential elements of questionnaire design and development', *Journal of Clinical Nursing*, vol. 16, no. 2, pp. 234–43

REED, DAVID L. *et al.* 1991 'Development and validation of the Physical Appearance State and Trait Anxiety Scale (PASTAS)', *Journal of Anxiety Disorders*, vol. 5, no. 4, pp. 323–32

ROBERTS, ALAN, *et al.* 2006 'Are black–white differences in females' body dissatisfaction decreasing? A meta-analytic review', *Journal of Consulting and Clinical Psychology*, vol. 74, no. 6, pp. 1121–31

RODIN, JUDITH, SILBERSTEIN, LISA and STRIEGEL-MOORE, RUTH 1984 'Women and weight: a normative discontent', *Nebraska Symposium on Motivation*, vol. 32, pp. 267–307

ROGERS WOOD, NIKEL A. and PETRIE, TRENT A. 2010 'Body dissatisfaction, ethnic identity, and disordered eating among African American women', *Journal of Counseling Psychology*, vol. 57, no. 2, pp. 141–53

RUBIN, LISA R., FITTS, MAKO L. and BECKER, ANNE E. 2003 '"Whatever feels good to my soul": body ethics and aesthetics among African American and Latina women', *Culture, Medicine, and Psychiatry*, vol. 27, no. 1, pp. 49–75

SANTIAGO-RIVERA, AZARA L., ARREDONDO, PATRICIA and GALLARDO-COOPER, MARITZA 2002 *Counseling Latinos and la Familia: A Practical Guide*, Thousand Oaks, CA: SAGE

SATORRA, ALBERT and BENTLER, PETER M. 2001 'A scaled difference chi-square test statistic for moment structure analysis', *Psychometrika*, vol. 66, no. 4, pp. 507–14

SCHOOLER, DEBORAH *et al.* 2004 'Who's that girl: television's role in the body image development of young white and black women', *Psychology of Women Quarterly*, vol. 28, no. 1, pp. 38–47

SLADE, PETER D. *et al.* 1990 'Development and preliminary validation of the body satisfaction scale (BSS)', *Psychology & Health*, vol. 4, no. 3, pp. 213–20

SMEDLEY, AUDREY and SMEDLEY, BRIAN D. 2005 'Race as biology is fiction, racism as a social problem is real: anthropological and historical perspectives on the social construction of race', *American Psychologist*, vol. 60, no. 1, pp. 16–26

SPITZER, BRENDA A., HENDERSON, KATHERINE A. and ZIVIAN, MARILYN T. 1999 'Gender differences in population versus media body sizes: a comparison over four decades', *Sex Roles*, vol. 40, nos. 7–8, pp. 545–65

STEPHENS, DIONNE P. and FERNANDÉZ, PAULA 2012 'The role of skin color on Hispanic women's perceptions of attractiveness', *Hispanic Journal of Behavioral Sciences*, vol. 34, no. 1, pp. 77–94

STICE, ERIC 2002 'Risk and maintenance factors for eating pathology: a meta-analytic review', *Psychological Bulletin*, vol. 128, no. 5, pp. 825–48

STOJEK, MONICA, FISCHER, SARAH and COLLINS, BRITTANY 2010 'Thinness and restricting expectancies mediate the influence of ethnic identity on bulimic symptoms', *Personality and Individual Differences*, vol. 49, no. 2, pp. 102–6

SYPECK, MIA F., GRAY, JAMES J. and AHERNS, ANTHONY H. 2004 'No longer just a pretty face: fashion magazines' depictions of ideal female beauty from 1959 to 1999', *International Journal of Eating Disorders*, vol. 36, no. 3, pp. 342–7

THOMPSON, J. KEVIN *et al.* 1999 *Exacting Beauty: Theory, Assessment, and Treatment of Body Image Disturbance*, Washington, DC: American Psychological Association

TURNAGE, BARBARA F. 2004 'Influences on adolescent African American females' global self-esteem: body image and ethnic identity', *Journal of Ethnic & Cultural Diversity in Social Work: Innovation in Theory, Research & Practice*, vol. 13, no. 4, pp. 27–45

WARREN, CORTNEY S. *et al.* 2005 'Ethnicity as a protective factor against internalization of a thin-ideal and body dissatisfaction', *International Journal of Eating Disorders*, vol. 37, no. 3, pp. 241–9

WILDES, JENNIFER E., EMERY, ROBERT E. and SIMONS, ANNE D. 2001 'The roles of ethnicity and culture in the development of eating disturbance and body dissatisfaction: a meta-analytic review', *Clinical Psychology Review*, vol. 21, no. 4, pp. 521–51

Mediators of stereotype threat among black college students

Douglas S. Massey and Jayanti Owens

Abstract

We hypothesize that the manner in which stereotype threat affects college-grade achievement is mediated by institutional context as well as individual characteristics. Drawing on a sample of black students from the National Longitudinal Survey of Freshmen, we find weak and inconsistent evidence that institutional characteristics influence the operation of stereotype threat. We find more consistent evidence to indicate that the effect of stereotype threat is conditioned by individual factors such as skin colour, multiracial origins and an integrated upbringing. Most of the effect on grade achievement occurs through the internalization pathway, in which the internalization of negative stereotypes leads to disinvestment manifested by a reduction in academic effort. The reduction in work effort, in turn, lowers grades. We also find evidence that immigrant origin confers protection from the negative effects of stereotype threat through both internalization and externalization mechanisms, although the ultimate effect of grade achievement is rather small.

Stereotype threat is a widely recognized social-psychological phenomenon and is well established in both the sociological and psychological literatures. The potential for stereotype threat arises whenever: (1) a negative stereotype exists about a social group in society; (2) members of that social group are aware of the stereotype; and (3) group members are required to perform in a domain where the stereotype is relevant. Originally developed by Claude Steele (1988a, 1988b), the stereotype threat model has been validated in many laboratory experiments (Major and O'Brien 2005; Inzlicht and Schmader 2012). In the laboratory, stereotype threat is created by priming a negative stereotype for members of an experimental social group to whom the stereotype applies while offering a countervailing prime, a neutral prime, or no prime to a control group of otherwise comparable individuals. With the negative stereotype threat primed and in mind, members of the experimental group perform systematically worse with respect to the stereotyped outcome than members of the control group.

Steele originally developed this model to explain black under-performance in educational settings. The stereotype of black intellectual inferiority is widely known in American society (see Herrnstein and Murray 1996; Tucker 2002) and deeply embedded in American social cognition (Sniderman and Piazza 1993; Schuman et al. 1998; Bobo and Johnson 2000). African American students are keenly aware of the stereotype, of course, and whenever they are called upon to perform academically they put themselves at risk of confirming this very negative stereotype about themselves and their group.

The effects of stereotype threat are not confined to African Americans, of course. Indeed, stereotype threat can undermine the performance of any stigmatized group whose members are negatively portrayed with respect to a domain of ability or performance (Lovaglia et al. 1998). Members of stigmatized groups underperform because they fear living up to negative group stereotypes about themselves and their group. If this fear is strong enough, it interferes with performance and leads to 'disidentification', a psychological defence mechanism in which the domain where the threat occurs is dropped as a basis for self-esteem (Steele and Aronson 1995; Aronson et al. 1998).

Although the concept of stereotype threat was originally developed by psychologists and validated in laboratory experiments, more recently others have supported the hypothesis using field experiments (Stricker and Ward 2004), observational studies (Cullen et al. 2004) and survey-based statistical analyses (Massey and Fischer 2005; Owens and Massey 2011). With respect to academic underperformance by minority students, survey researchers have been notably successful not only in confirming the existence of stereotype threat outside the laboratory (Charles et al. 2009; Owens and Massey 2011), but in demonstrating its potency as an explanation relative to other hypothesized social and psychological mechanisms (Massey and Probasco 2010).

Survey researchers have elaborated two distinct pathways by which stereotype threat influences minority student performance (Massey and Fischer 2005). The basic model is summarized in Figure 1, which is taken from Owens and Massey (2011). The *internalization pathway* occurs when minority students themselves subscribe at some level to negative stereotypes about their group, in effect internalizing the invidious beliefs to create a potentially serious threat to self-esteem. To reduce the threat, such students *disidentify* with academic achievement

Figure 1. *Conceptual Model of Stereotype Threat with Expected Direction of Relationships between Concepts.*

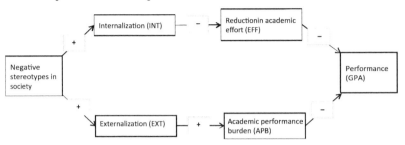

Note: The boxes overlaying arrows contain '+' or '−' signs that indicate the expected direction of the effect based on the theory of stereotype threat. '+' represents an expected positive relationship between the two concepts, whereas '−' represents an expected negative relationship.

as a domain of self-worth by *reducing their academic work effort.* In this case, if they perform badly in a class or an exam, they do not confirm the negative stereotype to themselves because they know they did not put in their best effort. They *could* have done better if they had tried harder.

The *externalization pathway* occurs when minority students expect *other* social actors, in particular white students and teachers, to hold negative stereotypes about their group and to make malicious judgements based on these prejudices. This expectation creates anxiety about performing badly before an audience of invidious judges (e.g. white peers and professors), yielding a psychological *performance burden* that undermines achievement. These two path-ways have been found to operate independently to reduce grade performance among blacks and Latinos attending selective colleges and universities in the USA using both standard structural equation estimates and latent variable models (Massey and Fischer 2005; Owens and Massey 2011).

In this paper we build on earlier work by assuming the validity of stereotype threat in survey settings and moving on to test whether the severity of the threat varies according to social context and personal characteristics. In the following section, we derive a series of hypotheses about how different institutional and individual factors might exacerbate or mitigate stereotype threat. We then describe the data and methods used to test these hypotheses and present results indicating that certain institutional settings and individual character-istics do indeed produce a greater stereotype threat than others. We conclude with a consideration of the theoretical and practical implications of our research.

Social context and stereotype threat

Our overall hypothesis is that the severity of stereotype threat varies systematically with respect to characteristics of the academic institution that students attend and the personal traits they bring with them to college. In general, we expect that those institutional and individual characteristics that heighten minority status, underscore negative group attributions and accentuate the stakes of academic performance will produce greater internalization and externalization of negative stereotypes and thus greater disidentification and heavier performance burdens, which ultimately will lead to lower academic performance.

Among the institutional factors that we consider are public versus private sector, school selectivity, emphasis on affirmative action, and black student representation on campus. In general, we expect private colleges and universities to be more exclusive and place a greater emphasis on scholarly credentials and academic performance, both before and after admission. Hence, we hypothesize that the basic mechanisms of racial stereotype threat will operate more powerfully on the campuses of private than public institutions. We also consider the effect of institutional selectivity, arguing that more selective colleges and universities are more likely to highlight indicators of academic achievement such as course grades, exam outcomes, honours and awards, thus focusing attention on scholarly performance to heighten the potential for stereotype threat. With respect to affirmative action, we hypothesize that institutions emphasizing minority inclusion may inadvertently stigmatize them as being less qualified than other students, especially if they are slotted into 'special' or 'remedial' programmes on the basis of race, thus exacerbating stereotype threat (see Fischer and Massey 2007; Massey and Mooney 2007). Finally we consider group size, arguing that other things equal, a relatively large number of minority students on campus will reduce the visibility of any individual minority student, thus mitigating the potential for stereotype threat.

At the individual level, we consider a student's skin colour, racial origins, immigrant background, parental education and origination in a segregated versus integrated environment. To the extent that light-skinned and multiracial African Americans are less sure of their identity and confident in their blackness, they may be more susceptible to stereotype threat. Blacks of immigrant origin grew up in households headed by at least one immigrant parent (and usually two), which means that parental socialization occurred primarily outside the racist environment of the USA, usually within a predominantly black society in Africa or the Caribbean. Prior work indicates that immigrant-origin students are less aware of and less affected by stereotyping and discrimination in American society and are less likely to have internalized feelings of inferiority and victimization from their parents (Waters 2000; Kasinitz 2002; Deaux 2006), and hence are hypothesized to be less vulnerable to stereotype threat (Owens and Lynch 2012). An immigrant ideology of grit and effort also helps them respond positively to any prejudice and discrimination that they encounter (Portes and Rumbaut 2006).

With respect to parental education, we hypothesize that first-generation college students are more vulnerable to the predations of stereotype threat owing to a lack of familiarity with the college-related human, social, and cultural capital that is second nature to the children of parents who have gone to college. Finally, we argue that coming of age in a segregated school environment confers some protection on black students, who were not so conscious of their minority status or exposed to the judgements of white peers while growing up, thus yielding less susceptibility to stereotype threat. Indeed, Massey and Fischer (2005) found that minority students who had predominantly minority-peer networks, attended minority schools and lived in segregated neighbourhoods experienced less stereotype internalization and externalization.

Data and methods

Our data come from the National Longitudinal Survey of Freshmen (NLSF), a stratified random sample of college students who entered twenty-eight selective colleges and universities throughout the USA in autumn 1999 (see Massey et al. 2003; Charles et al. 2009). Students were interviewed in person during the autumn of their freshman year and were re-interviewed by phone every spring from 2000 to 2003 to learn about their social and academic experiences in college. Here we draw upon data gathered at baseline and in the first two follow-up surveys, which had respective response rates of 86, 96 and 90 per cent. We selected black students for study because, as the nation's stigmatized minority of longest standing and greatest severity, they are likely to be most susceptible to stereotype threat. Multiple imputation was used to deal with item non-response (which ranged between 0.5 and 5 per cent) and to conserve degrees of freedom, yielding a final sample of 918 black students.

The ultimate dependent variable in our analyses is academic performance, which we measure as the grade point average (GPA) earned by students during the spring and autumn of 2000 – or the spring of their freshman year and the autumn of their sophomore year. Following Owens and Massey (2011), we developed estimates of the theoretical constructs pertaining to stereotype threat shown in Figure 1 using multiple indicators, which are listed in Table 1. The Owens-Massey latent variable analyses firmly validated this measurement

Table 1. *Indicators and dimensions of stereotype threat used in the analysis of immigrant- and native-origin black students*

Internalization (INT, $\alpha = 0.703$)
Own group is intelligent (0–6)
Own group is hard working (0–6)
Own group perseveres (0–6)
Externalization (EXT, $\alpha = 0.680$)
Whites treat other races equally or discriminate (0–10)
Asians treat other races equally or discriminate (0–10)
Instructors' stereotypes do not affect evaluations of members of stereotyped groups (0–10)
Students' stereotypes do not affect evaluations of members of stereotyped groups (0–10)
Academic effort (EFF, $\alpha = 0.630$)
Average number of hours studied in a seven/day week/10 (0–12)
Importance of learning course material (0–10)
Self-reported [academic] effort during past year of college (0–10)
Average hours of recreational activities during a five-day week/10 (0–10, reverse-coded)
Academic performance burden (APB, $\alpha = 0.763$)
Instructors think less of me for having difficulty in class (0–10)
Excelling academically reflects positively on my racial/ethnic group (0–10)
Doing poorly academically reflects negatively on my racial/ethnic group (0–10)
I don't want to look foolish or stupid in class (0–10)
If I don't do well, people will look down on others like me (0–10)
Self-conscious about the way white students perceive me (0–10)
Self-conscious about the way Asian students perceive me (0–10)
Self-conscious about the way teachers perceive me (0–10)

---

model and demonstrated its robustness under different configurations of the data set and different equation specifications.

We operationalize the internalization construct (INT) by taking the sum of three items that assess the degree to which respondents believe that members of their own group are lazy, unintelligent, and give up easily ($\alpha = 0.703$). Externalization (EXT) is indexed as the sum of four items assessing whether respondents think whites and Asians discriminate and the degree to which they think other instructors and students base academic evaluations on group stereotypes ($\alpha = 0.680$). We measure academic effort (EFF) by combining three items: the average number of hours studied per seven-day week during the academic year); how important the respondent believes it is to try hard to learn the course material in college courses; and how much self-reported effort they put into their studies over the past year ($\alpha = 0.630$). Finally, academic performance burden (APB) is assessed by adding together five items that ask respondents to report the degree to which: instructors will think less of them if they have difficulty in class; their individual performance reflects positively or negatively on their group; they have apprehensions about appearing foolish or stupid before others; they believe not doing well academically will cause people to look down on others like them ($\alpha = 0.763$).

Whereas Massey and Fischer (2005) and Owens and Massey (2011) included a large number of control variables in their final equations, here we will be dividing a limited sample of black students into categories based on institutional and individual characteristics, so we conserve degrees of freedom by including as controls just three variables that prior work has shown to be relevant in influencing academic performance in these data: cognitive skills as measured by SAT score, prior academic achievement as measured by high school GPA, and socio-economic status as measured by the share of college costs borne by the student's family (Massey et al. 2003; Charles et al. 2009).

Means, standard deviations and ranges for variables used in the analysis are summarized in Table 2. As can be seen, the average GPA lies on the border between a B and a C grade, with a value of 2.97 and a range extending from failing (0.43) to straight As (4.0). With respect to the internalization pathway, the index of negative stereotype internalization displayed an average value of 6.59 on a 0–14 scale

Table 2. *Means, standard deviations and ranges of variables used to analyse contextual effects on stereotype threat*

Variable	*M*	SD	Minimum	Maximum
Academic achievement				
Grade point average (GPA	2.969	0.468	0.433	4
Internalization measures				
Internalization score	6.591	2.292	0	14
Academic effort	16.729	4.828	0	30
Externalization measures				
Externalization score	22.722	6.498	0	34
Performance burden	30.947	12.531	0	63
Institutional context				
Private sector	0.678	0.467	0	1
High selectivity	0.484	0.500	0	1
High affirmative action	0.472	0.499	0	1
Large percentage black	0.698	0.459	0	1
Individual context				
Light skin tone	0.497	0.490	0	1
Foreign-born parent(s)	0.284	0.451	0	1
Multiracial	0.164	0.370	0	1
Parent college educated	0.676	0.468	0	1
Segregated schools	0.121	0.326	0	1
Control variables				
SAT score	1,292.086	145.419	840	1,600
High school GPA	3.708	0.330	1.667	4
% college paid by family	0.357	0.342	0	1

with a standard deviation of 6.59, whereas the index of academic effort averaged 17.73 on a 0–30 scale with a standard deviation of 4.83. In the externalization pathway, the index of stereotype externalization averaged 22.72 on a 0–34 scale with a standard deviation of 6.50 and the average performance burden stood at 30.95 on a 0–63 scale with a standard deviation of 12.53. Thus our core theoretical variables display ample variation. With respect to control variables, the range of SAT scores was 840–1,600 with a mean of 1,292; high school GPA ranged from 1.67 to 4.0 and averaged 3.71; and the proportion of college costs paid by family members ran the gamut from 0 to 1.0 with a mean of 0.357.

The institutional factors that we consider potentially important in mediating the potency of stereotype threat are sector, selectivity, affirmative action and black student representation. As one might expect given a sample of elite colleges and universities, the institutions are weighted towards the private sector, with 68 per cent of respondents at a private college or university and 32 per cent at one of the 'elite public' institutions (such as University of California Berkeley or the University of Michigan). To capture institutional selectivity, we divided the sample at the median institutional SAT score and defined those schools above this point as more selective and those below it as less selective. By this criterion, around 48 per cent of respondents attended more selective institutions. Following Massey and Mooney (2007), we assessed an institution's emphasis on affirmative action by taking the difference between the average SAT score for black and all students at each institution and then dividing the sample at the median value of this difference. In schools above the median, black SAT scores lie closer to the institutional average than in schools below the median, suggesting that other criteria (such as race) were given greater weight in the admission decision. According to this metric, around 47 per cent of students attended a college or university where the emphasis on affirmative action was high. Finally, we assessed how the relative number of black students affected academic outcomes by dividing the twenty-eight institutions into two categories above and below the median percentage of black students. By this measure, around 70 per cent of the students in our sample attended a college or university with a relatively high black percentage.

The individual-level mediators we considered are skin tone, parental birthplace, multiracial origins, parental education, and degree of school segregation experienced while growing up. Skin tone was measured using an interviewer-assigned scale of darkness that ranged from 0 (extremely light) to 10 (extremely dark) with a mean of 4.97. To dichotomize the sample into relatively equal-sized groups for comparison, we divided students into segments above and below the average darkness level, yielding two categories that we simply labelled 'light' and 'dark'. According to this classification, roughly half of all black students were classified as light skinned. Turning to parental birthplace, some 28 per cent of the students reported a foreign-born parent, whereas 16 per cent reported multiracial origins and 68 per cent of the sample had at least one parent who was a college graduate. Students who attended schools that averaged more than 50 per cent black while growing up were considered to have come from a segregated background, which was true of 12 per cent of the students.

Contextual effects on stereotype threat

To assess the effect of institutional context on stereotype threat, we divided the sample into two groups with respect to sector, selectivity, commitment to affirmative action, and the relative number of black students. Using ordinary least squares (OLS) models we then estimated equations associated with each of the pathways shown in Figure 1, yielding measures of the effect of stereotype internalization on academic effort, academic effort on GPA, stereotype externalization on performance burden, and performance burden on GPA, all controlling for the individual's SAT score, high school GPA, and the percentage of college costs paid by family. Table 3 presents coefficients associated with the internalization and externalization pathways across the various institutional contexts. In general, the coefficients follow expectations derived from the hypothesis of stereotype threat.

Table 3. *Effect of stereotype threat on academic performance of African American students in selected institutional contexts*

	Internalization pathway		Externalization pathway	
	INT →EFF	EFF →GPA	EXT →APB	APB →GPA
Sector				
Public	−0.159	0.030	0.111	−0.003
Private	−0.137	0.019	0.072	−0.001
Selectivity				
Low	−0.176	0.023	−0.004**	−0.003
High	−0.112	0.020	0.163**	−0.001
Affirmative action emphasis				
Low	−0.101*	0.019	0.187**	−0.002
High	−0.207*	0.025	−0.032**	−0.002
Black student representation				
Low	−0.126	0.035**	−0.071**	−0.003
High	−0.146	0.015**	0.154**	−0.001

* $p < .10$, ** $p < .05$

Note: All models control for student SAT score, high school GPA and family economic status.

The internalization of negative stereotypes leads to a reduction of academic effort while the externalization of stereotypes increases the academic performance burden, with both effects lowering grades for black students.

With respect to the internalization pathway, however, we observe few differences in the strength of effects by institutional context. In those institutions characterized by a stronger reliance on affirmative action, the effect of internalization on effort is marginally stronger than in those placing less emphasis such programmes, consistent with our stigmatization hypothesis. In terms of black representation on campus, students attending institutions with a relatively low black percentage appear to translate academic effort into grades with greater efficiency than those attending schools with a high black percentage, but the effect of internalization in reducing academic effort is virtually identical.

Turning to the externalization pathway, we find that among black students at more selective institutions, the effect of externalization on the academic performance burden is significantly greater than among those in less selective institutions, consistent with our hypothesis. More selective campus environments thus appear to highlight academic achievement in ways that focus attention on scholarly performance, thus heightening the potency of stereotype threat. Contrary to expectations, however, a greater emphasis on affirmative action was associated with a *less powerful* externalization effect on performance burden. Also contrary to our hypotheses, a higher representation of black students produced a *stronger* externalization effect.

In general, then, we uncover relatively little evidence of systematic differences in the potency of stereotype threat across institutional settings. Consistent with expectations, the internalization of negative stereotypes appears to produce marginally greater disinvestment (reduced academic effort) for black students at high affirmative-action institutions, but contrary to expectations, the externalization of stereotypes translates into a greater performance burden for black students attending low affirmative-action institutions. Moreover, although greater institutional selectivity does appear to heighten the effect of stereotype externalization on performance burden, a high proportion of black students on campus is associated with a greater rather than a lesser effect of stereotype externalization on performance burden, in contrast to what we expected. For the most part, our hypotheses about contextual effects on stereotype threat are not borne out by the data.

Table 4. *Effect of stereotype threat on academic performance of African American students in selected individual contexts*

	Internalization pathway		Externalization pathway	
	INT →EFF	EFF →GPA	EXT →APB	APB →GPA
Skin tone				
Light	−0.310	0.021	0.105	−0.006
Dark	−0.047	0.024	0.058	0.000
Racial origins				
Mono-racial	−0.096**	0.022	0.042**	−0.002*
Multiracial	−0.397**	0.020	0.198**	-0.004*
Immigrant origins				
Native	−0.209**	0.025**	0.017**	−0.004**
Foreign	−0.021**	0.014**	0.238**	0.002**
Parental education				
1st-generation college	−0.132	0.027	0.073	−0.002
2nd-generation + college	−0.155	0.020	0.089	−0.002
School origins				
Integrated	−0.166**	0.023	0.105**	−0.001**
Segregated	−0.029**	0.023	−0.070**	−0.010**

*$p < .10$, ** $p < .05$
Note: All models control for student SAT score, high school GPA and family economic status.

Individual influences on stereotype threat

Table 4 tests whether the potency of stereotype threat varies by selected individual-level traits. Although parental background clearly has no effect, we do find results consistent with our hypotheses for three of the mediating variables. The translation of stereotype internalization into reduced academic effort is significantly stronger for multiracial than mono-racial students and the effect of externalization on performance burden is likewise stronger among these same students. Similarly, students who attended integrated schools are more prone to translate internalization into academic disinvestment and externalization into a performance burden than those from segregated schools. Finally, the effect of internalization on academic effort is significantly greater among light-skinned than dark-skinned students; although the effect of externalization on performance burden is not significantly greater for those with lighter skin tones, the contrast is nonetheless in the expected direction.

In sum, the data suggest that black students who have a non-black parent, a light complexion and who attended integrated schools while growing up are more vulnerable to the negative influences of stereotype threat. In order to show more concretely the effect of stereotype threat on grade performance, we generated predicted GPAs by letting both the internalization and externalization scales run from

Figure 2. *Effect of internalization and externalization of negative stereotypes on college grade point average by skin tone*

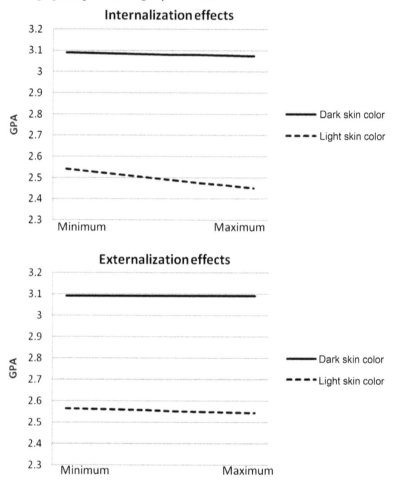

their minimum to maximum values while holding SAT scores, high school GPAs and the share of college costs paid by family members constant at their means. Figure 2 shows the effect of internalization and externalization on grade achievement for light- and dark-skinned students, while Figures 3 and 4 perform the same operation for mono-racial versus multiracial students and for students from integrated versus segregated school backgrounds, respectively.

As shown in the top panel of Figure 2, dark-skinned students generally earn higher grades, on average, than light-skinned students, but as the internalization of negative stereotypes runs from minimum to maximum, the gap grows larger. At the minimum, dark-skinned students display a GPA of 3.09, whereas for their light-skinned

Figure 3. *Effect of internalization and externalization of negative stereotypes on college GPA by racial origins*

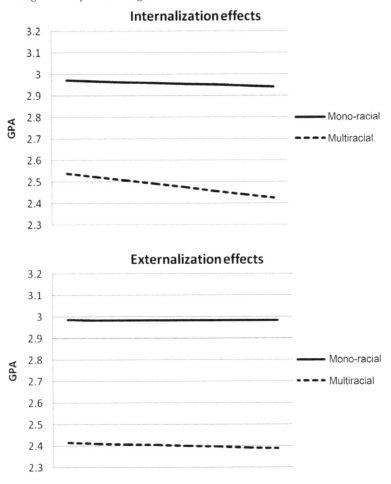

counterparts it is 2.54 – a gap of 0.55 grade points. At the maximum level of stereotype internalization, however, the GPA of dark-skinned students remains relatively constant at 3.07 but that of light-skinned students has declined to 2.45, raising the gap to 0.62 grade points. Although the same pattern prevails when stereotype externalization proceeds from its minimum to maximum value, the gap is only marginally increased and the two lines are close to parallel.

We see much the same pattern in Figure 3, where the GPA gap between mono-racial and multiracial students widens as internalization increases but does not change much as externalization increases. Thus at the minimum level of internalization, mono-racial students display a predicted GPA of 2.97 compared with 2.54 for multiracial students,

Figure 4. *Effect of internalization and externalization of negative stereotypes on college GPA by school origins*

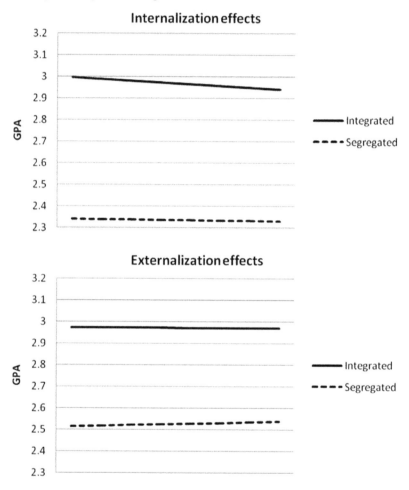

yielding a gap of 0.43 grade points. At the maximum level of internalization, however, the GPA for mono-racial students declined slightly to 2.94 but the GPA for multiracial students fell to 2.43, raising the gap to 0.51. At the same time, however, moving stereotype externalization from minimum to maximum leaves the gap virtually unchanged.

The situation depicted in Figure 4 is somewhat more complicated. Whereas students from integrated educational backgrounds earn higher grades than those from segregated backgrounds, they are more affected by stereotype internalization so that the gap narrows as the degree of internalization rises. At the minimum level of internalization, students from integrated schools display a GPA of 3.00 compared with a value of 2.34 for students from segregated schools, yielding a gap of 0.66 grade points. At the maximum level, however, the predicted GPA for students from an integrated background drops to 2.94, while that for those from a segregated background remains almost constant at 2.33, reducing the gap slightly to 0.61 grade points. The gap between integrated and segregated students also falls very slightly as stereotype externalization increases, going from a differential of 0.46 at the minimum to 0.43 at the maximum.

In the end, therefore, it seems that the internalization pathway is more important in determining grade achievement than the externalization pathway. In general, light-skinned, multiracial black students from integrated educational backgrounds are more susceptible to the internalization negative stereotypes, which translates into disinvestment through a reduction in academic effort. Although the ultimate effects on grades are not huge, they are significant and in the hypothesized direction, serving to widen the GPA gap between multiracial and mono-racial students and between light-skinned and dark-skinned students, but narrowing the gap between students from integrated and segregated schools.

The one individual-level factor we have not yet considered is immigrant origins, and with respect to this mediator we obtain anomalous but interesting results. Although the internalization results are consistent with our hypotheses, the findings for externalization are not. As expected, native-origin black students display a significantly stronger connection between negative stereotype internalization and disinvestment. As seen in Table 4, the effect of internalization on academic work effort is -0.209 for native-origin students but just -0.021 for those of immigrant origin – a mere 10th of the effect for natives. On top of this differential, academic effort is more strongly connected to grade achievement among native-origin than foreign-origin students, thus exacerbating the ultimate effect on GPA.

Contrary to expectations, however, stereotype externalization is translated into academic performance burden to a much greater extent among immigrant-origin students. Whereas the effect of externalization on performance burden is 0.238 for those of immigrant origin, it is just 0.017 among those of native origin. Adding to the anomaly, immigrant origin students respond to a heightened performance burden in a way that is opposite to that predicted by theory. Whereas among native-origin students, and in all other comparisons we considered, performance burden has a negative effect on grade performance, among students of immigrant origin the effect is *positive*. Rather than undermining performance, a greater subjective performance burden in response to the perceived negative stereotyping of their abilities by others seems to spur greater academic achievement in children of immigrants. In the end, therefore, immigrant origins end up conferring a protective effect in response to the externalization of stereotypes.

Figure 5. *Effect of internalization and externalization of negative stereotypes on college GPA by immigrant versus native origins*

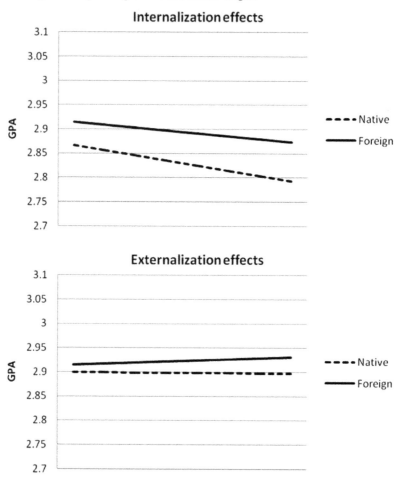

Figure 5 shows the effects of stereotype internalization and externalization on predicted GPAs for native- and immigrant-origin students. As can be seen, foreign-origin black students generally earn higher grades than native-origin students and the gap widens as both internalization and externalization increase. At the minimum level of stereotype internalization, foreign-origin students display a predicted GPA of 2.92 compared with 2.87 for those of native origin, for a gap of 0.05 grade points. At the maximum level of internalization, however, the gap grows to 0.08 points as GPA falls to 2.87 for foreign students but to 2.79 among native-origin students. Likewise, at the minimum level of externalization, students of immigrant origin display a predicted GPA of 2.91 compared with 2.90 for natives, whereas at maximum externalization the respective figures are 2.93 and 2.90, raising the gap from 0.01 to 0.03 grade points. Although these differentials are obviously small, they are once again significant and suggest that immigrant origins somehow confer some resistance to stereotype threat.

Conclusion

We began our analysis by hypothesizing that certain institutional and individual characteristics mediate the relative influence of stereotype threat on the academic performance of black college students, either exacerbating or mitigating the potency of the threat through the internalization and externalization pathways identified by earlier studies. In the former pathway, the internalization of negative stereotypes translates into disidentification and a reduction in academic effort and consequently lowers grades. In the latter pathway, the externalization of stereotypes (expecting to be judged invidiously by others on the basis of negative stereotypes) yields a higher academic performance burden that detracts from grade performance.

Drawing on data from the NLSF, we tested whether these mechanisms were affected by institutional characteristics such as public versus private sector, selectivity, commitment to affirmative action, and the relative representation of black students on campus. We found little evidence of strong or consistent effects of institutional context on the operation of stereotype threat among black college students. Although a few institutional characteristics produced differentials that were consistent with hypotheses, others yielded results that were opposite to theoretical predictions.

Our analysis of the mediating influence of individual-level characteristics yielded more interesting results that were generally consistent with hypotheses. Our data suggest that students whose 'blackness' might be less certain – those educated in integrated schools, having a light skin tone or a non-black parent – were more susceptible to the negative influences of stereotype threat, displaying more of a tendency towards disinvestment and subjective performance burdens than black students who were mono-racial, dark skinned and educated in segregated schools. Of the two pathways, the internalization pathway ultimately had the greater effect on grade achievement, serving to widen the GPA gap between multiracial versus mono-racial and light-skinned versus dark-skinned students as the level of internalization rose, but reducing the gap between students from integrated versus segregated backgrounds. Although the effects of internalization on grades were not particularly large, they were significant.

Consistent with what other social scientists have found, we also found evidence to suggest that immigrant origins confer a protective effect with respect to the influence of stereotype threat. Although the ultimate effects on grade achievement were not large, being the child of an immigrant significantly reduced the negative effect of stereotype internalization on academic effort; and although stereotype externalization produced more of a performance burden among immigrant-than native-origin students, their reaction was opposite to that of all other black subgroups we considered. Instead of lowering grade achievement, a greater performance burden spurred immigrant-origin black students to earn higher grades. As a result, as stereotype internalization and externalization rose, the GPA gap between immigrant- and native-origin students widened.

The foregoing conclusions suggest that stereotype threat is not a homogenous phenomenon that affects all people equally, but varies systematically according certain individual traits, underscoring the fact that today's black college students are far from a homogenous group. Diversity with respect to background characteristics such as skin tone, multiracial origins, immigrant background, and an integrated versus segregated upbringing can influence the operation of psychological processes and their behavioural manifestations. In this sense, researchers need to pay more attention to diversity within the black student population than they have in the past.

References

ARONSON, JOSHUA, *et al.* 1998 'The effects of stereotype threat on the standardized test performance of college students', in Eliot Aronson (ed.), *Readings about the Social Animal*, 8th edn, New York: Freeman, pp. 400–12

BOBO, LAWRENCE D. and JOHNSON, DEVON 2000 'Racial attitudes in the prismatic metropolis: identity, stereotypes, and perceived group competition in Los Angeles', in Lawrence D. Bobo, *et al.* (eds), *Prismatic Metropolis: Inequality in Los Angeles*, New York: Russell Sage Foundation, pp. 83–166

CHARLES, CAMILLE Z., *et al.* 2009 *Taming the River: Negotiating the Academic, Financial, and Social Currents in Selective Colleges and Universities*, Princeton, NJ: Princeton University Press

CULLEN, MICHAEL J., *et al.* 2004 'Using SAT-grade and ability-job performance relationships to test predictions derived from stereotype threat theory', *Journal of Applied Psychology*, vol. 89, no. 2, pp. 220–30

DEAUX, KAY 2006 *To be an Immigrant*, New York: Russell Sage Foundation

FISCHER, MARY J. and MASSEY, DOUGLAS S. 2007 'The effects of affirmative action in higher education', *Social Science Research*, vol. 36, no. 2, pp. 531–49

HERNSTEIN, RICHARD and MURRAY, CHARLES 1994 *The Bell Curve: Intelligence and Class Structure in American Life*, New York: Free Press

INZLICHT, MICHAEL and SCHMADER, TONI 2012 *Stereotype Threat: Theory, Process, and Application*, New York: Oxford University Press

KASINITZ, PHILIP 2002 *Caribbean New York: Black Immigrants and the Politics of Race*, Ithaca, NY: Cornell University Press

LOVAGLIA, MICHAEL J., *et al.* 1998 'Status processes and mental ability test scores', *American Journal of Sociology*, vol. 104, no. 1, pp. 195–228

MAJOR, BRENDA and O'BRIEN, LAURE T. 2005 'The social psychology of stigma', *Annual Review of Psychology*, vol. 56, pp. 393–421

MASSEY, DOUGLAS S., *et al.* 2003 *The Source of the River: The Social Origins of Freshmen at America's Selective Colleges and Universities*, Princeton, NJ: Princeton University Press

MASSEY, DOUGLAS S. and FISCHER, MARY J. 2005 'Stereotype threat and academic performance: new findings from a racially diverse sample of college freshmen', *The DuBois Review*, vol. 2, no. 1, pp. 45–68

MASSEY, DOUGLAS S. and MOONEY, MARGARITA A. 2007 'The effects of America's three affirmative action programs on academic performance', *Social Problems*, vol. 54, no. 1, pp. 99–117

MASSEY, DOUGLAS S. and PROBASCO, LIERIN 2010 'Divergent streams: race-gender achievement gaps at selective colleges and universities', *The DuBois Review*, vol. 7, no. 1, pp. 219–46

OWENS, JAYANTI and LYNCH, SCOTT M. 2012 'Black and Hispanic immigrants' resilience against negative-ability racial stereotypes at selective colleges and universities in the United States', *Sociology of Education*, vol. 85, no. 4, pp. 303–25

OWENS, JAYANTI and MASSEY, DOUGLAS S. 2011 'Stereotype threat and college academic performance: a latent variables approach', *Social Science Research*, vol. 40, no. 1, pp. 150–66

PORTES, ALEJANDRO and RUMBAUT, RUBEN G. 2006 *Immigrant America: A Portrait*, 3rd edn, Berkeley, CA: University of California Press

SCHUMAN, HOWARD, *et al.* 1998 *Racial Attitudes in America: Trends and Interpretations*, rev. edn, Cambridge, MA: Harvard University Press

SNIDERMAN, PAUL M. and PIAZZA, THOMAS 1993 *The Scar of Race*, Cambridge, MA: Belknap Press

STEELE, CLAUDE M. 1988a 'The psychology of self-affirmation: sustaining the integrity of the self', *Advances in Experimental Social Psychology*, vol. 21, pp. 261–302

——— 1988b 'A threat in the air: how stereotypes shape intellectual identity and performance', in Jennifer L. Eberhardt and Susan T. Fiske (eds), *Confronting Racism: The Problem and the Response*, Thousand Oaks, CA: SAGE, pp. 202–34

STEELE, CLAUDE M. and ARONSON, JOSHUA 1995 'Stereotype threat and the intellectual test performance of African Americans', *Journal of Personality and Social Psychology*, vol. 69, no. 5, pp. 797–811

STRICKER, LAWRENCE J. and WARD, WILLIAM C. 2004 'Stereotype threat: inquiring about test takers' ethnicity and gender, and standardized test performance', *Journal of Applied Social Psychology*, vol. 34, no. 4, pp. 665–93

TUCKER, WILLIAM H. 2002 *The Funding of Scientific Racism: Wickliffe Draper and the Pioneer Fund*, Urbana: University of Illinois Press

WATERS, MARY C. 2000 *Black Identities: West Indian Immigrant Dreams and American Realities*, Cambridge, MA: Harvard University Press

Index